EAGLE BLUE

EAGLE BLUE

A TEAM, A TRIBE,
AND A HIGH SCHOOL
BASKETBALL SEASON
IN ARCTIC ALASKA

Michael D'Orso

BLOOMSBURY

Lyrics from "Anthem of the American Indian," by Tom Bee, copyright 1973 by Jobete Music Co. Inc., reprinted by permission (the SOAR Corporation). Excerpt from "Northwest Passage," © 1942 TIME Inc., reprinted by permission.

Published by Bloomsbury USA, New York
Distributed to the trade by Holtzbrinck Publishers

All papers used by Bloomsbury USA are natural, recyclable products made from wood grown in well-managed forests. The manufacturing processes conform to the environmental regulations of the country of origin.

The Library of Congress has cataloged the hardcover edition as follows:

D'Orso, Michael.
Eagle blue : a team, a tribe, and a high school basketball season
in Arctic Alaska / Michael D'Orso.—1st U.S. ed.
p. cm.
Includes bibliographical references.
ISBN-13: 978-1-58234-623-6 (hardcover)
ISBN-10: 1-58234-623-2 (hardcover)
1. Fort Yukon School (Fort Yukon, Alaska)—Basketball—History.
2. Fort Yukon Eagles (Basketball team)—History. 3. Basketball—Alaska—Fort Yukon—History. 4. Basketball—Tournaments—Alaska—History. 5. Basketball players—Alaska—Biography. 6. Fort Yukon (Alaska)—History. I. Title.

GV885.72. A4D67 2006
796.323'62097986—DC22
2005025430

First published in the United States by Bloomsbury in 2006
This paperback edition published in 2007

Paperback ISBN-10: 1-59691-115-8
ISBN-13: 978-1-59691-115-4

3 5 7 9 10 8 6 4

Typeset by Palimpsest Book Production Limited, Grangemouth,
Stirlingshire, Scotland
Printed in the United States of America by Quebecor World Fairfield

CONTENTS

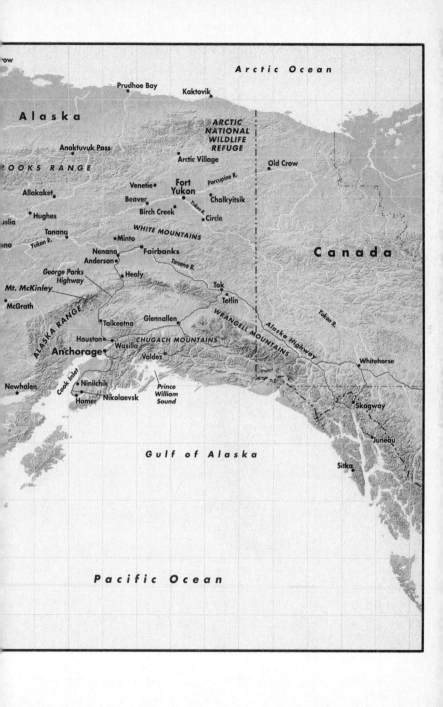

FORT YUKON BOYS BASKETBALL TEAM

Johnny Adams
Josh Cadzow
Aaron Carroll
Derek Carroll
Zach Carroll
Chris Engler
Tim Fields

Wade Fields
Bruce James
Justin James
Wes James
Kyle Joseph
Matt Shewfelt
Tim Woods

PEOPLE OF FORT YUKON

Adlai Alexander (Village Chief)
Dacho Alexander (Vocational Education instructor)
Dave Bridges (Boys basketball coach)
Diane Bridges (Dave's wife)
Cheryl Cadzow (Girls basketball coach)
Earl Cadzow (Cheryl's husband)
Clifton Cadzow (Josh's father)
Jay Cadzow (Earl's and Clifton's brother)
Mandy Cadzow (Girls basketball team star, Cheryl's daughter)
Jerry Carroll (Zach's and Derek's father)
Georgie Engler (School secretary, Chris's mother)
Willie Fields (Tim's father)
Delbert "Doc" Lantz (School principal)
Deb McCarty (Clinic director, Aaron Carroll's aunt)
Brian Rozell (Teacher)
Paul Shewfelt (Matt's uncle)
Jack Shewfelt (Matt's father)
Ryan Shewfelt (Matt's brother)
John Shewfelt (Matt's brother)
Gina Shewfelt (Matt's sister)
Anthony Shewfelt (Paul's son)
"Trader Dan" Teague (Storekeeper)

PROLOGUE
Spring 2004

THE BOY STANDS alone by the door of the cabin, in the radiant warmth of the bright Arctic sun. Strewn in the mud at his feet are the heads of a half-dozen mallards, their eyes gazing skyward, their scalps slick with blood, their necks hacked clean through.

He's been at it an hour now, at a small makeshift table, plucking and gutting and wielding his blade in the sharp April light. His cousins, the young ones, are heaving a ball at the hoop by the road. The backboard is battered, the rim bent and twisted. The torn netting flaps in the afternoon breeze.

From within the log walls of the cabin comes music—singing, a bass line, the thumping of drums. His father's old music. Hard rock. The boy's white high-topped Reeboks, spattered with offal, keep time with the rhythm as he slices the meat.

A jersey hangs loose from his thin, bony shoulders. The name on the back is a name the boy worships. Iverson. Number 3. "The Answer" is what they call Iverson, and sometimes, when he's sleeping, the boy imagines that he is the Answer himself. The crossover dribble, the lookaway feed, the thunderous roar of an NBA crowd—they belong to the boy, in the night, in his dreams.

But then he awakes, and he's still here, in the village, his People around him but nobody else, not one human soul for as far as the eye can see, and the eye can see so very far out here on the Flats.

Now, the Elders would differ. There are souls everywhere, say the old men and women, and not just the souls of the People alone. In the stands of white spruce and willow that circle the village. In the silvery shoals of the Porcupine River. Up the snow-quilted ridges that rise to the west, where the lynx and the fox and the wolf roam the woods. To the north, on the plains where the caribou graze by the dozens of thousands and the killing is good when the migration begins. And down there, to the south, where the pond-speckled Flats are laid out like a rug to the gleaming horizon, to the ice-packed foothills of the sparkling White Mountains.

There are souls all around, say the Elders. There are Spirits. In the earth, in the air, in the blood that still runs through the veins of the People.

The boy wants so much to believe them, to know that it's true. But it's hard to hear tales of the ancients on foot, with their sleds and their spears and their tents on their backs, braving sixty-below in the dead of the winter, bringing down bears with their wits and their hands. It's hard for the boy to hear stories like those, then to look at the men of the village today. There are some who still run their traplines the time-honored way, tracing the trails of their fathers through silent white forests with trained teams of huskies and hand-fashioned sleds. But the rest of the tribe, those who still call themselves woodsmen, saddle sleek snow-machines powered by NASCAR-grade engines, fiberglass beasts that blast over the ice at the speed of a Lexus.

The boy thinks of the stars and the wind that showed the way home when the Elders were young, then he looks at these men—the friends of his father—with their GPS bearings and satellite cell phones with signals that slice through the worst winter storm, and he asks himself: Where are the Spirits in any of this? He asks it while watching the men in the village who no longer run traplines at all, who no longer hunt moose in the fall or net salmon come summer. He looks at the husbands and fathers and brothers with pints in their pockets and dope on their breath, slumped on the stoops of their worn, weathered shacks. He can feel their surrender, soaked in whiskey and weed. He can feel their confusion, one foot in the old world, the world of the Elders, and one foot in the new, the world of the white man, with food wrapped in plastic, and color TVs, and lawyers and judges and government checks.

Trapped. That's the sense the boy sees has enveloped his People.

Trapped like a wolverine locked in the jaws of a number two set, sinking its teeth through its own flesh and sinew in its rage to get free. There is nothing, they say, like a trapped wolverine, thrashing the limbs off the trees that surround it, shrieking in pain and at the loss of its freedom. But there's no breaking free. And it finally tires, slumping down in the snow, exhausted, defeated, numb, nearly dead.

The boy looks around at the men and the women and too many children his own age and younger who drink themselves witless, who lash out in anguish at their friends, at themselves. He can feel it, the fog of that pain and despair. But he keeps his eyes down, moves ahead, does his work, splits the wood for the drum stove that warms this small cabin, heats a snack for himself when he gets home from school, trims the meat that his father and brothers will share when they come home tonight. And he doesn't waste time on thoughts of the future, of where all this will lead. He's seen what such thoughts have done to his brother John, who's consumed by an anger that eats him alive. John watches the people in charge of this village, the dopeheads and addicts scattered among them, who forsake their neighbors for their own narrow needs. John knows who they are, how they scheme to hold on to their slivers of power, how they funnel the money that flows in from outside, and how some like to spend it, on cocaine and grass hidden in freight on the airplanes that fly up each morning from Fairbanks.

John knows who's selling and buying, for how much and how often. He knows because he did his share of all that, back before he found Christ. Thank god for Jesus, says John, and thank god for the music, the one thing John clings to that offers him hope. His band, Native Pride, has scored paying gigs as far south as Fairbanks, as far southeast as Dawson, as far downriver as Nulato, where the crowds at the dances raise their bottles and beer cans to these Fort Yukon boys with their guitars and drums and their covers of Creedence and the Doors and the Stones. John's got dreams of his own, of music school somewhere Outside, beyond Alaska, someplace like Juilliard, maybe. He's got a brochure from Juilliard, dog-eared from handling, stashed in a drawer in the back of the cabin he shares with his girlfriend, Samantha. But those dreams are on hold now—the music, a college, his notions of turning this village around. Because Samantha is pregnant. She found out just last month. She's due in December, so John's got to find cash-paying work, make the money he'll need to take care of this child. But cash-paying work is not easy to come by, not here in the village. Loading trash. Hauling sewage. Mopping the floors at the Fort Yukon School. This is the work that one finds in the village, and these jobs are taken. Moving to Fairbanks is always an option, but that would mean leaving this world for the world of the white man. It may come to that, as it has for so many. But for now John is staying.

The boy has watched what the lostness is doing to John. He's watched what it's doing to Ryan as well, the oldest of all of them, the number one son. There was a time, not long ago, when Ryan was the pride of the village, the heart and the soul of the Fort Yukon Eagles. He could run like the wind, scored like a machine, outrebounded boys who were half a foot taller. But those days are gone, and now Ryan is just like so many in this town—an ex-player who lives for the night pickup games at the gym, still running the court like the star he once was. And when the gym's empty, he sits on a stoop like the others, or holes up in his cabin, stoned and wet-eyed, like them. Like them, he sometimes turns dark when the liquor takes hold, punching out at whatever might get in his way. Just this past Friday night someone in the village attacked the school's windows, shattering forty-two of the custom-made, double-paned, winterproof sheets of glass. Word is repairs will run thirty-five thousand dollars, more than most villagers make in four years. The town's three-man police force has been out all morning, knocking on doors, taking notes, asking questions. In a town of six hundred, it's not hard to find answers. News travels fast, door to door, phone to phone. The word by this morning was the cops in their red SUV were looking for Ryan, among others.

The boy hasn't seen Ryan since yesterday evening. He hasn't seen anyone since he woke up today. His father took off before dawn with his buddy, Mike Peter, out to one of Mike's duck blinds upriver, toward Circle. The shooting was good, and so was the drinking, by the sound of the laughter and man-to-man cursing as the two friends dropped off their kill sometime late this morning, while the boy was still curled in his bed.

He's not sure where they are now, his old man and Mike. Soon half the homes in the village will be empty and padlocked, the People moving upstream to their riverside fish camps, where they'll sleep in their huts and their tents for the next five or six weeks, tending their fish wheels for salmon and grayling, slicing and cleaning and stringing their catch from lines hung between trees, the smoke from their smudge fires turning back the mosquitoes as they sit by the swift-flowing Yukon and tell jokes or share stories or just bask in the glow of the warm midnight sun.

There are some who go south, for the work down in Fairbanks, construction jobs mostly, filling their pockets with seasonal cash before autumn arrives and freezeup begins and the outside jobs stop as the white world moves indoors. August, September—that's when the People return from the city and come home from the fish camps to hunt moose for the winter, store their salmon in caches, haul from the forest wood that they'll saw, split and stack to the roofs of their cabins to keep themselves warm in the dark months to come.

That's the time of the year the boy lives for, the dark months, when the rivers freeze solid and the landscape turns white and the gym opens each evening and the practices start, then the season begins, and the school's ice-crusted parking lot fills Friday nights with snow-gos and pickups, and the gym's three rows of bleachers are jammed with the townspeople, some who chant Gwich'in, the tongue of the Tribe, and the boy leads his teammates out onto the floor in their blue satin warm-ups and their white Nike headbands, while the Tanana Wolves or the Minto Lakers or the Tok Wolverines warm up at the visitors' end of the court, and the radio play-by-play man, the boy's uncle Paul, sits at a rough wooden table broadcasting the game on a five-watt transmitter, beaming its signal out into the clear Arctic night, out over the Flats, into clusters of cabins in hamlets like Chalkyitsik and Birch Creek and Beaver, places that make Fort Yukon look like a city.

Last season was magic, the boy draining three-pointers, and John leading the feverish press with his lightning-quick hands, and the six-foot-two kid, Aaron Carroll, the sophomore, starting out clumsy, hardly able to run up the court without tripping. But by midseason Aaron was no longer stumbling, and by March the big kid was posting down low like a pro. No one expected the Eagles to do much, but something began clicking, and they started to roll. Then came the Regionals, which Fort Yukon had won five years in a row. No one gave them a chance to do it a sixth, not with a record of more losses than wins. But when the State Tournament opened in Anchorage, with eight Regional champions left in Alaska from the sixty-one Class 1A teams that started the season, the Eagles were among them, unranked but still kicking.

When they won their first game, edging the Noatak Lynx, the village took notice, some stepping outside to shoot guns in the air. And when they took out the Aniak Halfbreeds in the semis, the eight boys from Fort Yukon awoke the next morning to see their names in large print in the Anchorage papers, the first time a Fort Yukon team had made it that far since the school's fabled squad back in '76, the one the boy's uncle Paul played on.

They lost that night in the finals to Wainwright, from up north near Barrow, but even that loss could not dim the luster of what this team had achieved. Both the boy and his brother were named All-Tournament. The boy was named first team All-State, something no one from Fort Yukon had ever achieved. The runner-up trophy the team carried home to the village was the most elegant anyone there had ever laid eyes on.

That was all just last month. Now it's over for John, nothing ahead but those long hollow nights in the dead of the winter, when the boys' practice is finished, and the town's men take the floor in that small, dingy gym, running full court in work pants and T-shirts and ball caps turned backward, some still wearing their jackets and heavy snow boots, replaying the days when those white satin jerseys with royal blue numbers were theirs.

The rumors have already started again, as they do at the end of each season up here. Is Coach Bridges quitting, or will he be back? Like the young wide-eyed teachers who fly up each fall from Wisconsin or Texas, who find more than they bargained for here in the Arctic and fly back south for good when the school year is over, or turn tail even sooner than that, around Christmas, taking off without notice, leaving ungraded papers stacked high on a table, the dishes from their last meal still piled unwashed in the sink—just like a good teacher, a good basketball coach in the bush is a hard thing to find and even harder to count on for more than one year.

Every spring the rumor mill kicks in again. Will Coach Bridges be back? Coach Bridges does nothing to stem the confusion. Truth is he seems to enjoy it, to keep everyone guessing, wondering if this is the year he'll decide to retire. The seven seasons he's put in now are already more than any coach the town's had since that gym was first built back in '71, the only gymnasium the town of Fort Yukon has ever had.

The boy thinks of all this as he trims the plump meat in the warm April sun, meat that will become tonight's dinner, a pot of duck soup rich with juices and fat. He thinks of his brothers. His father. His teammates. The Elders. The coach. Most of all, he thinks of next season, when he'll be the captain, the senior they count on, the hopes of the village carried on his slim back.

The boy welcomes that burden. He wants it. He wishes the season was starting tomorrow.

The ball bounces toward him from the kids by the hoop. It rolls into the wet mess that has pooled at his feet. He sets down his knife, his hands dripping with blood, bends and picks up the ball and takes aim at the basket.

The shot bangs off the rim, caroms into the road. The kids scurry to chase it. The boy shrugs, picks up his knife, turns back to the meat, and his thoughts, and his dreams of the season that's just eight months away.

PART ONE
Preseason

ONE

Dave

THE FIRST OF November, almost a week since the Sox won the Series, and Dave Bridges still can't wipe that grin off his face. It's his birthday today, his fifty-first, but that's not why he's smiling. The door to his hutch of an office is festooned with photos of Pedro and Manny, of Damon and Schilling, the hugging and weeping that swept across Boston, the sweet taste of redemption that only someone who grew up in New England could possibly fathom, much less feel. They're showing highlights on ESPN, and Bridges is soaking it in, the sound muted on the little TV he keeps in a corner as he files a form for some outgoing freight.

He hears the faint drone of an approaching aircraft. The late-morning Wright Airlines flight up from Fairbanks. He grabs his work gloves and hunts for his hat. Winter won't be here for seven more weeks, but the temperature's already dipped below zero and the limbs of the spruce trees that circle the airstrip are thick with a coating of soft autumn snow.

Bridges zips up his Carhartts, all weathered and ragged and torn at both knees. His wife, Diane, shakes her head whenever she sees them, says they make him look like he's homeless, asks him why not buy new ones. Bridges just smiles. Why waste money on new overalls when these are just fine? They're warm, and they're sturdy, and who cares how they look? He knows it sounds corny, but his Carhartts are like a dependable friend, same as that beat-up Ford van parked out front, the junkheap he picked up for 450 bucks at a school district auction some five years ago. Sure, the thing looks like a wreck, dented and rusted, cracks in the windshield, a paint job the shade of a jar of cheap mustard. But it gets the job done, just like the Carhartts. And what Bridges likes best is there's not one thing phony about either of them.

A knock at the door, and an old man shuffles in. Bridges has never seen him before. He's Native, probably visiting family or friends in the village. The old man says he'd like a seat on that plane coming in, says he needs to get over to Birch Creek. He fishes a torn, wrinkled check from his coat pocket, hands it to Bridges and asks, "Is that enough?"

Bridges studies the worn piece of paper, a government check for seventy-five dollars. He adjusts his eyeglasses, touches his mustache with the tip of a finger, glances back at the man. He prefers not to hassle with two-party checks, but in this case he says it's okay. Something about the old man's eyes tells Bridges he can trust him. Not like the woman who pokes her head in the office a few seconds later. She's Native, too. Her breath smells of bourbon. She talks fast and too loud. She says she's left some packages on a bench in the terminal's front waiting room. Says she has to run uptown for a couple of minutes, asks Bridges to keep an eye on her stuff till she gets back. Bridges picks up his keys, says nothing to the woman, who leaves as abruptly as she appeared.

"A couple of minutes?" he says, shaking his head and pulling his office door shut. "Who is she kidding? Don't pee down *my* back and tell me it's raining."

He walks into the front room—the "lobby," as outsiders might call it, the tourists who show up every couple of weeks, often doing no more than step out onto the ice of the runway to pose for each other, snapping some photos to prove they were actually here, above the honest-to-god Arctic Circle, then hurrying back to their seats on the plane, huffing and rubbing their hands to get warm. The more daring among them might actually climb off until the next flight, make their way into the village, ask where they can get a hot cup of coffee and learn that there's no place in Fort Yukon that sells coffee like that, no place that sells anything hot to drink or to eat besides Cheryl's Café, which is down toward the river. But good luck finding Cheryl's unless someone shows you the way, past the school and the town's old Episcopal church, through the woods, up a couple of snowmachine trails, beyond Kevin Solomon's place with its yard full of dogs and its outhouse a couple of steps from the door. Take a left just past Kevin's, where the trail bends toward the banks of the Yukon, another hard left and you're there, at the green clapboard house with a satellite dish the size of a Volkswagen perched on its roof. Cheryl will fry you a burger on her countertop grill—the same plug-in kind they sell on TV—or she'll fix you some chicken fingers and fries. She's got cold cans of soda she keeps in the fridge. You can sit at your choice of two tables, unless Cheryl's kids are doing their homework at one. If your timing is right, her husband, Earl, might spoon you a bowl of his homemade moose soup or give you a piece of some dried caribou. And, yes, she has coffee, though it's not on the menu.

The old man takes a seat in a hard straight-back chair by the window, scanning the gray late-morning sky for that incoming plane. Another man slumps on a bench by the door. His eyes are shut, his jaw stubbled, unshaven, his hair dirty and matted, his coat held together by swaths of duct tape. He hears Bridges walk into the room, turns his head toward the sound. He grunts, gathers his thoughts. His tongue is heavy, his words slurred by liquor.

"What . . . time . . . does the plane . . . leave for . . . Chalkyitsik?"

"Kenny," says Bridges, "I've told you three times now. It doesn't get here till one thirty. It won't leave till about one forty-five. And if you're not sobered up by then, you ain't getting on it."

The man's chin drops back down to his chest. Bridges has known Kenny for more than two decades, all the way back to when Bridges taught school in Chalkyitsik. Kenny was a nonstop drinker back then, and little has changed. He stunned Bridges one summer, showing up unannounced at the wedding of Bridges's big sister, in Maine. This was back in the pipeline boom days, when money was flowing like oil up here, and Kenny got a wild hair to surprise his friend Dave. No question it was a surprise. Kenny showed up with the best of intentions, but promptly got plastered. He was still three sheets to the wind when the weekend was over and Bridges was packing his truck for the drive back to Fairbanks. How could he not offer Kenny a lift? They didn't get far, though, before Bridges could see that this just wouldn't work. Kenny couldn't stop drinking, and when he drank, more often than not it turned ugly. Bridges finally dropped him off on the roadside just past Montreal.

To this day he's not sure exactly how Kenny got home. He figures he must've just stuck out his thumb till he made it clear across Canada to Whitehorse, then up the Alaska Highway to Fairbanks, some 3,500 road miles in all. Then the last leg, of course, as always, by air, with a stop in Fort Yukon, then on to Chalkyitsik. However he did it, Kenny's still here some twenty years later, still drinking, still flying, still finding his way home.

Kenny turns to the old man, asks if he'd give him a dollar for a drink from the soda machine. The old man looks at Kenny, turns and gazes back out the window. The old man is Native, like Kenny, but that's where the bond ends. It's Natives like Kenny who give the old man a bad name. In the eyes of the white people living downstate—not all the whites, certainly, but more than a few—those sad, sorry drunks stumbling out of the bars on Two Street in Fairbanks or Fourth Avenue in Anchorage, passing out on park benches, panhandling passersby for spare change or a cigarette, they're all just alike. Savages. Hopeless. Better off back in their villages where they belong.

The old man wears a ball cap with the legend NATIVE PRIDE stitched on the crown. Eskimos, Athabascans, Yupiks, Aleuts—Natives all over Alaska wear those words on their shirts and their hats and their jackets. For some, the words mean very little. For others, like the old man, they are holy. They're righteous. And they're slandered each time a Native man is arrested for beating his wife. Or the wife goes to prison for knifing her husband. Or someone like Kenny shows up like this.

Bridges stops for a second to check his geraniums. They're under a grow light, on a table set up by the door to the bathroom—two rows of clay pots aligned like sentries. Come next May they'll be ready to put in the ground, along with the cabbage and carrots and onions, and nasturtiums and marigolds, impatiens and snapdragons and whatever else Bridges might find a good deal on at the greenhouse sales they throw every April in Fairbanks. The small yard surrounding his cabin, just up the road from the airport, is bare at the moment, bone-white with its blanket of snow. By the end of the winter that blanket will be close to four feet deep, maybe five. Then, come late spring, the melt will begin, the ice in the river will break, the sounds of its bucking and heaving resounding like dynamite throughout the village, and Bridges's front yard will explode with the colors and blossoms and tendrils of spring.

His bees will arrive about that same time, the two boxes he orders each year from a dealer in Fairbanks, who buys them himself from a bee farm in California. They come about five thousand bees per container, each container roughly the size of a shoebox. It's like Christmas for Bridges, the day those boxes show up. He loves the exquisite ritual of it all, preparing the two hives he keeps in his yard, each with its broad wooden platform and fitted tin top and interior network of brood rooms and frames. He loves fishing out the lone queen in each of those boxes, each queen encased in a small plastic bulb. He soaks the queens down so they won't fly away, then places each one into her hive, where the other bees follow—the workers and drones. Then he sets up a chair just outside his back door, where he sits every day after work, through the spring and the summer, mesmerized by the show. Who needs TV, he asks, when you've got something like this? The worker bees hovering over the garden, floating off toward the blossoms in the shade of the forest, feeding on willow and lupine and the purple-red fireweed that bursts up from the ground in the warm July sun. And the drones, coming and going with nothing to do but have sex with the queen. He never gets tired of watching the bees flying back to their hives so laden with pollen and nectar they can hardly stay airborne, banging smack into the fronts of their boxes, where they fall to the platforms by the dozens, stunned for a moment, then stand and stagger into their hives like drunks coming home from an overnight binge.

Some of his neighbors think Bridges is nutty, Old Dave sitting out there for hours just watching his bees. But nobody laughs when the honey starts flowing, sometime around August. It's all Bridges can do to find enough jars to keep up with the syrup oozing out of those frames. One season he jarred nineteen gallons. Nineteen gallons from only two hives. He's got friends back in Maine who refuse to believe it. But that's how everything is up here in the Arctic. So extreme. Everyone knows how cold it can get this far north—the record low for the village is seventy-five below zero. But what most people don't know is how hot it can get in the summer. The highest temperature ever recorded in the state of Alaska was right here in Fort Yukon, in August of 1915, when the thermometer hit one hundred degrees on the nose. A neat trivia fact Dave will sometimes lay on visitors is that Hawaii's record high temperature is the same as Alaska's—one hundred degrees.

The flow of honey he gets at the end of bee season is just another example, Dave says, of the climatic extremes up here. Think about it, he says. Bees work and they mate in the day, when there's sunlight. Well, there's always sunlight in the summer up here, twenty-four hours a day in mid-June, so the bees just keep going and going, breeding and feeding all day long, every day. At the end of August it reaches its peak. The honey flow is insane, and so is the bees' birthrate. By the first frost of September those ten thousand insects Dave began with in April have become fifty thousand.

The sad part is having to kill them all after that first frost sets in. They'd eat all the honey if he let them remain. Besides, there's no way they could live through a Fort Yukon winter. So come each September Bridges puts on his sweatpants and netting and gloves, and he smokes down the hives. Then he pulls out each frame, thick with thousands of bees, sprays them down with a mixture of water and sugar so they can't fly away, then scrapes them into a large tub of water and soap, where they sink to the bottom and drown.

He can hear the naysayers now, the animal rights people, PETA and such, outraged at the slaughter of innocent bees. There's so much for those people to protest up here in Alaska. The netting of salmon. The shooting of bears. The trapping and skinning of beaver and mink. Just last week there were marchers in Anchorage dressed up like wolves, dispatched by a New England—headquartered group aroused by a government plan to thin the state's wolf packs by shooting the beasts from the air. What Bridges wants to know is how many of those marchers have had to hunt a moose to put food on their table. How many have seen what a lone wolf can do to a caribou herd or to a cow moose and her calf? Bridges has seen it. He's watched a wolf kill, and he'll tell you it's not pretty. No swelling strings, he says with a half smile. No strains of "Born Free." How many of those people, those protesters, understand life as it's lived in a place like the Arctic? That's what he'd like to know. How many could make it through one winter up here? Make it the way that the Natives do, the ones who still live the traditional way. Bridges has lived among the Athabascans for nearly three decades now, more than half his life, and his awe and respect for the skills and the knowledge the Elders pass on to the younger among them, those who still choose to live off the land—his respect for that process, far from fading with time, has continued to deepen with each passing year.

The plane's overhead now, circling the village to bank in from the north. Bridges hopes there's not too much freight aboard. He'd like to get this load done, then stop at the school to check in on Gavin. It's been a hell of a morning already with Gavin. The school office called around nine to tell him Gavin had run off again. This time it was his hat. A teacher told him to take it off. Gavin refused. She told him again, and next thing they knew he'd stormed out of the classroom, stormed out of the building altogether, throwing a few punches on the way. He didn't have time to grab his jacket. Five below zero and he was out there on the streets, wearing only a T-shirt.

So Dave had to go hunt him down. Again. How many times has he had to do this over the years? It's the worst in warm weather, when Gavin goes deep in the woods, hides for hours, sometimes all day. In the winter he never gets far. Especially wearing only a T-shirt. This morning Dave caught up to him just past the post office, on the side of the road. Drove him back to the airport, turned him loose in the garage on a busted snowmachine engine. That calmed Gavin down. They shared a bite to eat, then Dave drove him back up to the school.

No question Gavin's been more than a handful, for both Dave and Diane. The kid's strong for a twelve-year-old, and there's no telling when he'll explode. One minute everything's fine; the next he's putting his fist through a wall or, worse, through a window, which is not a small problem when it's forty below.

Dave and Diane had no idea it would be like this when they took Gavin in seven years ago. Diane's sister—Gavin's mother—couldn't handle him anymore. Dave and Diane were already raising five kids of their own—Diane's three children from her first marriage and Dave's two girls from his. Gavin turned out to be more work than all five put together. That's what fetal alcohol syndrome is like. Bridges had struggled with kids like this for years, back when he was teaching school in Dillingham and Venetie and Chalkyitsik, before he ever even got to Fort Yukon. Kids whose behavior was way out of bounds. Impulsive. Irrational. Violent. Kids who looked different, their eyes and their ears not aligned quite normally. There was something a little bit off with these children, but Bridges didn't know what, until a colleague came in one afternoon and handed him a book, told him he needed to read this. *The Broken Cord*, it was called. Bridges took the thing home and devoured it in one sitting. All he could see as he turned every page were the faces of all those kids he'd been teaching for all those years. FAS. That's what the book was about. It was about every one of those kids. It was about Gavin. The strange facial features weren't there for Gavin, but everything else fit the bill. The anger. The cursing. The horrible dramas that didn't make sense. Fetal alcohol effect—FAE is what the doctors called this milder form of the same awful condition, the result of a fetus soaked in the liquor and beer of a mother who drinks while she's pregnant.

By the time Dave drove Gavin back to the school, the boy was fine, back to normal. Doc, the principal, set him to work washing the library's windows, to atone for the punches Gavin had thrown at Doc during his tirade this morning. As Dave was leaving, Doc mentioned that the girls' basketball team raised a cool seven hundred dollars at their fund-raising auction last night. They plan to spend the money on new jerseys, Doc said, with each girl's name stitched on the back.

Dave can't believe it. New jerseys? His boys have been wearing the same jerseys for the past five seasons, and they'll be wearing them for at least the next five as well. It's the same ritual at the start of each winter. He passes each player a complete uniform: two jerseys, home and away, two pairs of shorts, one set of warm-up pants and a pullover. After the last game of the year he collects every piece, washes and folds it and puts it away till the next season begins. It cost five thousand dollars to buy fifteen of those uniforms five years ago, and every one of those dollars came out of somebody's pocket in town. Bridges can't count the number of bake sales and cakewalks, auctions and scrimmage games against the village men's team that his boys have to play every year in order to cover the gap between the school's budget for basketball and what it actually costs to put a team on the floor. There is no road to Fort Yukon, no road to any bush village, so every "away" game begins with a flight, which in Fort Yukon's case runs about $2,500 just to get the kids and the coaches—himself and whoever's in charge of the girls—down to Fairbanks and back. If they fly direct to another bush village, say Nulato, the price can climb as high as $8,000. Then there's the cost of the vans that they rent whenever they travel downstate—one for the boys' team and one for the girls'. Whenever they can, they sleep in the school where they're playing, pushing the desks to the side of a classroom and spreading their gear on the floor. If they're lucky, the host school will offer to feed them. If not, Dave stocks up on cases of Cup O'Soup and big jars of beef jerky, and Sam's Club–size pallets of pastries and juice. Once in a while they'll stop for a sit-down meal at an actual restaurant—an Applebee's, maybe—but most often they'll line up for dinner at Subway or, god forbid, Taco Bell. Dave hates Taco Bell, but the kids love it, so sometimes he relents.

When you add it all up—the airfare, the vans, the gas, the meals, the occasional motel room with fourteen boys squeezed into one suite and seven girls in another, the thirty bucks a pop for some new practice balls, the cost of flying a visiting team and a couple of refs up to the village for two or three home stands a season because who can afford to pay airfare to Fort Yukon?—when you total those numbers, it runs about $50,000 or so to field a boys' and girls' team for one season. The school budget covers less than half that amount. The remainder comes from the six hundred people who live in this village, some in the form of donations from the Tribal Council and the town government, and the rest from the villagers themselves, who are willing to pay, over and over again, five and ten bucks at a time, to put their kids out on the basketball court.

With all that, the idea of waste is appalling to Bridges. Putting names on new jerseys—meaning the jerseys will be good for only one year—is a waste, pure and simple. There was a time, not long ago, when waste was unheard of in this village. This tribe has always been one that used everything, threw nothing away. The caribou, for instance, whose antlers adorn every cabin in town, a symbol of the proud Gwich'in, the People of the River. The caribou's meat and organs are still eaten, of course. But once, so were the undigested greens in the animal's stomach. And the muscles in its jaw. And the tongue and the cheeks. And the soft glutinous fat found behind the caribou's eyes. The remains of the head were boiled down into soup. The hides were sewn into blankets and ground cloths and boots. Tools were fashioned from legbones. Rawhide rope—what the Gwich'in call *babiche*—was braided from strips of tanned caribou hides and laced into snowshoes and the webbing of sleds.

There are a few men in Fort Yukon—grandfathers, mostly, of the boys Bridges coaches—who still follow the caribou herds in the fall, as the migrating packs cross the plains to the north. But most of the villagers now depend on the canned and shrink-wrapped food and factory-sewn clothing and machine-fashioned tools that are sold at the Alaska Commercial store next to the school—the "AC," as it's called. You don't have to look farther than the AC, Bridges says, to see signs of the waste that's infected the village. Not too long ago the AC stopped bagging its customers' groceries in plastic, because the bags wound up strewn all over town, snagged in the branches of trees, blown by the breeze into the surrounding forest. Just like the empty beer cans and cigarette packages tossed in the snow, the bags were a sign of these don't-give-a-shit times. The village's Elders asked if the store might switch to paper, so at least some of that trash would be able with time to rot back into the landscape, unlike plastic, which stays there forever.

It's a little thing, sure, but to Bridges that trash is the tip of an iceberg, the sign of a throwaway culture creeping into this place. There are those fighting hard to cling to the old ways, taking care of the Elders and raising the children, sharing the wealth when a moose is brought down or a fish wheel is full. Bridges himself does his part at the airport, when those chartered Cherokees with their white, well-heeled hunters and guides stop through on their way back from the Brooks Range to the north. The holds of the planes will be heavy with five or six hundred pounds of raw moose or caribou meat. The head of the kill is typically all that these sportsmen are after, a trophy they can bring home to mount on their living room wall. They're happy to give Bridges the rest, which he unloads in large plastic bags, then calls Diane to spread the word around town. "Got meat," he tells her, and in a matter of minutes four-wheelers and pickups from all over the village have pulled up at the airstrip, dividing the bounty to take back to their homes.

That's the Gwich'in tradition, this interdependence, the reliance on one another, the sharing. This is what Bridges does his best to instill in the boys he coaches. He would never say such a thing out loud. He'd never be that overt. But that's the way his teams play, the way that he shapes them. Ask Bridges which kid's averaging how many points, and he couldn't tell you. Ask him how many wins he's amassed in the seven years he's been coaching, and he has no idea. The game's not about numbers, individual scores, not the way Bridges approaches it. It's about the beauty of five players moving as one, the feel for each other, the flow. Maybe that's why the idea of players' names stitched on jerseys bugs the hell out of him. Beyond being wasteful, it defies the idea of a team, of the whole being so much more than the mere sum of its parts.

But hey, he says, shaking it off, it's the girls' money to spend any way that they want. He's got enough to worry about with his boys. The first practice is less than four weeks away, and he has no idea who's coming out and who might be quitting—quitting basketball, quitting school alto-gether. Wade Fields, for example. The boys tell him they haven't seen Wade for a week now. It's not just that Wade hasn't shown up at school. They haven't seen him around town at all, have no idea where he is. Which is just like Wade, dropping out of sight with no signal. He's as quick as any player Bridges has ever coached, and that's saying a lot, as quick as the Fort Yukon teams always are. Wade would be penciled in right now as a starter, but there's no way Bridges can count on him even showing up from one day to the next. It's the same with a few of the others. If it wasn't for basketball, they wouldn't even be going to school anymore. And the fact that they're going doesn't mean that they do what's required. Some days even the best of his boys will just slump in the classroom, their hats pulled down over their eyes, ignoring the teacher, ignoring their work. And Bridges won't hear about it until it's too late, until the weekly grades are posted and he finds out three or four of his players aren't eligible for that weekend's games.

The plane has touched down now, a Cessna 208 loaded with close to a ton of mail and groceries Bridges has to unload and haul to the post office and AC. The pilot leaves the propeller turning, keeping the engine warm, as Bridges backs up his van and starts pulling off freight.

The old man climbs aboard, buckling himself in for the ten-minute trip to Birch Creek.

And inside the terminal, Kenny sleeps on, awaiting the next flight.

TWO

Matt

EVENING, AND THE sky over Fort Yukon is dancing. It shimmers with waves of diaphanous light. They billow and bend, celestial ribbons of green, blue and violet swirling in from the north, arcing over the village and whirling off toward the mountains that lie to the south.

Beyond those mountains, some 160 miles away, in the hills around Fairbanks, tourists from all over the planet pay top dollar to sit in hot tubs at various spas and gaze up at what the city's chamber of commerce calls "the greatest Northern Lights show in the world."

In Fort Yukon, the show's even better. The lights seem so close you could touch them. The Gwich'in believe that the lights are the spirits of the dead and departed. If you whistle, they say, the lights will come even closer.

But no one is whistling this evening. The village is silent. The school-house, the AC, the post office, the little Assembly of God chapel tucked into the trees—they're all darkened, shut down for the night. Trader Dan's place is still open, the bare bulb above his front steps casting a yellowish glow on his single gas pump. He'll be there till nine, selling spark plugs and candy bars, the warmth in his hut of a service station a welcome relief from the ten-below-zero darkness outside.

Smoke curls from the stovepipes of the homes along Third Street, Fort Yukon's main drag. Every five seconds a flash of white light sweeps over the squat snow-banked yards—the beam from the airport's rotating beacon a half mile away.

The front stoop of one of the homes is littered with freshly split fire-wood and crushed Budweiser cans. Inside the cabin, the heat is stifling.

A fire blazes orange-hot in the woodstove by the door. The floor is bare plywood. Damp clothing hangs on a line strung from the front of the room to the back. A pair of worn, beat-up sofas are shoved against one wall. A TV set sits by another. The door to the cabin's lone bedroom is open. So is the makeshift door to the bathroom—a curtain pulled back on a jerry-rigged shower stall and a toilet.

A boy busies himself in the kitchen. He's heating a couple of slices of pizza. He wears a loose T-shirt and low baggy jeans. A crystalline stud glimmers in the lobe of one ear. His close-cropped black hair sets off the tone of his skin, its delicate paleness like porcelain china.

There is much about the boy that seems delicate, almost frail: his thin shoulders and arms, his long bony fingers, even the feathery lashes that frame his dark eyes. There's a tenderness to his movements, a sensitivity. He's a caretaker, no question, keeping this place together, picking up the loose ends whenever he has to. "Mother Matt," that's what his brothers call him when he's washing their clothes or cooking them food or picking up the trash that they've left on the floor. Anything they don't do for themselves, they know Matt will take care of it.

But look past those lashes and into his eyes. There's the hint of fierceness, an edge, a warning that says don't push too hard. He's a kid who speaks phrases like "holy cow" and "cripes," all wide-eyed and innocent, and the next minute he'll sprinkle his sentences with "fuck" and "bad-ass" and "bitch." Some of it's the testosterone posing of any seventeen-year-old boy. Some of it's mimicking his two older brothers and dad. Some of it's simply holding his own in an Indian culture where the macho code still reigns supreme. Whatever the reason, he's got it, that edge that separates survivors from casualties, winners from losers—in the wild, on the streets, or inside a gym, on a basketball court.

They should be here any minute now, Ryan and John. It's almost time to play ball, to head across the road to the locked, darkened gym, and Ryan's the one with the keys. He's out in his shack-sized back cabin at the moment, playing video games with his sidekick, Simon. Two years ago they were lightning and thunder, little five-foot-three Simon at point guard, breaking the press and getting the ball to Ryan, who took care of the rest. Thirty, forty points a night was routine for Ryan. The

Anderson Grizzlies, the Nenana Lynx, the Tri-Valley Warriors—they were all fodder for number 33's dips, spins and insane fallaway jumpers.

The two have been back there a couple of hours now, smoking Ryan's dope and eating Matt's pizza. There's plenty left from the twenty or so pies Matt and the other seniors cooked up this afternoon in the school cafeteria and delivered around town to raise money for their class trip this spring. They'd love to go to Europe, all five of them, but they realize they might have to settle for Hawaii. It seems more Fort Yukon senior class trips wind up in Hawaii than anywhere else.

Matt pulls his food out of the oven and flips on the TV. The Nuggets are playing the T-Wolves. Carmelo against Kevin Garnett. His dad would love to watch this one, but he won't be home anytime soon. He was out at the wood yard all day, and now he and Billy Gjesdal have gone uptown someplace, spending what's left of their Permanent Fund Dividend checks. The checks aren't that large anymore—nine hundred dollars or so, less than half what they were only three years ago—but it's free money, it comes every October like clockwork, mailed by the state government to each and every resident of Alaska, and as long as the oil keeps flowing down that pipeline from Prudhoe Bay, the state will keep putting those checks in the mail.

And Matt's dad, Jack, will gladly keep spending them. People around town call him "One-Eyed Jack," because of that thing he does with his left eye, squeezing it shut when he's had a few too many. There's no one in the village knows how to party harder than Jack. There's no one the boys up at the wood yard or out on the fire line would rather work beside, either. He's funny as hell, all day long, can drink every one of them under the table, and he works his ass off, too. He'll tell you himself; that's one thing about the Gwich'in—when their back's to the wall, when there's no other choice, they will rise to the challenge and do what is needed. Even the worst drunks in town can still kill and clean a moose if absolutely necessary. They can cut wood, like Jack does, to put cash in their pockets. They can build a fish wheel out of birch limbs and spruce. And when somebody dies, they all head to the cemetery down near the river, every able-bodied man in the village, with pickaxes and shovels, working in shifts for two full days hacking a grave out of that concrete-hard permafrost ground, building a fitted pine coffin in the shop at the school, and finally, at the funeral itself, after the box is lowered into the hole, covering it with soil, one spade at a time, each man taking his turn.

God knows, Matt can work when he has to as well, chain-sawing firewood like his father, shoveling snow off the roofs of his neighbors' cabins, washing trucks in the summer, borrowing a four-wheeler from one of his friends and hauling trash to the dump at the north edge of town—the same chores his dad did when he was Matt's age. The only thing Matt doesn't do that his father did when he was a boy is pack water. He's heard Jack and his buddies talk about what a nightmare that was, lugging two five-gallon buckets hung from a yoke over their shoulders, hiking down to the river with an ax in one hand, chopping a hole in the two-foot-thick ice, filling the buckets and hauling them back, doing it over and over until the home's fifty-five-gallon barrel was filled. Matt can't imagine what that was like. It's hard to imagine that most of this village was doing it through the mid-1990s, when half the homes in Fort Yukon still had no indoor plumbing.

He found out today he'll be taking the SAT next month, just before Christmas. He's been thinking about going to college, maybe to the University of Alaska down in Fairbanks. That or small engine repair school. Like most of his friends, he loves nothing more than working on snowmachine engines. Wednesday and Friday nights the school's vo-tech center stays open for kids to come work on their machines. The "Snow-Go Mojo," that's what Dacho Alexander, the vo-tech instructor, calls it. Matt used to show up every night with his little Elan. He still lights up just talking about it. He had that thing souped. Welded some bad-ass exhaust pipes to the sides, spray-painted it metallic black, mounted some sweet boogie wheels on the base, spray-painted them gold—that machine was hot, no doubt, he says. It was no match for the neon-green Ski-Doos and bloodred Arctic Cats his friends blast around town or take out to the airport at night, gunning them 130 miles an hour down that ice-packed runway. Next to those two-and-a-half-ton monsters, Matt's two-hundred-pound Elan looked like a toy. But it got him where he needed to go, and in style, if he might say so. He sold it last summer, though, for $250, and now he has to bum rides from his friends. Or walk. Which is not that big a deal in a village that's just two miles long by three miles wide.

He hasn't given much thought till now to this college thing. He wouldn't mind going away, but it's not as if he's never been anywhere. Back in third grade he and a group of ten boys from Fairbanks flew down to San Diego for a youth boxing tournament. Matt lost both of his fights "to some fast-ass Mexican kids." But he got to see the zoo, which was cool. Just two years ago he and Chris Engler won a trip to Minneapolis with their science fair project from school. "How to Trap and Tan Martens." That was the title. They mounted some skins and fur on some poster board, even made a video. They sold eight hundred dollars' worth of pizzas to raise spending money and blew almost all of it on the first two floors of the Mall of America. They never even got to the other four levels. Matt had never seen anything like that place. It made the Bentley Mall in Fairbanks, with its ten stores or whatever, look pathetic.

The school's guidance counselor, who only shows up once a week or so—she lives in Fort Yukon but has to hop by lightplane to eight village schools sprinkled across the Yukon Flats, a region the size of New England—met with Matt not long ago and told him about a couple of colleges in Kansas that looked interesting. One is a Catholic school called St. Mary's that offers some good scholarship money. The other is a place called Haskell Indian Nations University, where Matt could go for free if he wanted. Fort Yukon's Tribal Council would pay his way. He checked out the Haskell Web site, and they've got a basketball team—NAIA Division II—which is nice, although Matt's not fooling himself about his chances of playing ball beyond high school. At five-ten and 145 pounds, he might make it as a walk-on, but that's about it.

The only Native Alaskan Matt's ever heard of who actually got a scholarship to play men's college basketball was an Eskimo kid named Butch Lincoln from Kotzebue, on the Chukchi coast, close to Russia. Lincoln played point guard in the mid-1990s for the University of Alaska in Anchorage. There's a girl playing right now for UA—Fairbanks—another Eskimo named Adrienne Taalak, from Nuiqsut, on the North

Slope. She's supposed to be UAF's best player this season, from what Matt's read in the papers. But that's about it. People in the Lower 48 talk about Carlos Boozer and Trajan Langdon as Alaskans who made it all the way to the NBA. But neither of them is Native. And they definitely did not play ball in the bush. Christ, says Matt, Boozer played for Juneau-Douglas, a school fifty times the size of Fort Yukon's. Langdon played for East Anchorage. About 2,300 kids go to East Anchorage, compared to the 32 who go to Fort Yukon.

Basketball aside, Matt's not sure he's ready to make the commitment it would take to stick it out in a place like Haskell—or at any college, for that matter. Forget the homesickness, which drives so many bush kids back to their villages when they try to go away for school or a job. Or culture shock, which is a huge issue for Natives from towns like Fort Yukon. None of that would be much of a problem for Matt. He's been around. He knows what the world's like beyond the village. Fairbanks is practically a second home to him, with his mother living there and all. And thanks to the basketball team's success the past several seasons, he's been able to take at least one trip a year down to Anchorage, for the State Tournament. No, what worries him about college is his tendency to, well, if he's frank about it, his tendency to, as he puts it, fuck off.

It's like this, he explains. When his friends aren't around, he truly gets into his schoolwork. He's got a 3-point-something GPA to prove it. There are stretches of time when he does nothing but go to school, come home, take care of the house—do the laundry and whatnot—walk uptown to watch old westerns on TV with his grandpa Stanley, then come back and finish his homework. And he's perfectly happy. But so many of the kids around here—most of them, actually—don't give a shit about school, he says. Hanging around them, he starts to not give a shit either.

That's one thing that really sucks about life here in Fort Yukon, Matt will tell you straight up. Whenever someone tries to do something worthwhile, to make something of themselves—and this is true for the grownups as well as the kids—it seems like everyone else tries to pull them back down. It's hard to explain, he says, but it's true. He's heard it compared to a bucket full of crabs. If one crab gets a claw-hold on the edge of the bucket and starts to pull itself out, the others will reach up and grab it and pull it back down. That's how it seems to be with so many things in Fort Yukon. People putting each other down, pissing on somebody else's good fortune, whatever. The basketball team seems to be about the only thing in town that's not polluted by that kind of crap. And even the basketball gets a little cloudy sometimes, with some of the older guys in the village resenting the success of the boys, claiming their teams were better than the kids playing today. Ryan and John get into that all the time with Matt. So does Jack. And Matt's uncle Paul, he's one of the worst, still living in the winter of '76, still replaying that state championship series against Nome.

Sometimes it's all Matt can do to keep from laughing out loud when he hears some of the older guys get going about their days on the court. They all brag about what bad-ass players they were. They talk about how they could almost dunk it. But what ever happened to them? Where are they now? His dad, his uncle, the Cadzow brothers, the Solomon boys. All those stars of the past. Even Matt's cousin Anthony, Paul's son, who made honorable mention All-State four seasons ago. What's he doing today? Raising dogs in the yard beside Paul's house and playing pickup ball at night. That's about it.

Some of those older guys truly had skills. Matt's seen it himself. Jerry Carroll, for instance. He was a Fort Yukon legend in the late 1970s, on the same team with Matt's dad. Jerry is still tearing it up today, in the city league down in Fairbanks. Just last winter he flew up with some of his friends to play a team of Fort Yukon men, including Ryan. Fort Yukon beat them the first night, in front of a packed house, and Ryan was talking some serious trash to Jerry after the game, giving him a very hard time. That was a mistake. The next night Jerry Carroll lit up the gym for sixty-three points, the most Matt's ever seen anyone score, anywhere, even on TV. Jerry torched the place, nailing threes from all over the floor. He would have scored even more if he hadn't blown out his ankle in the middle of the fourth quarter. His team still won by fifteen, which shut Ryan up good.

It seems like Ryan still hasn't gotten over the loss to Noorvik two winters ago, the climax of his senior year, the climax of his career. The team was 23–1 headed to the state tourney in Anchorage, ranked first in the state. Matt was a sophomore, thrilled just to be there. Fort Yukon won its opening-round game. Then, in the semifinals, they were up by a point with the clock ticking down when a Noorvik player, with Ryan draped over him, threw up a fourteen-foot leaner, a prayer, at the buzzer. Matt couldn't believe that fucking ball went in the basket. None of them could believe it. Ryan was crushed. Devastated. Back at the motel that night, somebody snuck a bottle of Smirnoff into the boys' room and Ryan pulled out some dope he'd brought with him, and he and some of the other guys on the team got blasted. They took turns in the bathroom, smoking the weed through an empty pop bottle stuffed with a couple of sheets of fabric softener to cover the smell. Old Dave never had a clue.

Of course Ryan knows every trick in the book about weed. No one in the village smokes more than he does. He doesn't hide it at all anymore. His favorite ball cap has a neon-green cannabis leaf plastered on the crown. He's got a huge black-light poster of the same leaf in his room. Jack's got no problem with that—herb is his substance of choice as well. As for Matt, he can take it or leave it. The first time he smoked was about three years ago, with his dad. Jack sat him down and told him he'd rather have Matt trying this stuff with him than with somebody else. His only warning was don't get addicted. And Matt hasn't. His approach to getting high is the same as to alcohol: He'll enjoy it if it's around, but he doesn't miss it when it's not. The fact is, he can think of better things to do with his money. The magic number in Fort Yukon is thirty—thirty bucks for a fifth of rum or whiskey or gin from one of the town's bootleggers; thirty bucks for a night of cash bingo up at the Elders' lodge; thirty bucks for a gram of marijuana from whoever's got some; and thirty bucks for a "black magic" pill to hide the dope in your system if you happen to work for the city or the Tribe and have to take a piss test the next day. A gram of grass gives you about three to five joints, says Matt, depending on how thick you roll them. The only way he and his friends can afford that kind of price tag is to pool what they've got in their pockets at any one time. Someone decides it's time for a party, and the shout will go up: "Any Gwich'in wanna pitch in?"

The only thing Matt's come close to getting hooked on is cigarettes. He started smoking two years ago, while his dad was in jail down in Fairbanks, doing nine months for blowing up Pierre Tremblay's car. That was not a good time for Matt. Shannon and Mike Hardy took him in, cared for him as if he were their own son. But they could do only so much, what with their own lives to live—both young, in their twenties, each with a nine-to-five job down at the Native Village offices. Matt was essentially on his own, and he fell through the floor. His grades went to shit. There was pot and some drinking. But most of all, there were cigarettes. He couldn't understand it. He'd never been drawn to chewing tobacco, which is like mother's milk to most Fort Yukon kids. Not long ago one of the teachers at the school took a head count of how many students in the high school chewed. Twenty-eight said that they did. Twenty-eight out of thirty-two kids, including the girls. Matt was one of the four who did not. So this cigarette thing felt confusing. Every time he lit up, he found himself thinking, "Why am I doing this?" But every time he was around cigarettes, he'd feel the urge and he'd light up again. Finally, last winter, just before basketball season, he decided to stop, just like that. It really wasn't too hard, he says. He kept himself busy, a few days went by, and one morning he said to himself, "Holy Cow, I haven't had a cigarette in a *week*!" And that was it. He was unhooked.

It bothers him watching so many little kids around town these days smoking and drinking and dipping chew. They're doing it younger and younger, it seems. Elementary school kids, for Christ's sake, says Matt. He watches these little boys, fourth and fifth graders, holding a lit cigarette, and it just looks so . . . *weird*.

That's one reason his dad sent Matt's kid sister Gina, the youngest, the only girl in the family, away to Mount Edgecumbe, the Native boarding school down in Sitka—to get her away from all this. She's a sophomore there now, and not doing so well. She says the Eskimo girls treat her like dirt, that they're making her life miserable. She's talking about moving back home to the Fort, maybe as soon as next month.

Girls. It's safe to say at this point that if Matt's got one addiction, that's it. His dad and his brothers call him "Matt the Cat," because of his way with the ladies. He's got an e-mail address book filled with the online names of girls he's met downriver on basketball trips. *Lady Wolf. Gwichin Injun. Sexy Native Biatch.* He's got pages of names. His own address is *AK_Baller*. Ask every guy on the team why they play basketball, Matt says, and they'll tell you the main reason is to meet girls. You'd feel the same way, he says, if you grew up in a place like Fort Yukon, where every girl in the village is a cousin, or sister, or half sister. He admits that so far all his e-mailing hasn't led to much more than just that—writing. The closest he came to actually hooking up with one of these girls was two seasons ago, at the State Tournament. Nulato had a pair of bad-ass sisters on its team, the Hildebrand girls. They could shoot the lights out, says Matt, and the younger one, Ashley, was his age, a sophomore. They hung out together a lot that week, he and Ashley, had a good time. That spring Matt burned through three or four eight-hundred-minute calling cards talking to her on the phone. That summer, John's band played at a dance down in Nulato, and Matt got John to take him along—passed him off as the sound man—so he could get to see Ashley. But it just didn't click, which was a letdown after the thrill of Anchorage and all those late-night phone calls. There's no way to explain it, Matt says with a shrug. It was just "different."

But that was more than a year ago. Now he's got his eye on a couple of girls on the Tanana team. He can't wait to see them when Fort Yukon plays there this season. The schedule's almost set. Coach Bridges and Doc have been making phone calls the past week or so, trying to fill the last empty slots on the calendar. They know the Eagles will be playing in late January in the Nenana Invitational Tournament—the "Little NIT," as it's called. And they're booked for the Tok Round-Robin in late February. They'll open the season at the Tri-Valley Tournament down in Healy, near Mount McKinley, followed by a long trip to the Kenai Peninsula for a rematch with that school of Russian kids who blew them away last year.

And, as always, they'll be playing downriver at Tanana. Matt heard through the grapevine that the Tanana boys were talking trash all summer about what hot shit they're going to be this season, how they're going to kick Fort Yukon's ass. They've got the sophomore Tyler Hyslop back, with that nasty hop-step of his and those dunks. And they've got the transfer from Galena, Norman Carlo, with his crazy-ass left-handed shot. Carlo can be deadly when he gets hot, but he doesn't know how to stop pulling the trigger, even when he's ice-cold. And his defense is sketchy at best, just like Tyler's.

That's one thing Matt's bought into in his three years of playing for Dave—that scoring is fun for the players and fans, but defense wins ball games. Period. And nothing feels better than winning. Matt's learned that from Dave as well. Defense and winning. That's what Fort Yukon has come to be known for since Old Dave took over seven seasons ago. That's what Matt and the guys love to call him—Old Dave. They tease him all the time, cracking Viagra jokes, rolling their eyes when Dave tells them for the umpteenth time to pull down the hoods on their jackets when they walk into a restaurant. There isn't one line Dave says that Matt hasn't heard a hundred times over the past three years. And now it's their last go-around together, Matt and Dave.

Matt's brothers and dad haven't let him forget that this is his last shot. And theirs. They remind him almost every day that this is the last chance a Shewfelt will have to win a state title for Fort Yukon. At least this generation of Shewfelts.

They want Matt to win it, no doubt. That shelf mounted on the wall above the TV set, sagging with basketball trophies and ribbons and plaques won over the years by Matt, John and Ryan—Jack would love to add a State Championship medal to that.

But at the same time, there's a chafing with all three of them—Matt's brothers and dad—a pang of resentment that any success Matt has will be his and not theirs. He knows it's not right, that his closest flesh and blood should feel that way. But he doesn't waste time thinking about it. He's always been about keeping his eyes on the business at hand. And right now that business is getting those lights turned on at the gym.

Whenever Ryan gets here with the keys.

THREE
Paul

THE DOGS SIT on top of their houses, each on the roof of its own straw-bedded box. Their silvery fur shines in the moonlight. The rhythmic puffs of their breathing hang frozen, suspended in the subzero air. The forest around them is dark. A large blackened pot simmers over an open wood fire, cooking a mixture of salmon and grease and food scraps from the garbage.

A truck pulls up, and the dogs begin barking. The driver shuts off the engine, steps out onto the snow. It crunches under his feet, like sand. He balances a paper bag in one hand, opens the door to his cabin with the other. The stink of the dog yard follows him in.

A heavy blanket is nailed over the doorframe inside, holding back what it can of the cold. The door's inside knob is caked with white ice. A few feet farther in, the cabin is toasty, the heat from the roaring wood-stove filling the room.

A guitar sits in a corner. And a harmonica. A radio by the window is playing a Hank Williams tune. A female voice comes on as the music fades out.

"*That was 'Honky Tonkin',*" the voice says with a halt. There's a clutch in her throat. A stammer.

"*This is KZPA, 900 AM, Fort Yukon. Don't forget, tomorrow night we'll be having an auction and raffle here at the station for Brewster Fields. There'll be good stuff to bid on, and Willie and Chester and Gordon will be here to play some songs, so come on over. It's for a good cause.*"

The music starts up again. Merle Haggard.

The man takes off his jacket and gloves, pulls a bottle of Riunite out of the bag. An identical bottle, drained empty, sits on the kitchen table, beside a fresh pack of Marlboro Lights and a glass tumbler.

He twists the top off the wine, pours some into the glass, lights a cigarette and takes a seat by the radio. The morning's newspaper sits on the floor by his chair. The sports section highlights an upcoming basketball tournament hosted by the University of Alaska in Fairbanks.

"Top of the World," the man says, reading the tournament's title aloud. He shakes his head, takes a deep drag and exhales through his nose.

"If that's the top of the world, we're *over* the top up here."

He takes another drag, smiles, sits back. His eyes are half lidded, clouded by wine and fatigue. He reaches for a side table, picks up a folder, pulls out a worn typewritten sheet of paper.

"Let me read you a poem I wrote," he says.

He sets down the glass, stubs out the cigarette, turns off the radio and begins.

> *I try not to hate you.*

He stops, adjusts himself in his seat, then resumes.

> *But when the freedom torch shines for you*
> *And flickers for me,*
> *Burning its way through the pages of history*
> *With free men writing with Eagles' feathers*
> *Dipped in blood*
> *Of a land so beautiful, so free*
> *From sea to shining sea,*
> *My heart beats the sound of an ancient war dance.*

A pause. A sip of wine.

> *You never looked up to God*
> *In whom you trust and printed on your green heart.*
> *Instead your eyes looked northward.*

Seven point two million beats later
The flow attempted to thaw
The icebox of the last frontier.

Another pause. Another sip.

When you encountered my ancestors,
Did they try to kill you? Or rob you?
Or feed you?
The God who took care of my grandfathers
Made you believe we never heard or knew of him.
This ignorant mockery turned miracle
Whom you named the "heathen."
Indian names cannot be pronounced
By forked tongues.

The howl of a dog outside the window.

Truth was not the serum riding on that famous sled
Down the Iditarod Trail
To the golden streets of Nome.
Nor is it with your sister, Juneau,
Who hides in the panhandle.
Nor with your brother, Fairbanks,
The golden heart of Alaska.

The howling stops.

Before you spoke, you coughed and cleared your throat.
Your words entered and destroyed the circle.
Your cough brought sickness and death.
Break your back when you slip and fall
On the oil . . .
That greased the gears . . .
Of assimilation.

He sets the folder aside. Lights a cigarette. Points out that "seven point two million" was the price the United States paid to buy Alaska from the Russians in 1867. Seward's Folly. The Iditarod dog race, he explains, commemorates an emergency shipment of diphtheria serum delivered to Nome by dogsled in 1925. He coughs, takes a slug of wine, notes that the year he was born, 1959, was the same year Alaska achieved statehood. Maybe that's why he's always been so involved, he says. Maybe that's why he's always been such an activist. Indians' rights. Tribal lands. The Native Question. Red Power. The Canoe Vote. Standing up to the man. Blocking the federal government's plan to build a dam on the Yukon, which would have put this village beneath thirty feet of fresh water. Opposing the oil deals that traded so much Native land and authority for the "mailbox money," as he puts it, on which most bush Alaskans now depend. Raising hell right this minute, as a member of Fort Yukon's city council, about the government's plans to drill in the Arctic National Wildlife Refuge (ANWR), in Fort Yukon's own back-yard. To hear him tell it, he's been on the front lines all along.

"Political Paul," he says, stubbing his cigarette butt in a used piece of foil. "That's what they call me."

His wife, Cindi, is out for the evening. So is his daughter, Natasha, who would have been a starter this year as a junior for the Fort Yukon Lady Eagles but found out last spring she was pregnant and dropped out of school. Her baby's due in a month, around Christmas.

His son, Anthony, isn't here either. He's up at the gym, playing ball. The dogs in the yard belong to Anthony. He takes them out almost every day, on the trails in the woods surrounding Fort Yukon, chasing his dream to someday race in the Yukon Quest. There's no way a lone musher raising his dogs in the woods by himself stands a chance anymore in the Iditarod, explains Paul. That's become a businessman's game, with corporate-bankrolled drivers and handlers breeding and training hundreds of huskies and malamutes full-time, all year round, in state-of-the-art kennel compounds. They look like Formula 1 racing teams when they arrive at a starting line in their one-piece jumpsuits plastered with sponsors' logos. That's what the Iditarod has become, says Paul, a big-money show for tourists and TV.

Which leaves the Yukon Quest as the last bastion of balls-to-the-wall dog mushing left in the world. It's a tougher race than the Iditarod. Colder. Darker. More severe. An average of two dogs die every year in the Quest. Frostbite and injuries for drivers and dogs alike—breaking through bad river ice, or snagging a tree root, or plunging off a mountainside cliff in the midwinter darkness, or being blown off the trail by ninety-mile-an-hour winds—are common. All of which simply increases the allure of this race for the hard-core traditionalists left in the world of dog mushing, the ones who still live by themselves in the bush and consider it a point of both honor and pride to do it the hard way, alone.

Natives from villages all over Alaska—Nenana, Two Rivers, Kotzebue, Eagle, Ninilchik—consider the Quest their baby, unlike the Iditarod, which few of them can afford to enter. The only Fort Yukon man to ever finish the Quest in the money was Jay Cadzow, who placed third in the 1993 race. His prize was a check for eight thousand dollars—hardly enough to pay for the kibbles he flew in that year to supplement his dogs' daily diet of fish and food scraps. If there's a first family of mushing in Fort Yukon, it's the Cadzows—Jay and his brothers, Clifton and Earl.

The Shewfelts, on the other hand—Paul, his brother Jack, and their sons, all except Anthony—know next to nothing about dogs or trapping or the Indian ways of the wild. Music and basketball, that's what the Shewfelts are known for. Ask Paul about this, and he points to his father, who was an Air Force staff sergeant stationed here in Fort Yukon in the mid-1950s, when the 709th ACW Squadron manned a radar base in the woods past the east end of town. It was Sergeant Dave Shewfelt's marriage to a young Gwich'in woman named Addie that produced Jack and Paul and six other children, all of whom grew up like so many kids produced in Fort Yukon during that time—as white as they were Indian. "Our dad was from Chicago," Paul says, laughing. "He didn't know a fucking *thing* about trapping or dogs, so how could he teach *us?*"

The base at Fort Yukon was part of the military's "White Alice" system, a network of radar stations posted across Alaska during the Cold War as a backup to the fabled DEW Line, built to detect a nuclear missile attack from the Soviet Union. The sweeping sixty-foot-high White

Alice radar shields rose out of the white tundra and forests throughout the Arctic like something out of a Godzilla movie, looming over villages like Nome and Galena and Fort Yukon until the turn of the 1990s, when the Soviet Union finally collapsed and the bases were shut down.

Paul gets up, pours another glass of wine. He's grown beefy in his forties, nowhere near the lean, lanky teenager he was back in high school. His hair, jet-black and gleaming, hung down between his shoulder blades back then. Now it's thinning, trimmed and combed like a sensible middle-aged man's. There are women his age in other villages today whose eyes still light up when Paul Shewfelt's name is mentioned. They remember the boy from high school, the dreamboat who used to play for Fort Yukon's basketball team.

"Yeah, the base," he says, smiling and settling back into his seat. He and his friends grew up playing ball with the GIs at the Air Force base gym, he says, years before the Fort Yukon School got its own basketball court. "The black guys," he says, "they taught us how to play. They couldn't believe how quick we were, just as fast as them. They also couldn't believe how the hell they wound up in fucking Fort Yukon. We used to tell them they must have done something seriously wrong to be stationed here."

He lights another cigarette.

"We used to give them a hard time. We'd say, 'All you guys are doing up here is making us a fucking nuclear *target*.' They had something called 'Air North' that would fly their supplies up. '*Scare* North,' that's what we called it. 'Three *Frights* a Day.'"

The blue smoke from his cigarette curls toward the ceiling. A stack of green MRE boxes—government-issued Meals Ready to Eat—is piled on the floor by the kitchen counter, left from his firefighting work this past summer. Half the men in Fort Yukon earned most of their income this year flying around rural Alaska from June to September, helping hundreds of firefighters brought up from the Lower 48 to battle the worst wildfires in the state's history. An uncanny season of thunderstorms and lightning strikes—as many as eight thousand strikes in one day—sparked blazes that burned close to seven million acres of Alaskan wilderness, an area the size of New Hampshire. It cost the state and

federal governments more than $106 million to combat the flames. That
included the fifteen to twenty dollars an hour paid to Native volunteers
from villages like Fort Yukon, who welcomed the work as a gift from
the gods. "You know what we say up here," Paul says, tapping his ash
into the foil. "Keep Alaska black and our pockets green."

He takes another sip of wine and gets back to the subject of the base.
There was a small movie house there when he was a kid, he recalls.
And a bar, where the soldiers were allowed to bring women in from the
village. One of the base trucks served as a bus, ferrying GI's and Fort
Yukon women back and forth from the village several times a day. Some
of the village's men would hit that bar as well, with more than a few
fistfights erupting at the sight of the Fort Yukon women making out
with these soldiers. "The 'Hug and Slug,'" says Paul, laughing. "That's
what we called that place."

More than a hundred GIs at a time were stationed at the base in its
heyday, including a young enlisted man from Texas named Alberto
Gonzales, who spent two years there in the mid-1970s before moving
on to the Air Force Academy. The front page of the newspaper lying at
Paul's feet features a story on newly reelected President George W. Bush,
who has just announced his nominee for U.S. attorney general: Alberto
Gonzales.

Paul cringes at the sight of George Bush's name. The war in
Afghanistan, the invasion of Baghdad, the federal government's plans to
drill in ANWR—it's all the same story to him, the same insatiable thirst
that brought the pipeline to Alaska thirty years ago.

"Why don't they just drop the pretense," he says, "put another star
on the flag, make Iraq the fifty-first state and start sucking the oil out
from under their sand like they've done it with us from under our snow?"

The way he sees it, the money that trickles down to Alaskans from
that pipeline oil—and Paul emphasizes it's now down to a virtual
trickle—has been as addictive as alcohol or cigarettes. And just as debil-
itating.

"I read about a laboratory experiment they did with some mice," he
says. "They dropped these mice into an aquarium tank filled with water.
The mice struggled like crazy to stay afloat before they finally started

to sink and the scientists pulled them out before they drowned. That was after about two minutes. The next day, the scientists put the mice in the water again. This time they started sinking after a minute and a half, and the scientists pulled them out again. The next day they started sinking after a minute. The next day, after thirty seconds.

"See what was happening? The mice *knew* they were going to be saved, so they stopped struggling as much.

"That," he says, stabbing the air with his cigarette, "is what the Permanent Fund Dividend does to people."

Yet Paul is happy to cash his own PFD check every year, as well as the additional money he receives thanks to ANCSA—the Alaska Native Claims Settlement Act—which pays every Native Alaskan an annual dividend stemming from the 1971 deal in which Alaska's various tribes settled for one billion dollars and forty million acres of wilderness from the federal government in exchange for signing over the rights for oil companies to drill and build pipelines on what had always been Native land. What resistance there was to the deal at that time came mostly from the Interior tribes of Alaska, from Athabascan Indians including the Gwich'in right here in Fort Yukon, who have always felt ignored and dismissed by the more visible and politically prominent Eskimos, who live out on the coast.

"We've never gotten along," Paul says of the Indians and Eskimos. They are two different peoples; the shorter, rounder Eskimos live off the bounty of the sea—whales and seals—and the taller, leaner Gwich'in roam the Interior's rivers and forests, hunting and trapping and fishing for salmon. The Gwich'in's bloodlines run south all the way to Arizona and New Mexico, where Navajo and Apache share the same Athabascan genes. The languages of Alaska's Indians and Eskimos are different. So are their customs. Nothing pisses off an Athabascan more than to travel somewhere outside the state and have people ask if they live in igloos and hunt polar bears. "They're talking about goddamn *Eskimos*," says Paul, "not about us."

There is more than a little resentment about the political advantages gained by the Eskimos through the historical course of Alaskan Natives' encounters with white men. The Eskimos, by virtue of living along the state's coastline, were, naturally, the first Natives encountered by the early white seafaring explorers—Russians in the 1700s. The Indians, on the other hand, lived in Interior forests and along rivers rimmed by the soaring snow-covered peaks and crags of such mountain ranges as the Brooks, the Kuskokwim, and most imposing of all, the Alaska Range, where Mount McKinley—Denali—touches the clouds. Those mountains, made even more forbidding by their year-round Arctic conditions, were a wall that kept most of the white world out of Alaska's Interior until well into the twentieth century.

"Most people still don't even know we exist," says Paul. "They've made most of their deals with the Eskimos."

It's true. The oil pumped down that pipeline comes from Prudhoe Bay, on the state's northernmost coast, where the Inuit Eskimos live. Those North Slope tribes and villages have become wealthier and more politically powerful over the past thirty years than any of the Interior communities. The segment of ANWR that is currently the focus of plans for new drilling lies along that same north Alaskan coast, nearer to Prudhoe Bay than to Interior Gwich'in villages like Fort Yukon. The caribou herds that migrate to ANWR's coastal plain every spring to give birth to their young begin their annual journey here in Gwich'in territory, to the south, and they return to the south every autumn. Those herds and the land they roam over have always meant more to the Gwich'in than they do to the Eskimos, who are mostly happy to sign it away. "There aren't any bowhead whales in ANWR," explains Paul.

To the eight thousand members of the Gwich'in Nation, extending from Alaska into Canada, the plains of ANWR represent the Tribe's last fading shreds of identity and autonomy. This is the land their ancestors roamed, the land they lived off to survive, the land that defines their religious beliefs, that defines who they are. It's that lifeline, that legacy, say the Indians opposed to this deal, that matters more than mere meat to put on the table or skins and fur to put on their backs. Yet there are many Gwich'in—most who have moved away from bush communities like Fort Yukon and Venetie and Arctic Village to the suburbs of Fairbanks and Anchorage, some who have never lived in the bush at all, a few who have never lived in Alaska but are counted as members of the tribe by their blood—who are eager to see this drilling begin.

"There are people in fucking South *Carolina* who get a vote on this," says Paul.

These people are happy to put some cash in their pockets in exchange for land that means nothing to them. Their votes, through tribal corporations set up by ANCSA, count as much as the votes of the Natives who still live up here in the wild, where those wells and pipelines and haul roads will be built. What the "wallpaper Indians," as the Natives opposed to this deal call their urbanized brethren, don't seem to understand or to care about is that whatever money they might get for however much oil is found in ANWR will mean nothing when that oil eventually runs out and the Gwich'in are left with even less of themselves and their land than they have now—which is already so little compared to what they had and who they were before the white man arrived, before their world became what some Natives today call "colonial Alaska."

"It's forty acres and a mule all over again," says Paul. "It's stealing Manhattan for a handful of beads."

If there's any inconsistency between his moral outrage and the fact that he cheats his neighbors whenever he can in terms of the firewood he cuts and delivers to their front yards ("wood fucking," he and his brother Jack and their pals call it with lighthearted glee), or that he did forty months in prison ten years ago for sexual assault after taking liberties with an unconscious woman who had passed out from drinking at a village house party, a woman who was Jack's girlfriend at the time— if he has any issues reconciling those facts with his sense of Native honor and pride, Paul doesn't show it.

He stands up, fishes a dusty cassette from a drawer and pops it into his stereo system. The tape is from the early 1970s. The band is called XIT. They were renegades, a group of fiery young New Mexicans— Navajo, Sioux, Pueblo, Cree—who funneled their political fury into guitars and amps, fusing the wail of a Stratocaster with traditional Native American music. Their albums had titles like *Plight of the Redman* and *Silent Warrior*. To young Natives coming of age across the continent at that time—young Natives like Paul—XIT was as big as the Beatles.

The beat of an Indian drum thumps out of the speakers, then a

Hendrix-like guitar riff and chanting. Paul's eyes well up as the song's words begin.

> *Oh Great Eagle, king of the sky,*
> *Lift our spirits and carry us high,*
> *Wings of strength that float along,*
> *Take away the weak and make us strong*
> *Make us strong, strong,*
> *Make us strong, strong.*

"That was our warm-up song," he says, pulling a box down from a shelf and taking out a small black-and-white photograph. He cradles the photo as if it's a crucifix. And now the shift is complete. He is there once again, at the apex of his life, twenty-eight years ago, when he was a starting forward for the Fort Yukon Eagles.

Eleven boys appear in the photo, standing and kneeling in the Fort Yukon gym. They wear tight jerseys and basketball shorts. Ten are Native, their ink-black hair spilling down past their shoulders. They could be warriors—Cherokee, Sioux or Cheyenne. They are fifteen, sixteen, seventeen years old. They are ageless. It's the winter of 1976 and their world is on fire. Flames of unrest are raging throughout the land. Indian uprisings. Drumbeats of protest. Marches on Washington. Natives in blue jeans and braids confronting FBI agents and soldiers with rifles. They've raided the prison at Alcatraz Island. Painted the Plymouth Rock red. Seized the Bureau of Indian Affairs headquarters in downtown D.C. Hearts have been buried at Wounded Knee—two Natives dead, one FBI agent shot down. The cry of Red Power resounds down the long Trail of Tears, across the Great Plains, up and over the ice and snow of Alaska into the heart of the Arctic, into Fort Yukon.

"It was our *time*, man," Paul says, tracing a finger over the photo. "We were the first ones, the first generation that didn't conform. We didn't buy into any of it. The values that were coming in with the oil. The money. The bullshit. We saw it for what it was, and we didn't buy it."

He points to the faces in the photo, one by one, who they were then and where they are now.

Norman Carroll, living upriver today, in the village of Circle, raising a family there.

David Solomon, living upriver as well, near Glenallen, where he's raising a family, too.

Willie Salmon, now in Chalkyitsik, whose brother Woodie was just elected to the state house of representatives.

Ricky Solomon, dead, from cancer.

Sonny Williams, dead, too, from pneumonia.

Warren Carroll, the best man at Paul's wedding. He still lives in Fort Yukon, still fishes with Paul every summer.

And the starting five:

Donald Carroll, who lives in Fort Yukon today with his wife and three kids.

Rick Hardy, who works with Trader Dan up at Dan's store.

Bobby Solomon, who works at the school as a part-time janitor.

Bob Halverson, the tall blond-haired center, the only six-footer, the only white kid on the team. His dad was Fort Yukon's chief of police at the time. He's long gone now, moved away with his family soon after graduation.

And finally, number 42, his hands at his side, his long shining hair parted straight down the middle, a sly, half-wicked smile on his face, like he's just stolen something and nobody knows.

"I was probably stoned," says Paul, putting the photograph down and reaching for something else in the box. It's a videotape of that season's state title series against the Nome Nanooks.

He pops the tape into the player, sits back down and stares at the screen, mesmerized, as if he's watching this game for the first time. The echoing shouts of the crowd in the packed Fort Yukon gym. The four cheerleaders leaping onto the floor during time-outs. The Fort Yukon boys' hair pulled back in tight ponytails, their movements slow and methodical, as archival as the black-and-white footage itself.

But they're efficient. Effective. Their passes are crisp. Their cuts are precise. They call out their plays and run them like disciplined soldiers.

Bobby Solomon swishes a jump shot from the left side of the key.

Shewfelt chases a loose ball into the corner and knocks down a left-handed set shot.

"That would have been a three if they had them back then," he says, his eyes glued to the screen.

This was the beginning, the dawn of basketball in the bush, and Paul Shewfelt was there. The signing of ANCSA in '71 prompted a wave of construction of new schools and gymnasiums in Native villages throughout the Arctic, most of which had neither till then. The gyms became de facto community centers—clean, well-lighted spaces where the villagers could gather in the darkness of winter to meet, share a meal, get warm, take showers, wash laundry. And, naturally, play basketball.

The game swept through the bush like those summer wildfires. From Point Hope, far up on the north Chukchi Sea, to Bethel, down in the southwestern delta, to Unalaska, out toward the tip of the Aleutians, everyone played. The grown men in their "Huff 'n Puff" leagues. The grown women as well. Even the Elders, shuffling across the hardwood in their new store-bought sneakers. And the teenagers, both the boys and the girls, suiting up in their school colors on Friday and Saturday nights to put their village's honor on the line against teams from other towns, other tribes. Eskimos. Yupiks. Tlingits. Aleuts. It became a phenomenon, these little bush hamlets with their high schools of thirty or forty kids, packing their gyms to the rafters with wild, cheering Natives wherever they played. It was, quite literally, in the cold dark perpetual night of the long Arctic winter, the only game in town.

It was a different game from the one that was played down around Anchorage and Fairbanks. In those cities and freshly hatched suburbs, high school basketball at the turn of the 1970s looked much like it did in Dubuque or Fargo or Saint Paul—a winter diversion played by teams of mostly white kids. It was just one among many pleasures and distractions in lives increasingly filled with pleasures and distractions. With the influx of oil by the middle of that decade, Alaska's only two true cities were suddenly growing as never before, shirking their rough frontier roots and becoming much like the rest of mainstream America, with new highways, subdivisions and shopping malls. For those urban and newly suburban Alaskans—tens of thousands of them transplants from the Lower 48 come to cash in on the pipeline bonanza—life was blooming, booming, unfolding with promise and possibility as never before. Not even the gold-rush days were this heady.

But up in the bush, something was slipping away. Natives throughout the Arctic were torn between who they had once been and what they were now becoming, between where they could once turn to feel pride and connection and where they now felt little but lostness and shame. They were fragmenting—as families, communities, even as individuals. Amid such upheaval, this simple game, basketball, gave them something to turn to to pull them together, and they threw themselves into it with a passion close to religious.

It was that way in Fort Yukon. When the school's gym was built in 1971, a tile floor was laid over plywood—it's been replaced with hard rubber since then—three rows of bleachers were squeezed against one side wall and two locker rooms were constructed, with two showers apiece, one room for the boys and one for the girls. The school fielded its first team that winter, led by juniors Earl Cadzow and David Englishoe and twelfth grader Johnny Wallis. Their first road trip was to Tanana. Earl's dad and a friend flew them down in a pair of Cessna 207s. They played four games that weekend, men from both villages mixing in with the boys. Fort Yukon's coach, a teacher named Frank Adreon, suited up for one of the games.

The Fort Yukon kids had strong lungs and legs, thanks to their god-given genes and, for the ones whose families still lived the traditional way, winters of snowshoeing and running traplines and dogs. They were short—five foot six and five foot seven—but they ran like flushed rabbits and, with practice, they learned to shoot basketballs as well as they shot rifles. When they ventured downstate over the next several years—to Talkeetna and Glennallen, to Tetlin and Tok—they held their own against schools much larger than theirs. The only out-and-out rout in those early years came at the hands of Valdez, which had swelled overnight from a small fishing village of a few hundred people into a port city of ten thousand, most of whom had come to finish the pipeline that would soon pour its oil into the holds of the tankers parked there in Prince William Sound. Those mechanics and welders, roughnecks and truckers, up from Iowa and Kansas, Missouri and Texas, brought their wives and their tall corn-fed children along with them. The Fort Yukon kids, as fast as they were, stood no chance against those tall white Valdez boys, who could actually dunk.

Paul ducks into the bedroom, returns with a blue-and-white, leather-sleeved Fort Yukon letter jacket. The name CINDI is scrawled on one shoulder in blue ballpoint pen.

"She's still my wife," he says, setting the jacket down and refilling his glass. He wrote a poem about that jacket, he says. "I used to *shoplift* in that jacket." He laughs.

No question, says Paul, those years were the best of his life. The coach by the time Paul was a senior was a teacher from L.A. whose wife, it was said, had once dated Elvis. "The King put the *boot* to her," notes Paul, with a cackle. "That was her claim to fame."

The road trips, as Paul recalls them, were one long chance to play ball and party—not necessarily in that order. One weekend, he says, the team flew down to play Healy, southwest of Fairbanks, near Mount McKinley.

"The first night, just before the game, me and Bobby and David went out to, um, get some air. I had a joint in my pocket. We were about to fire it up when Ernst—Bob Ernst, the assistant coach—came out. 'Holy *shit!*' I said. 'There's *Ernst!*' We put it away just in time. Never did light it.

"So we go out and play these fucking coal miners' kids. *Big* kids. Six-six. Six-seven. All white guys. And we beat them. Beat them bad.

"The next night, just before the game, coach comes over, kind of winks and says, 'Why don't you guys go take a walk?'

"We couldn't fucking believe it. He thought we had gotten stoned the night before, and he wanted us to do it *again*.

"Which we did."

Pause.

"And we beat them again."

He smiles, shakes his head, bemoans the fact that it's not like that anymore.

"Shit, we had so much *fun*," he says. "We put on a *show*. When we played, it was an *event*. The basketball games *and* the parties afterward. Home games, we'd have a dance both nights, Friday and Saturday, and the whole town would come. Other villages couldn't wait for their teams to come play Fort Yukon, so they could come here and party."

He gets up, shuts off the tape. He knows how it ends. Fort Yukon wins the game. Nome wins the series.

"It's not like it was back then anymore," he continues. "There's no dances because they're afraid there'll be trouble. They're afraid something bad might happen. They're worried about liability. And they say it would cost too much."

He takes a deep drag on his cigarette, shakes his head.

"It sucks. I hate it. They don't give the kids a chance to have fun anymore, to be *young*."

He pours the last of the wine.

"And the way they play now, this apeshit run-up-and-down-the-court basketball, it's so crazy, so ragtag. They never run any offensive plays at all, not like we did."

He picks up the guitar, slides the harmonica into a neck holder, slips the brace over his head and sits back in his chair.

"People say how great it is that Fort Yukon's gone to the State Tournament the past six years in a row," he says.

He adjusts the harmonica.

"Shit, they haven't *won* it *once*. They should have won at least a couple of times by now."

He clears his throat, fingers the fretboard, shuts his eyes and begins strumming two chords. B-minor and E. Back and forth. Slowly. Mournfully.

He starts to sing, his voice plaintive, yearning, achingly sweet.

> *Think I'll pack it in*
> *And buy a pickup.*
> *Take it down to L.A.*
> *Find a place to call my own*
> *And try to fix up.*
> *Start a brand new day.*

The wine bottle is empty.

> *The woman I'm thinking of,*
> *She loved me all up,*
> *But I'm so down today.*
> *She's so fine, she's in my mind,*
> *I hear her calling.*

The cigarettes are gone.

> *See the lonely boy,*
> *Out on the weekend,*
> *Trying to make it pay.*
> *Can't relate to joy,*
> *He tries to speak*
> *And can't begin to say.*

The dogs begin howling again.

FOUR

First Practice

THE FORT YUKON gym should have burned to the ground ten years ago, the night the school went up in blazes. Just about everyone in the village turned out that midwinter evening, pulled from their beds by the sounds of shouting and phones ringing and frantic knocking on doors, by the sight of flames licking into the night and the smell of burning roof tar. There had already been one fire in the village that week, a blaze that destroyed Denise James's house, killing her three-year-old son, Chance. And now this.

They did all they could, the men of the village, aiming the volunteer fire department's canvas hoses at the flames, as the subzero wind whipping in from the north turned the spray from the water to ice. The heat was ungodly. The school's iron flagpole out by the parking lot softened and sagged in the face of the flames, drooping till it bent toward the ground.

The fire began at one in the morning. By four they knew it couldn't be stopped. The question at that point was whether the blaze might spread to the gym right next door. More than a few looking on hoped that it would, especially those who played basketball. Twenty-four years they'd been running the court in that gym, feeling the floor buckle and heave, watching the walls crumble and the ceiling sag with the passage of time. No way was the state going to build them a new one, not with the budget cuts schools were now facing each year, not with the oil money dwindling to nothing at all. The only way the state would even consider building Fort Yukon a new gym was if the old one were destroyed in some way. Say, by a fire.

It didn't happen. By the time the fire marshals flew up from Fairbanks late that afternoon, the flames were under control. The school was a total loss, but the gym was untouched. A year later Fort Yukon's kids were seated in brand-new classrooms, eating their lunch in a new cafeteria. But the PE classes were still taught in the same decrepit building.

They're in there this evening, four days past Thanksgiving—Aaron and Derek and Tim Woods, lounging on the bleachers, watching the girls finish their first night of practice, waiting their own turn to begin this new season.

There's not much to watch. Only three girls are out there, along with their coach, Cheryl Cadzow, the four of them running a ragged game of two-on-two. Cheryl's more a den mother than a coach. Her daughter, Mandy, is the girls' star, which is the only reason Cheryl is doing this. She doesn't know a lot about basketball, but she's organized, she gets the girls to their games on time, and she's willing to act as their shepherd through the course of those long drawn-out road trips. There aren't a lot of volunteers in the village for such a position. There are just seven girls on the team.

The boys look immensely bored. They're wearing their street clothes—heavy jackets, hooded sweatshirts, ball caps, baggy jeans, sneakers. Beneath the clothing, they're wearing their practice gear—shorts, jerseys, socks, jocks. The gym's locker room is next to useless, with only two showers, one of which runs just cold water, the other which runs nothing at all.

Several of the ceiling's caged metal light fixtures hang loose, dangling, dangerously close to falling thirty feet to the floor below. A trapeze is roped to the ceiling near the far wall. No one remembers it being used. The same with the rock-climbing wall in the corner. Word is some teachers with an Outward Bound bent put that stuff up about ten years ago. The teachers are long gone, and now the wall and trapeze are just something for the kids to heave balls at.

The gym's lone scoreboard is mounted on the wall across from the bleachers, directly above half-court. It tends to blink on and off during games, because of loose wiring. Sometimes it goes dark altogether, causing the refs to whistle time-out while one of the janitors or someone in the crowd jiggles the connections.

There's just room enough on that side of the gym for a player to stand between the wall and the sideline. The words to the Fort Yukon fight song are etched to the right of the scoreboard in large hand-drawn letters. None of the boys on the team knows that the words come from Paul Shewfelt's old cassette tape, the one by the band XIT. None of them has ever heard of a band called XIT. When they come out to warm up for home games, their song of choice is "Thunderstruck" by AC/DC, or anything at all by Disturbed, blasted at full volume on the score-keeper's sound system. That gets them pumped. Once in a while Paul will try playing some of that old shit, and the boys will look over at him like he's crazy, till he finally gets the point and puts their music back on.

Five on the dot, Dave comes through the door. A blast of icy night air trails him in. The sun, no more than a tangerine smudge on the southern horizon at this time of year, went down nearly three hours ago. It won't rise again until half past ten tomorrow morning. By the middle of next month, the village will have maybe two hours of daylight, if it can be called that. And the temperature will dip into the fifties—fifty-below.

Tonight's relatively warm—around zero. Dave's wearing his work parka over a ragged gray sweatsuit. He's got on a lush ear-flapped fur hat over his Red Sox ball cap. The fur is top-of-the-line marten—smoother, softer and more supple than the more commonly found beaver. In the fashion district of New York, they call marten "sable." No one in Fort Yukon could afford to buy a sable hat in Manhattan. But here, half the village wears marten headgear, sewn from the copper-toned furs that they've trapped for themselves. It took Diane three pelts to fashion this hat for Dave, including the tails sewn to the back—a Fort Yukon tradition.

It's been a long week for Dave. He's still recovering from the holiday crush. On a typical workday he unloads and delivers four thousand pounds of freight off those airplanes. Last Wednesday, the day before Thanksgiving, he moved three and a half tons—seven thousand pounds—almost all of it fresh fruit and vegetables, breads and cakes, meat and ice cream and soft drinks bound for the AC and the villagers' holiday tables. Cripes, says Dave, it almost killed him. Two days after that, he had to deal with twice the normal load of freight and mail, since he took Thanksgiving off. Then, Friday night, he had to deal with a drug search on the late Wright Airlines flight.

Such searches have become almost routine, not just here in Fort Yukon but throughout the bush. This morning's Fairbanks paper featured a front-page story headlined MARIJUANA SMUGGLING SEIZURES UP. The piece reported record numbers of drug seizures in villages throughout rural Alaska, and Dave knows that it's true. He can't count the number of times the Fort Yukon police have arrived at the airstrip to meet and search an incoming plane. They've found baggies of grass tucked inside homemade birthday cakes, buried in jars of mayonnaise, hidden in frozen hamburger meat, stuffed into oversized sacks of corn chips. Once in a while they'll come across some coke or crystal meth, but marijuana is by far the drug of choice in Fort Yukon, and in all of Alaska, for that matter. Just two months ago the state's supreme court ruled that adults could legally possess up to four ounces of pot in their homes for personal use. The rub is that it remains illegal to sell or buy it. A proposition to completely decriminalize both the sale and possession of marijuana in the state was on the ballot in the election earlier this month. The initiative had strong support in bush communities, including the backing of many village Elders and even police officers, who said there was no comparison between the problems they face from people who smoke pot and the problems they face with drinkers. "Liquor is so much worse," said one elderly voter. "If a man gets drunk, he beats his wife. If he smokes marijuana, he eats her dinner." A cop from the village of Gambell, on Saint Lawrence Island, concurred, calling any prohibition of pot "a waste of time." Pot smokers, he explained, aren't as prone to become as violent as people who drink. "Not once have we ever had to arrest anyone who was stoned and causing trouble," he said. "It doesn't happen."

With all that, 57 percent of the state's voters, the vast majority of them from the cities, cast their ballots against the initiative. And so the cat-and-mouse game between the cops and the smugglers continues, as it did just three nights ago at the airport.

What happened was this. Someone in the village called the police station with a tip that some dope was coming in on the late Wright flight. When the aircraft landed, the department's drug-sniffing black Labrador—his name's Raven—was there to greet it. Dave pulled the freight off the plane, and Raven circled it, stopping each time at a nondescript cardboard grocery box. The officer asked Dave to bring the box into the terminal, where it was opened, revealing a thirty-two-ounce resealed coffee can containing thirty-one ounces of coffee and one ounce of high-grade marijuana tightly sealed in cellophane. The name and address on the box were, naturally, fictitious. Whoever intended to pick up the package clearly thought better of it upon seeing the police SUV parked at the airstrip.

The drug seizure was big news around the village, but the talk of the town remains last week's suicide attempt. Dave was at work Tuesday morning when he saw the town's ambulance shoot past, lights flashing, headed toward the clinic, up past the airport. The thought crossed his mind that this might have something to do with Gavin. But within minutes, Gerald James stopped in to check on a flight and told Dave he'd heard that one of the town's girls had just tried to kill herself. A couple of phone calls later, Dave had the whole story.

It was a neighbor, a teenage girl, a student up at the school. Dave knows her well, better than most of the girls in the village. She lives with her grandmother, just around the corner from Dave's home. She played basketball as a freshman but didn't come out for the team last year. Dave talked to her about that, tried to get her to change her mind. He could see what was happening with her, what happens with so many girls in the village. "She was trying to grow up too fast," he says. She was starting to drift. "Starting to party," says Dave, "and we're not talking about cake and ice cream."

The girl had been hanging out the evening before with a crowd of kids over at Ryan Shewfelt's back cabin. There was drinking, and who knows what else? Sometime past midnight she left to walk home along one of the dozens of foot trails that cut through the woods of the village. The temperature was ten-below. Somewhere along the way she passed out. If Levi Ginnis hadn't happened to have come by, picked her up and carried her home, that would have been it right there. She would have been dead.

Apparently the girl woke up the next morning agitated, upset, got into an argument with her grandmother, and swallowed an overdose of pills. The paramedics arrived, rushed her to the clinic, where she was stabilized then medevaced out of the village on an air ambulance down to the Native hospital in Fairbanks.

It's nothing new, this problem of suicide up here in the bush. Tribal leaders have been calling it an epidemic for years now. Native Alaskans have long had the highest suicide rate of any group of people in the United States. Recently it climbed to four times the national average. The rate among Native Alaskan teens is even higher. The rate in bush villages is the highest of all. A torrent of government studies and newspaper reports with titles like A PEOPLE IN PERIL and INDIAN ARMAGEDDON have trumpeted the suicide issue, along with the myriad other crises pressing in on Alaska's indigenous tribes. There are so many factors to look at, say the experts, so many root causes that lie behind the problems. The state's rural villages are all struggling with cultural upheaval. They're all making the rocky transition from one way of life to another. They're all riddled with poverty, violence, despair, addiction of one form or another—the same bleakness found on any Native reservation in the Lower 48, the same ills festering in any inner-city neighborhood in America. But one factor that dwarfs all the others, say the studies—and it seems to be worse here in Fort Yukon than anywhere else—is alcohol.

The history speaks for itself. Fort Yukon has always been bush Alaska's Interior hub, the central location for the network of smaller villages scattered across the surrounding Yukon Flats region—a wilderness area twice the size of Ireland. When Canadian and British fur traders first crossed the mountains and reached the Interior in the mid-nineteenth century, it was here, at the confluence of the state's two largest rivers—the Porcupine and the Yukon—that they built their first settlement, the first English-language community in all of Alaska. They called it Fort Yukon, though the actual fort, fashioned from spruce logs in the summer of 1847, turned out to be unnecessary. It was built to protect the traders not from the local Indians, who were friendly, who posed no threat at all, but from the Russians, who owned the territory at the time. No Russians had yet penetrated this far up the Yukon— they were still several hundred miles downriver, working their way through the wilderness—and they never would get their chance. Twenty years after the fort was constructed, Alaska was bought by the United States. Twenty years after that, the fort was torn down, its logs sold to feed the engines of the commercial steamboats that had by then begun plying the Yukon.

Though the fort was gone, the village remained, awash in more fur than the traders could dream of, mountains of fur stacked high on the sleds of the nomadic Indians who moved through the surrounding forests. From the beginning, the traders sent breathless dispatches back to their parent companies in Canada and the United States: SEND BEADS AND GUNS, NOTHING BUT BEADS AND GUNS. Before long the traders were bartering with something that overshadowed the trinkets and weapons. That something was booze.

Anyone who works with alcoholism is aware of the amplified biological effect liquor has on the sensitive systems of what experts call "special populations"—most notably Asians and Native Americans. Because of differences in enzymes and rates of metabolism, people from these cultures tend to become inebriated faster and more forcefully than the typical drinker. Not only does booze hit them harder and more immediately, but its hook tends to sink deeper, prompting addiction. Those early traders and trappers saw this and exploited it as thoroughly as they could. In many bush villages, the traders passed through only occasionally, leaving the local Natives to retain something of their culture in the face of this onslaught. But in Fort Yukon, the white men put down roots, establishing themselves and the tools of their trade—most notably liquor—as a permanent presence.

All Native villages in Alaska struggle with the legacy of booze, but in Fort Yukon and hamlets surrounding it, the history is particularly ugly. Well into the twentieth century, there existed a club of white men in the region who called themselves the Squaw Humpers Union. Their express purpose was to introduce young Gwich'in women to liquor in order to have sex with them. By the turn of the twentieth century there was already a movement throughout Alaska to ban alcohol from such communities. In Fort Yukon, those efforts were led by a white man, an Episcopal missionary named Hudson Stuck, who settled in Fort Yukon in 1905 and made this "squalid looking little place," as he called it, his base of operations for the entire Interior. The Episcopal church that stands in the village today was where Stuck preached his sermons. In summers, he boated up and down the Yukon, bringing his Bible and robes to the Natives in their fish camps. Stuck is buried in the Fort Yukon cemetery today, where he lies for eternity among the Gwich'in who adored him.

Stuck was a champion of Native rights long before the phrase was even in use. He journeyed from Fort Yukon to Washington, D.C., in 1911 to urge the U.S. Department of the Interior to outlaw the sale of liquor to Alaska's Native people. He wrote several books on the plight of the Indians and his efforts to help them. His titles include *Ten Thousand Miles on a Dogsled*. Maxwell Perkins—muse to Ernest Hemingway and F. Scott Fitzgerald—was one of Stuck's editors. Stuck was the first man to summit Mount McKinley, North America's highest peak, which he insisted on calling "Denali"—the Natives' name for the mountain, meaning "Great One." He made a point of sharing the glory of that 1913 ascent with his Native sherpa, an Athabascan companion and guide named Walter Harper, who was actually the first member of the climbing party to reach the top. The reason Stuck made that climb— made it the Indian way, wearing moccasins fashioned from moosehide (with five pairs of socks), eating pemmican cooked down from caribou— was to draw attention to the plight of the Gwich'in. "They are the rightful owners of this land," he wrote, "simple, kindly, honest people who are being made into drunkards, wastrels and thieves under our 'civilizing' influence."

It's a straight line from there to what Fort Yukon faces today. Four out of five calls to the village's police department involve drinking. Beyond outright acts of intentional violence, almost every "accident" to which the town's cops and the clinic respond—snowmachine collisions, house fires from untended woodstoves, gunshot wounds, chain saw mishaps, bodies passed out in the snow, overturned boats in the summer, or, most common of all, seizures and severe dehydration from drinking binges that last for as long as three weeks—almost all of these "mishaps" are related directly to liquor.

It's not happening just here in Fort Yukon. It's happening throughout bush Alaska. But it seems to be worse in Fort Yukon than just about anyplace else. In the mid-1980s, the state legislature, responding to the devastation wrought throughout the bush by alcohol, passed a statute allowing individual villages to prohibit the sale and consumption of liquor. Today, more than half of the state's 170 or so off-road communities have voted themselves dry, banning the sale or possession of liquor. The village of Beaver, fifty-some miles downriver from Fort Yukon, went dry just this past summer—which simply brought even more customers to Fort Yukon, where the largest village-owned liquor store in the state does a booming business.

It's not much to look at, that windowless shed down near the river. Besides the plastic beer company banner mounted by the front door—WE HAVE YOUR NORTHERN LITES—there is no indication this is the address where the city gets roughly one-fifth of its revenue each year, more than it receives from any other source. It's such a small building. No more than three or four customers at a time can squeeze inside, where Dave's sister-in-law—Diane's sister Karen—is most often the cashier, fetching the twelve-packs of beer and bottles of whiskey stored on the shelves and coolers behind her.

The liquor store has been a magnet for controversy since it first opened its doors thirty years ago—with an opening-day giveaway of piggy banks in the shape of Schlitz beer cans for the village's kids. There have been numerous movements over the years to shut the place down. One actually succeeded, in the winter of 1984, when the store was padlocked after the townspeople narrowly voted to close it. Within weeks, snow-machines were roaring up the frozen Yukon to the village of Circle, seventy miles away, where the nearest liquor store was located. Bootlegging suddenly became Fort Yukon's most profitable private business, and nothing changed in terms of the drunken distress calls coming in to the police. Within a year the store was reopened, and it's been open ever since.

The prohibition movement in Fort Yukon crested one final time, nine years ago, when a crusade was launched by Diane's brother Richard after his teenage son Martin shot himself to death behind the family's cabin after a session of drinking. It was Richard who discovered his son's body. When Martin's best friend killed himself the following summer, Richard declared war on the store, which happened to be run at that time by Fort Yukon's city manager—Richard and Diane's own father, Richard Carroll Sr.

The spectacle of father squared off against son made headlines in newspapers across the state. Richard Carroll Sr. came straight out of central casting—a gruff, cigar-smoking kingpin of Fort Yukon politics. Before becoming city manager, he had been the town's mayor, a city councilman and president of the school board. He didn't give a damn about decorum or political correctness. To him this liquor store debate, like everything else, was a bottom-line issue. It's like this, he said at the time. That store's sales total about six hundred thousand dollars a year, of which the village government receives roughly a fourth. "You find us a hundred and fifty thousand dollars," he told his son and the others who wanted to shut the place down, "and we'll give you our license." Richard Jr. had no answer to that. His crusade, like the others before it, soon petered out. Today Richard Jr. is Fort Yukon's deputy mayor. His father is retired. Yet another sibling—Richard and Diane's sister Fannie—is now city manager. And no one is making a sound about shutting the liquor store down.

God only knows how any of this—the suicide attempt, the drug raid at the airport, the boys on the team who might still be out of town for Thanksgiving break—might affect who shows up for practice tonight.

The girls clear the court as Dave pulls five basketballs from a blue mesh bag and rolls them out on the floor. Aaron and Derek and Tim have already peeled down to their practice outfits. They each grab a ball, stick it under their jersey and start rubbing it up. The balls are like ice, with no bounce at all—they've been sitting all day in the subfreezing temperature of Dave's van. It's a daily beginning-of-practice ritual—warming the "rocks," as Dave calls them.

The three boys begin circling the court at a slow jog, bouncing the balls on the hard rubber floor as the rest of their teammates start filtering in.

Tim Fields—the bull of the team, built like a noseguard, five foot ten, nearly two hundred pounds, a junior, a starter at forward—trudges in with a grunt and a nod in Dave's direction.

Justin James, a junior as well and a backup last year, ambles in with Josh Cadzow. They're the two shortest and quickest boys on the squad—five-six and five-five, all ropy muscle and sinew, not an ounce of body fat on either of them. They each weigh all of 135 pounds. Josh is a wild card, a senior who's never played a minute of high school ball. He transferred to Fort Yukon this fall from Fairbanks, where his family moved when he was in junior high. His dad is Earl Cadzow's brother Clifton. Josh wants to graduate from his hometown school, he wants to work with his sled dogs, which is easier here than in Fairbanks, and he wants to play ball. Dave knows Josh is cat-quick, but that's about it. How well he can actually play this game remains to be seen.

Matt walks in by himself, followed by Wes James, the baby-faced freshman. Wes is soft, he's short—five foot six—and he speaks in a shy indecipherable mumble. But he's dying to play basketball. He's been living in the gym this entire fall, showing up every night for the men's pickup games, eager to learn all he can, willing to do whatever is asked of him. He's the kind of kid Dave counts on to keep the Fort Yukon tradition going. Wes may not play much this season, but Dave can see he's a comer. He's not one of those kids who will sit on the bench and bitch about why he's not in the game. He'll watch and he'll learn, trusting that his turn is coming. By the time he's a senior, Wes James will be a player, says Dave, maybe one of the better ones this town's ever seen.

That makes eight so far, circling the court as they continue to get loose, flinging mad shots at the backboards, hurling the balls off the walls, heaving the balls at each other. The squeak of their shoes on the hard rubber floor is sweet music to Dave, like the infield chatter and the crack of line drives at spring training in Florida, the dawn of yet another new season, ripe with promise and hope.

When Wade Fields walks through the door, Dave does a double take. He wasn't sure Wade was even in town. Wade mutters something about staying after school for some tutoring in math, which is why he is late. Dave nearly falls to the floor. Last season Wade didn't give a rat's ass about school. His grades were barely good enough to allow him to suit up for home games. He didn't come close to qualifying for road trips. Now he's a junior. Maybe he's seeing the end of the tunnel, his last two years of high school. Maybe he wants to get something out of this before it's too late. Who knows? This new version of Wade might not last long, but Dave's happy to see him tonight, all five foot eight of him, 150 pounds, all of it muscle.

Next through the door is Kyle—Kyle Joseph. He's got no practice gear on, which doesn't surprise Dave. Kyle strips off his jacket and sweater and jumps right in with the others, wearing jeans and a wife-beater T-shirt, thin wire-rimmed glasses and basketball shoes. He looks like a skinny dockworker playing ball on his lunch break. Typical Kyle. He's five-eleven, only a sophomore, one of the taller kids on the team, but he's so laconic Dave has doubts if he'll ever grow into the player he could potentially be.

Finally, in comes Jerry Carroll's kid Zach, the team's other freshman. He, too, transferred in this year from Fairbanks, along with his big brother Derek. Their dad wants them both to have the chance he had, to play ball for Fort Yukon. Derek had no chance at all down at North Pole High School in suburban Fairbanks, with its thousand or so students. He's an eleventh grader, a shade over six feet tall, which at North Pole meant nothing. Six-footers are a dime a dozen down there. But here he's a big man, the only boy his size on this team besides Aaron. Derek's got a sweet stroke, just like his father. No doubt both Zach and Derek can shoot. They've got their dad's genes. But whether they can do anything else is a question. Derek is rail-thin, polite, gentle almost to a fault—not the best traits for a rebounder, which is what he must become to find a place on this squad. As for Zach, he's one of the goofiest kids Dave's come across in his coaching career. Zach's like a big puppy—loud, impulsive, speaks and acts without thinking. "Chief Talks Too Much"—that's what the boys call him. He's built like his father—broad shoulders, thin waist, the thick-muscled legs of a boxer. His shot's like a heat-seeking missile, but shooting's the only thing he knows how to do. He plays defense like a sleepy matador waving at bulls. He's five-nine, has a crewcut, wears eyeglasses, has plenty of growing still to do. Look at his feet, says Dave. They're monstrous. No question, Zach's physical upside is huge. It's his head Dave is worried about.

So that's it. Eleven boys here for the first day of practice, and three no-shows: Johnny Adams, a five-eleven sophomore; Chris Engler, a junior, five-ten, a reserve from last season; and Bruce James, Wes's brother, a five-six sophomore who's never played organized ball.

Dave's never had this many kids come out for the team. Chances are a couple will drop off between now and the start of the season. Grades, home life, the withering of desire—there are all kinds of reasons kids quit. It happens. When Dave's got only seven or eight boys coming out, he sweats the loss of any one of them. With fourteen, he's at least got the luxury of knowing he'll have a full squad even if two or three quit or can't keep up their grades.

He blows his whistle, grabs a ball, sticks it under his arm, motions the boys to the bleachers. They flop in the stands, a couple sprawl on the floor, mopping their brows with their shirts. Aaron grabs a bottle of Gatorade from a backpack, takes a swig, passes it on. By the time it comes back, there's one swallow left. Aaron's one of the quietest kids on the team. He's a mute compared to the chatter of Justin and Josh, the wry comments of Tim Fields, and the boneheaded banter of Zach. But Aaron's the hub. Without him at center, even with Matt's all-around skills, this team is nothing. Aaron came out of nowhere last season. The Anchorage papers called him "the Greenhorn." But now he's established, the player the others depend on to clear rebounds and anchor the defense, protecting the hoop when his teammates get beat. He has the face of an altar boy, an eyes-to-the-ground shyness when he's in public. But he's ferocious on the offensive and defensive glass, he swats away shots like an NBA center, and he's developed a picture-perfect turnaround jump shot over the summer, spending hours on the blacktop outdoor court in back of the school.

"We've got a lot to accomplish before January thirteenth," Dave begins. "The first thing you've gotta do is get your lives together, get yourselves organized. If you have a girlfriend, I expect you to keep her. For the whole *season*."

The boys chuckle, glancing sideways at one another.

"If you don't have a girlfriend," he continues, "don't *get* one till April. I don't want any woman problems. I don't want any drama. We've got enough to deal with.

"Besides," he adds, "it's more fun when you travel if you don't have a girlfriend. Right, Matt?"

The boys crack up. Matt half smiles, gazes down at the floor.

Dave flips the ball in the air, begins pacing.

"We are not going to surprise anybody anymore, fellas," he says. "People know what they're going to get when they play us. Speed, quickness, an up-tempo game, defensive pressure. People expect these things from Fort Yukon."

He pauses. The boys are silent, their eyes fixed on him.

"And I've got my *own* expectations," he tells them. "I call it my annual migration to Anchorage. That's in March, every spring, and I don't expect it to be any different this year."

The older boys smile, nod. The younger ones stare intensely, straight-faced.

"I expect you to be here every night, unless you've got a good reason. Josh has got his dogs to take care of. He drove them this afternoon, but he still got here on time."

Dave turns to the subject of drinking, smoking, chewing.

"I've had players who did all that, had good careers. They say it never affected their game. My question is always how good *could* you have been? How much *better* might you have played without that stuff?"

He stops, stares silently at the boys for about five seconds, lets his words sink in.

"You've got four years for this right here," he says, spinning the ball in his hands. "You've got the rest of your life for that other stuff. But right now, *now* is for *this*."

He flips the ball in the air.

"Okay." He draws a deep breath. "Defense. Everything we do is about moving the other team out of their comfort zone, forcing them away from what they're familiar with. Every time you force them to be somewhere they don't want to be, to do something they don't want to do, to make them uncomfortable, we win. Making *them* change, making *them* adjust, dictating the tempo, the terms of the game—that's what our defense is all about."

He pauses, stares, gauges if they're paying attention.

"A team likes to walk it up the floor?" he continues. "We'll push them, make them hurry up, go faster than they're used to. We'll make them pass to someone who doesn't want the ball, someone who's not used to having it in that situation.

"We get a guy who *likes* to push it up the floor? We dog him. We ride him every inch of the way. We make him *work* every time he touches the ball. By the end of the third quarter, I guarantee we'll see a wet streak across the floor, and it's going to be that guy's tongue."

The boys laugh.

Dave turns to a story from a couple of years back. Matt's heard this one before.

"It was at the State Tournament," says Dave. "This coach was up in the bleachers, watching us play, scribbling notes, trying to figure out how to beat us. What's our secret? That's what he wanted to know.

"He came up to me after the game, and said, 'I understand from your boys that you just run 'em till they puke.'

"I said, 'No, that's not quite true. I run 'em till the *first* one pukes.'"

The boys crack up. With that, Dave claps his hands.

"Okay, let's get on the baseline."

It's time for what he calls "gassers"—sprints back and forth to the foul line, then to half-court, then to the far foul line, then to the other end of the floor and back again, over and over and over. They'll be doing this every day, from now till the last practice of the season. By tournament time they'll be doing sixteen of these in a row. Dave's teams may shift year to year in terms of the names and the faces. The teams that they face may be bigger than them. They may even be better. But one thing is constant, year in and year out. Dave makes sure of it. And that is that no one will be in better shape than the Fort Yukon boys. No one. Dave can't count how many games have turned around in the fourth quarter, when the other team finally broke under the relentless pressure of the swarming Fort Yukon kids. They keep coming and coming and coming. They don't tire out.

And this is why. This is where it begins, right here.

Dave watches Matt, Josh and Justin leading the way, pushing each other. Wade, Chris and Kyle are right there with them. And Aaron. They're fast, all of them. Scalded-dog fast. Hair-on-fire fast. As fast as any team Dave's ever had. And definitely deeper. There are nine boys out on that floor who could start right now, nine Dave can count on, and a couple of others who may well contribute as the season wears on. With that many bodies, Dave can press the other teams even harder, without worrying about foul trouble or fatigue. He can just cycle his guys in and out, keep them coming in waves, don't let up, push it, push it, push it.

He spins his whistle around his finger. There's a bounce in his step as he paces the sideline. He can't hide it. This just might be it, the team he's been waiting for, the one the whole town has dreamed of for thirty-three years, since this gym was first built. This just might be the year Fort Yukon wins the whole thing.

Dave would never say such a thing out loud. He'd never jinx it like that. And he knows there's so much that can happen between now and the Regionals, so much that can change, that can go wrong, on the court and, even more likely, off it.

But right now he's as pumped as the kids. From now until March the rhythm is set. Practice each weeknight from five to six thirty. Public scrimmages against the village men each Friday and Saturday night till the season begins in mid-January. Then it's games every weekend for nine solid weeks, at home or away, at least two games a week, sometimes as many as four. If all goes as planned—if all goes as hoped—these boys will play close to thirty basketball games by the time this season is done.

And it all starts right here.

One practice down, forty-nine more to go.

FIVE

The School

IT'S PEARL HARBOR Day, and the first cold snap of the season has set in—forty-eight below zero this morning.

A cottony low-hanging fog envelops the village, hovering at ground level, rising no higher than the tops of the trees. It's eerie, otherworldly. Ice fog, the villagers call it. When a trapper or woodcutter or anyone else who works outside in the winter awakes to see ice fog outside his or her cabin window, they go back to bed. It's simply too cold to be outdoors. The Elders knew how to deal with this kind of cold when they were young men and women. They had to. They'd stuff extra wads of rabbit fur into the toes of their canvas boots and the tips of their mittens and head out to check their traplines. They'd pay no mind to the pockmarks of frostbite that would erupt on the smallest patch of exposed skin. They knew how to keep moving, with air so algid it hits like a sledgehammer the moment you step into it. It's breathtaking, in the most literal sense of the term. It's visceral, as if you've been hacked with an ax. The nose and the cheeks, any unprotected flesh at all, sting as if scorched by a flame. The burn is followed by a deep throbbing ache, not just where the skin is exposed but down in the lungs, where the shock of the glacial air sucked into the body leaves it gasping and weak. Not only do you see your breath when it's this cold outside, but you hear it as it freezes and crackles in front of your face.

The slightest sound travels forever in this kind of cold. A twig snapping a quarter mile away sounds like a gunshot. The thrum of the village's generator, down near the river, can be heard all the way uptown, at the school. The smoke from the cabin stovepipes along Third Street, rather than rising, spills toward the ground like liquid nitrogen, feeding the fog, making it thicker.

It's eight A.M., pitch-dark outside. A smoky wisp of green northern lights arcs across the star-speckled sky as a slow-moving line of cars and trucks crawls up Third Street, the beams from their headlights cutting through the fog as the parents of Fort Yukon drop off their children for school.

An acoustic guitar version of "Away in a Manger" wafts out of a bent metal speaker mounted above the front door, as the bundled-up kids push their way into the brightly lit building. Inside the main office, the children are already queueing up to buy juice and cookies and chips from the school secretary, Georgie Engler, whose makeshift concession of snacks supplements the school's lunch program, which functions just three days a week because of budget cuts. Tuesdays and Thursdays the cafeteria is closed. The kids either bring their lunch on those days, or they buy something from Georgie, or they go without eating.

"Out, outta my office, *get*!" she says, shooing away a crowd of little ones who've collected around her desk. On the floor beside her, Matt and Josh are drawing posters for the school's Christmas Bazaar. They're two of five seniors in the school, the only two seniors on the basketball team. Being a twelfth grader has its privileges, which include spending a period each day as Georgie's assistants in the office. Josh, who resembles a pint-sized version of teen hearthrob film actor Josh Hartnett, has set a few hearts beating among the girls in Fort Yukon since returning to the village this winter. But he has no interest. Like the rest of the boys on the team, he can't wait till the season begins. Especially the road trips. Especially the road trip to Tanana. From what Josh has heard, the Tanana girls' team is supposed to be loaded this year. Loaded with lookers.

Matt's cracking up at the moment. Josh has just finished writing "Tacos and Nacos" in large script letters, listing the food they'll be selling at the bazaar. Matt loves it. Josh, the big bad honor student with his 3.8 average or whatever, can't even spell "nachos."

Josh stands up, realizes he's left out the *h* and silently accepts the ribbing.

Doc pokes his head out of the principal's office, asks Georgie to find him a phone number. He checks on two kids stewing in the detention room next door. "You doing that work?" he asks one, a laconic teenage girl drooped over a blank piece of paper and a closed textbook. She nods her head yes. "Cool," says Doc. "Cool."

When Delbert "Doc" Lantz says the word "cool," it's with a thick Okie accent. He's a good old boy and proud of it, raised in Texas and schooled in Oklahoma, where he graduated college back in 1970. "Oklahoma State," he says, stepping outside to light one of some twenty cigarettes he smokes in a typical day. He's fifty-seven, balding, crusty and lean, though he's put on a bit of a gut in the last couple of years. He spent a quarter century teaching high school science and shop class around the Midwest before heading up to Alaska in 1998. "I was divorced, my three girls were grown, and I was ready for some adventure," he says, "kinda like *Call of the Wild*."

He got what he was looking for, first down in Skagway, near Juneau, where he was hired as principal of the little town's 120-student school, grades K through twelve. He spent one year there before moving up to the Interior village of Huslia, about three hundred miles southwest of Fort Yukon. "Now that was *real* Alaska," he says, "just like here." Skagway, he explains, is a popular cruise-ship stop, a Disneyfied version of the raunchy gold-rush boomtown it once was. "It's a tourist town now," says Doc. Almost every student he had at the Skagway school was white. In Huslia, a village half the size of Fort Yukon, Doc took care of seventy kids, all but one of them Athabascan.

"I loved it down there," he says. "I'd probably still be there if they hadn't needed me up here."

He got the call last summer to come to Fort Yukon after the school's principal at the time learned he had cancer. Truth be told, says Doc, he would never have accepted the job here if not for the basketball team.

"All I ever heard about Fort Yukon when I was down in Skagway was horror stories," he says. "Fort *Yuk*, that's what everyone talked about. A town with a lot of troubles. Not a real friendly place, or so they said."

He's finished his smoke, fishes another out of his coat pocket and continues.

"But then, when I got to Huslia, we played them in basketball. And when those boys—Dave's boys—came to our school, well, they couldn't have been any more polite or better behaved. Very well disciplined. I was mighty impressed by that."

So Doc took the job. What he likes about running the school here in Fort Yukon, he says, is the same thing he liked about running the school down in Huslia. "On the whole they're good places, with good people. And their schools are the centers of both communities. Just about everything in the village revolves around the school."

What he doesn't like, and what every principal at every bush village school in Alaska must deal with, is the collision between cultures, which shows up in the schools more acutely than anyplace else. First there's the rub between the Natives' subsistence lifestyle and the school calendar. Doc still has parents who pull their kids out of school for a week or two each fall to help the family hunt moose for the winter. The same thing happens come spring when duck hunting begins. There are plenty of days in midwinter when a student is tardy or absent because he or she is needed at home to cut wood or take care of some other chore. That's life in the bush. Doc respects these traditions, these needs. He encourages his teachers to accommodate them. What he has deeper concerns about are the families who simply don't give a damn about their kids' schooling, who don't give a damn about school, period.

Doc understands why they might feel this way. The history of schools in Alaska's bush villages is rife with neglect, racism, gaps between cultures and outright scorn. Most of these villages had nothing but rudimentary church missionary classrooms until well into the 1950s. If a village child wanted a decent education, he or she had to move to the city to live with a friend or relative, or had to apply to one of several Bureau of Indian Affairs boarding schools located around the state. In either case, hardships ranging from homesickness to harsh mistreatment from teachers and fellow students sent the vast majority of these Native children back home. Some of the larger villages, including Fort Yukon, had their own bare-bones BIA schools, staffed mostly with white teachers who were, at best, ignorant of the cultural differences between themselves and their students, and at worst were blatantly hateful. Horror stories abound among parents and grandparents in Fort Yukon today who attended the village's BIA school when they were kids. They were punished for speaking Gwich'in. A sign mounted above the old school's front doors read SPEAK ENGLISH, TALK TO THE WORLD. Those who refused were spanked, shamed or even dismissed. Elders recall how embarrassed they were when they went to the village store as children and had to point silently to what they wanted to buy because they could not speak English and the white store owners weren't about to speak Gwich'in. They had little choice but to leave their own language behind, in school and out in the world—just one example, they say, of the ways in which their culture has been debased and displaced by the white world and its standards.

With the arrival of oil money in the 1970s, virtually every village in rural Alaska received a brand-new public school. The BIA system withered away, but the gaps between the two cultures remained. Standardized tests written for kids in New Jersey and Florida were befuddling to children in Alaskan bush villages who had never seen a fire hydrant or an elevator or a streetlight—all these odd objects referred to in the English and math sections of these exams. The scores that the bush kids received on such tests were abysmal, more evidence on the face of it that they were failures, inferior. The numbers today send the same message. Roughly one out of four students in Alaska's public school system are Native. Fewer than one out of ten go on to college, and the vast majority of those live in urban areas. College-bound students from bush communities like Fort Yukon are almost unheard of. Those who do make it to college are the ones whose families either leave the village and move to Fairbanks or Anchorage, or the ones who are shipped off to Mount Edgecumbe, the state's Native boarding school in Sitka, where three out of every four graduates go on to college.

It's not hard to see why the kids who remain in Fort Yukon might feel forsaken. They see so many teachers, most of them white, come and go every year. They know what these teachers are paid. Starting salaries run around $35,000 a year. The teachers who stay long enough can earn close to $68,000. The kids and their parents look at numbers like that, compared to the average per capita income for Native Alaskans today, which is $9,113, and it's easy to see why they might feel some resentment. It doesn't help matters when they watch a new white teacher move into one of the nicer cabins for rent in the village, maybe one with its own washer and dryer and cable TV and Internet access. Too many new teachers spend all their time either at the school or holed up in one of those cabins. They make no effort to get out into the village. They never show up at a potlatch, where tables are pushed to the walls, and guitars and fiddles are pulled out, and everyone dances and fills their bellies with home-cooked Native food: moose soup, fry bread, smoked salmon. These white teachers, too many of them, don't show up at birthdays or funerals. They don't come watch the dogsled races staged downtown on weekends throughout the winter. Some of them don't stay around at all for the weekends. They fly down to Fairbanks every Friday night, come back Sunday evening, and do it again the next weekend. It's not surprising, says Doc, that some of these teachers come home from those weekend excursions to find their cabin egged, or splashed with paint, or worse.

The good teachers, the ones who understand what it takes to do the job right up here in the bush, get out into the village every chance that they get, like Doc does. They show up at every fund-raiser, every auction, every event posted on that bulletin board outside the AC. They understand what it takes to break through the barriers of mistrust and suspicion that every outsider—but especially teachers—faces from the parents and kids in a community like this. They realize the wisdom of that old saw about 90 percent of life being just showing up. The good teachers show up, at everything, every chance that they get.

Doc does. He's got 144 students enrolled at the school at the moment, preschool through twelfth graders, all of them Native. "I know pretty much what's going on with every one of them," he says. "Here and at home."

His own home is at the airport, where he rents a room in the back of the terminal, behind Dave Bridges's office. He hikes the quarter mile or so up Third Street to the school every morning, wearing nothing to cover his head but his favorite camouflage ball cap, even in temperatures like today's.

It's been a crazy morning for Doc, and the day's hardly started. A mother just left with her seventeen-year-old son, whom she had to pull out of school to take to the courthouse, across the street. The magistrate is in town today, up from Fairbanks for his monthly visit to hear cases in the village's little state office building. His docket is loaded, including a morning appointment with the seventeen-year-old, who was picked up by the village police three weeks ago for underage drinking.

Doc's desk is cluttered with paperwork. He's got a stack of purchase orders to sign: supplies for the library, Play-Doh for the preschoolers, glue sticks, crayons and Magic Markers for the elementary school kids. He's looking at sick-leave applications from two of the sixteen teachers he's currently got on staff. Thank the Lord, he says, he's got three certified substitutes in the village ready to step in anytime: Dacho Alexander's mom, Ginny; Mike Mastel, who graduated here in the mid-1970s; and Shirley Thomas, who also grew up in this school. Mastel may join Doc's staff full-time any day now, to replace a science teacher Doc's been having "problems" with, as he puts it. Doc says he may just transfer the woman down to Stevens Village and replace her for the rest of the year with Mastel, who did the same thing last year when he stepped in full-time for a teacher who up and quit around Christmas. Doc appreciates Mastel's willingness to help out, considering how much is going on in Mastel's own life right now, not the least of which is he's about to become a grandpa soon—his son Mike Mastel Jr. is the father of Paul Shewfelt's daughter Natasha's baby.

Doc's also got the recent suicide attempt to deal with, the girl who lives near Dave Bridges. Doc went into emergency mode after hearing the news, called the Native Village and School District offices to see if he should bring in a crisis counselor for the kids. His first year in Huslia, eight people in that village died. "Eight," he says. "That's a lot of funerals in one year for a town of three hundred people." Two of those deaths were suicides. One was a student at the Huslia school, a teenage girl. The other was a village man who had had an affair with the girl. The man hanged himself not long after the girl was found dead. Yet another former Huslia student was killed that same year in a gunfight down in Fairbanks.

"It was awful," says Doc. "Them kids down there were walkin' around in a daze, wondering which of 'em would be next. Or which aunt, or uncle, or parent."

They wound up closing the high school for a couple of days and flew the entire student body, thirty kids, down to Fairbanks, where they stayed in a motel and took several hastily arranged field trips: to the university, to the offices of the Native Doyon Corporation, to tour the Alaska Airlines operation at the airport.

"We called it 'Career Exploration,'" says Doc. "We had to do something to get those kids' minds off that stuff. We needed to get them thinking about *life*, not death."

No such measures have been taken here, not yet, though Doc and some of the staff have organized a presentation to the junior high and high school kids about the dangers of alcohol and the statistics on suicide in Alaska. "But that's something we do pretty regular anyway," he says.

He's getting cold now, so he steps into the school's garage, takes a seat next to a truck jacked up with its front tires removed and lights another cigarette.

One thing Doc says he's missed big-time since moving to Alaska is football. He's been a diehard University of Oklahoma fan all his life, which he admits puts him at odds with his classmates from Oklahoma State, the Sooners' archrivals.

"Hey, I grew up back in the days of Bud Wilkinson," he says, referring to the fabled OU coach who won three national titles in the 1950s. There's no college football in Alaska, and only a smattering of high school teams, down around Anchorage and Fairbanks. Football in the bush is unheard of, as foreign as cactus. That leaves basketball as the sport into which Doc pours his passion. He's never played the game, couldn't tell you the difference between a 1–2–2 zone and a 2–1–2. But he's caught the fever of the villagers, he's seen how they live and breathe this game twelve months a year, and he has no doubt about its value as a tool to help him do his job. When he first got to Huslia, he says, the basketball program there was struggling. They hardly had enough players to field a team—and the school's attendance was plunging. He made it a priority to build both the boys' and the girls' programs back up. It's no coincidence, he says, that in the four years he was there, not only did the basketball teams' fortunes rise—the boys' team almost knocked out Fort Yukon in last season's Regionals—but the school's enrollment rose from forty-six students Doc's first year there to seventy-three when he left.

"No question basketball keeps a lot of these kids up here in school," he says. "We try to use that. We do everything we can to get 'em in and keep 'em here."

Doc's heard talk that there's been a movement among a number of people in Fort Yukon to decrease the school's focus on this game, to scale back the budget for basketball or even to eliminate it altogether. The way he understands it is there are some in the village who think all this money the school spends on basketball would be better spent on academic programs, on broadening the curriculum, on maybe putting a few new computers in the classrooms, anything but throwing it away on this silly game.

"Cut basketball?" He shakes his head. "Ain't gonna happen. *Ever*. Not here. It's too much of a tradition in this town, way beyond what I saw in Huslia or in any other village I've been to. Fort Yukon and basketball just go together. It means too much to the people who live here. I heard in the late eighties they didn't have a team, and I understand that was a pretty grim time in this town. That's when a lot of that 'Fort Yuk' stuff developed, I think."

Numbers don't lie, says Doc. All you have to do is look at the numbers this year: thirty-two students in the high school, fourteen of them on the boys' basketball team, seven on the girls' team. He can think right off the top of his head of five or six of those kids whose only reason for staying in school is to play ball. And he and his staff are doing everything in their power to make that possible. He's got three teachers right now staying after school every day to offer one-on-one tutoring to any player who needs special instruction. The kids know the rules of the game. To be eligible to play basketball, the state requires that each athlete pass all his or her classes for the first semester and maintain at least a 2.0 grade point average. Then, once the season begins, the Yukon Flats School District has its own rules. Students' grades are calculated on a week-to-week basis. In order to be eligible for each week's games, a student must sustain that 2.0 average and maintain a passing grade in every class. If the overall average dips below 2.0, or if the student is flunking a particular class, he or she is ineligible to suit up that week.

"There are a couple of 'em hanging on by a hair right now," says Doc. It's touch and go whether they'll make it. That's why he's asked for volunteers among his staff to help out with tutoring. Frankly, he says, the turnout among the kids has been disappointing, especially the turnout among the girls, who haven't shown up at all. If the season started tomorrow, adds Doc, only two of the seven girls on Cheryl Cadzow's roster right now would be eligible. In other words, they would have to cancel the girls' season entirely, which is not unheard of in bush villages. Every winter a couple of boys' and girls' teams in the state scratch their schedule at the last minute for lack of enough eligible players. That's why Doc and Dave have been on the phone the past couple of weeks, trying to nail down the teams that they've scheduled. The one from Minto, for example, a village west of Fairbanks, is a big question mark. Fort Yukon plays Minto every year. The Eagles are scheduled to open the season with a home game against Minto next month, as well as playing an away game against the same team in late February. But from what Doc's heard, Minto's in trouble. If they do field a team, it's going to be by the skin of their teeth, with just five, maybe six players. And that's only if they can get a couple of kids who are flunking right now to pull up their grades in the next couple of weeks. If they can't, Doc and Dave will have two holes in their schedule that they'll have to fill, with the clock ticking down to the start of the season.

It's almost eight thirty, time for classes to start. Doc ducks back into his office just as the day's first bell sounds. The scene in the high school wing of the building—two small hallways, wall-to-wall lockers, four classrooms—could be that in any school anywhere in the Lower 48, only less crowded. Some of the kids rush to beat the late bell. Others trudge nonchalantly in the general direction of class. A couple—a boy and a girl—lean against their lockers without moving at all.

In Brian Rozell's English classroom, the desks are arranged in a neat semicircle, to encourage the discussions he works so hard to inspire among his students each day. There are fourteen seats in the room, four tabletop computers, an overhead projector, a blackboard, a metal bookrack filled with sets of novels by George Eliot and the Brontë sisters, and a clock mounted over the door with the words TEMPUS FUGIT posted below it—"Time Flies."

Rozell whistles the theme from the film *Spider-Man* as each student picks up a spiral notebook from a stack by the door and takes a seat. All fourteen seats are filled, half with members of the boys' basketball team.

"We're going to write about our favorite movie today," says Rozell. "What's your favorite movie? Anyone?"

Silence.

Kyle Joseph gazes absently at the floor, clicking his pen. Ruby Thomas, daughter of Jack and Paul Shewfelt's sister Roberta and starting center on the girls' team—if she can stay eligible, which right now is in doubt—has her head on her desk and her eyes tightly shut. The glare from the ceiling's fluorescent lights glitters off the snow banked outside the room's windows. It's black as midnight out there and will be for two more hours.

Finally, Zach breaks the silence.

"*Spider-Man!*" he blurts out. He glances around for a response from the others.

Nothing.

"What's *your* favorite movie?" Zach asks Rozell.

Rozell stares him down.

"That's enough, Zach," he says.

Zach shrugs, slumps in his seat.

"I don't have a pen," announces one of the girls in the back of the room.

"Neither do I," chimes in another.

"Okay," says Rozell, unfazed. "How many people need pens?"

Five hands go up.

"Wes," he says, "can you go get some pens for us?"

Wes James, ever the compliant freshman, hops up and scurries out of the room.

"The rest of you, go ahead and start writing," says Rozell.

Zach raises his hand, begins asking a question.

"Does it have to be—"

Rozell cuts him off.

"Zach," he says, walking back to his desk, "just write."

Rozell would not look out of place in a New England prep school. His khaki slacks and long-sleeved polo shirt are crisp and creased. His coppery beard is trimmed short and precise. He's thirty-one, as is his wife, Stephanie, who teaches reading just down the hall. They both came to Fort Yukon last year, after teaching school for several years in their home state of Texas. Stephanie found out two months ago that she's pregnant with their first child, due this coming June. They live in a rented cabin near the airport, just across the road from Dave Bridges. The place is cozy, but it could use a little more furniture. They'd love to invite people over, but right now there's no place to sit other than a couple of chairs and a small kitchen table. Next weekend they may fly down to Fairbanks to order a dining room set they've had their eyes on for a while. Then they can start entertaining the way they'd like to.

They're two of the involved ones, Brian and Stephanie. Doc wishes all his teachers were like them. Brian's gone out with his neighbor, Fred Thomas, to run Fred's traplines in the woods east of town. It's incredible, says Brian, to watch this eighty-seven-year-old man still braving the cold and bringing back pelts. He loves sitting with Fred, hearing the old man recount what it was like living out in the "toolies" back in the 1930s and '40s; breaking trail with his dog teams through Yukon Flats woodlands with names known only to trappers like himself—Midnight Gulch, Windy Valley, Glacier Creek, Devil's Washboard—seeing no other humans for weeks at a time, living on boiled porcupine and beans, sleeping under a canvas tarp, looking up at the stars and considering himself one of the luckiest men in the world. It's men like Fred Thomas who lived Alaska the way Jack London wrote about it, and Brian Rozell feels truly blessed to have the opportunity to sit at this man's knee and hear him tell stories.

Wes returns with a handful of pens, and Rozell moves to the blackboard.

"Okay," he says, "put your journals away and pull out some paper. We're going to work on introductory paragraphs."

Half the class stares blankly. The other half picks at their nails, studies the grain on their desks, doodles on the backs of their hands. Ruby's head is still down.

Rozell writes a sentence on the board in large block letters: "WHY I SHOULD BE SELECTED TO GO TO JUNEAU."

The class has been working on this essay contest all fall, as have students in other classes in other villages across the state. The winners will earn an expenses-paid trip to the capital city.

Rozell reads the words on the blackboard out loud. Then he turns to the kids.

"Why would any of us want to go to Juneau?" he asks.

"Because of government?" offers a girl near the back of the room.

"What *about* government?" asks Rozell.

A boy in a wheelchair raises his hand. Ruben Jones. Ruben's been in that wheelchair since he was a tot, and he will be for the rest of his life. He was oxygen-deprived during his mother's pregnancy and was born with impaired motor functions. The condition is strictly physical. Ruben is one of the smartest kids in the school. Every morning a small yellow school bus picks him up and carries him here. Every afternoon the bus takes him back home. No other riders are allowed. The school ran two buses for all of the students last year, but budget cuts put both vehicles in the garage over the summer. Ruben's disability qualifies him for a ride, but the rest of the village's kids must find their own way to and from school. Most parents drive them, or they ride their snowmachines, or they walk.

"Is it the *importance* of government?" suggests Ruben.

"Yes, good," answers Rozell. "What's another one?"

Zach thrusts his hand up.

"Yes, Zach." Rozell's tone is weary, wary.

"Is it the *importance* of government?" asks Zach.

Rozell sighs. He's not going to let this kid get to him.

"We've already got that one, Zach," he says, drawing a deep breath. "Any other suggestions?"

"To talk about issues," says Tim Woods. Tim's one of Dave Bridges's more eager players, like Wes. He's a sophomore. His game is mediocre at best, and unlike Wes or Zach, it doesn't look like he'll get much better in the future. But he's upbeat, he hustles, and he never gives Dave any lip. Dave also knows he can count on Tim to pass all his classes.

"Yes, *issues*," says Rozell, clearly brightening. "Like what?"

"Marijuana," says Kyle. It's his first word this morning.

A titter runs through the class.

"Good," says Rozell, writing the word on the board.

"What else?"

"Abortion," says one of the girls.

"Yes," says Rozell, writing that word down, too.

"Bear baiting," shouts out one of the boys.

"Excellent," says Rozell.

Now he begins parsing the words on the board, suggesting how each of these topics might be arranged into an essay's introductory paragraph. No sooner does he begin than he sees that he's losing them. The kids are sinking down in their seats. Their eyes are glazed over. It's all too conceptual.

So Rozell moves to make it concrete.

"Think of a sandwich," he says.

The kids look at him, at one another.

"What do you need to make a sandwich?" he asks.

Silence.

"Bread?" says Derek. It's the first word he's spoken today. He's the opposite of his brother Zach. Derek is quiet, taciturn, shy. Here. In the gym. Everywhere.

"Exactly!" says Rozell, sketching a slice of bread on the board. "What else?"

"Tomato," says Tim Woods.

"Right."

Rozell makes a rough drawing of a wedge of tomato.

"What else?"

"Pickles?" says Ruben.

"Okay."

Rozell draws a pickle.

"Meat!" shouts out Zach.

"*Yes!*" says Rozell, adding on to the drawing.

Now there's silence.

"What else?" Rozell asks. "What's still missing?"

The kids study the board.

"Mustard?" asks one.

"No," says Rozell.

"Chips?" asks another.

"Unh, unh," he says, shaking his head.

Silence.

"Think about it," says Rozell.

Dead silence.

"What about *another* piece of bread?" Rozell finally says, drawing a second slice.

He steps back.

"This sandwich," he says, pointing up at the board, "is your essay."

A couple of the kids screw up their faces. The rest just stare blankly.

Rozell points at the first slice of bread.

"*This* is your introductory paragraph," he explains.

He points at the tomato, the pickle, the meat.

"This is the *body* of your essay, your supporting paragraphs."

Then he points at the last slice of bread.

"This is your *concluding* paragraph."

He turns back to the kids.

"Is everyone with me?"

Ruby lifts up her head.

"But I like *cheese* on mine."

The classroom erupts with laughter.

Zach can't resist.

"How come we can't make it a BLT?" he says.

"I like *peanut butter*," says a kid by the window.

Rozell sighs. Juneau has drifted far, far away.

"Zach," Rozell says, looking back at the sandwich, "does this make sense to you?"

"Yes."

"Do you understand it?"

"No."

Rozell turns away.

"Amanda," he says, addressing a girl sitting beside Ruby. Her head, like Ruby's, is down on her desk. Amanda could well be the most talented athlete on the girls' basketball team. But she completely lacks focus. She drifts in and out of games, tuned in one minute, performing like a star, then suddenly fading out, as if a switch has been flipped and her mind's gone somewhere else. It drives Dave Bridges crazy watching her, seeing how good she might be if she could only stay tuned in.

"*Amanda*," says Rozell again. The girl hasn't moved.

"Amanda, are you with me?"

She lifts her head, ever so slowly.

"Yeah," she replies. Her voice is barely audible.

"Good," says Rozell.

Her head drops back down to the desk.

It's almost nine twenty-five, time for the bell. The room fills with the sound of shuffling papers as the students put their work back into their folders and close their notebooks.

The bell rings. The kids rush from the room, each dropping a journal on the stack by the door. Ruben wheels past, waves good-bye to Rozell.

Rozell nods to Ruben, turns and starts wiping the board.

The second-period class filters into the room, grabbing notebooks from their own stack by the door.

"Okay," says Rozell, clapping his hands as the tardy bell rings, "we're going to write about our favorite movie today."

SIX

Dave and Diane

MICKEY THE CAT is not doing so well. Her kidneys are failing, she's been losing weight lately, and she's spending more time than ever in her hideaway under the tub in the bathroom. That's where she runs when strangers enter Dave Bridges's house, but these days she's been slinking back there even when no one's around but the family.

They've been through a lot, Mickey and Dave and the girls. They got Mickey when she was a newborn kitten, nineteen years ago, just after Dave and the girls' mother split up. They called Mickey the "Divorce Cat." "Something to help take their minds off of things," explains Dave. Every summer, he'd pack them all into the nineteen-foot RV he used to keep down in Fairbanks and they'd drive cross-country to Maine to visit his parents. Mickey would sit up front beside Dave as he drove, taking naps in the nook above the passenger's seat. Dave's dad loved Mickey. Six o'clock in the morning, everyone in the house would still be asleep, and you could hear Dave's dad in the bathroom, talking to the cat.

The girls have been gone for a couple of years now, Jamie to college in Colorado, Gabrielle to Fairbanks where she works as a dental assistant. Diane's kids are grown and moved out as well—her sons, Lewis and Andrew, and her daughter, Jolene. Now it's just Dave and Diane and Gavin and Mickey. And Mickey's not doing so well.

"I've always felt like I owed that cat one," Dave says.

It's Saturday afternoon, two weeks before Christmas. Gavin is slouched on the living room sofa, staring at the TV. Diane's at the dining room table, sewing tiny bright beads onto a pair of tan gloves trimmed with white fur. Dave sits beside her, waiting for the coffee to brew.

The gloves are a Christmas gift. Diane and her mother sew twenty-some pairs every year, along with half a dozen hats just like Dave's, for family and friends and holiday fund-raisers. The fur they use comes from skins trapped by Diane's dad, Richard Sr. Dozens of pelts from his old trapping days—rabbit, beaver, marten, lynx, wolf—are bundled and stored in a cache behind the cabin where he and Diane's mother live, not far from Dave and Diane's place. Just last month Diane's dad told her and the rest of her siblings to help themselves to whatever they'd like.

He's not doing so well, Richard Sr. He's seventy-four now. His eyesight's almost gone. He's got diabetes. And his heart's been giving him trouble the past couple of years. "All the classic symptoms of being an Alaska Native," says Diane.

Dave's making notes on a small pad of paper, preparing for tonight's scrimmage against the village's men. He's also thinking about the town's School Advisory Committee, which met this past Tuesday night. The antibasketball contingent—Buzzy Kelly and Dave's sister-in-law Jennie Carroll—went after the basketball budget again. They've become like a team, those two, out to bring down this game in Fort Yukon any way that they can.

Dave can understand Jennie's opposition. She's not from Fort Yukon. She's an academic, a white woman who came here in the mid-1990s to work on her master's thesis in anthropology after doing her under-graduate work at Harvard. She met Diane's brother Jim, married him and was hired to run the University of Alaska's rural education center down near the Episcopal church. What Jennie knows about basketball could fit in a thimble, says Dave. Her understanding of what basketball means to this village, to these kids and their families, he says, could fit in a container even smaller than that.

If there's one thing Dave's learned in close to three decades of bush village life—and he's learned many things—it's that turf battles can get viciously intense. Jennie Carroll's turf is that little university operation down by the church—that and the Fort Yukon School. The fact that she and Dave are family has made no difference in Jennie's crusade to cut basketball off at the knees, to shift the money the school spends on this game to more—as she put it in a letter made public last spring—

"academic" activities and programs. That letter, written in the wake of a mini-scandal involving the girls' team at last year's Regional Tournament in Fairbanks—they were spotted in their hotel's bar, watching a band from Fort Yukon play—proposed that basketball be suspended for one season so that the school might rearrange its priorities. The backlash among the pro-basketball forces in town was volcanic. Someone posted Jennie's letter, with less-than-kind comments scribbled across it, on the bulletin board outside the AC. Jack Shewfelt hung several handmade protest signs on the split-rail fence in front of his cabin. Paul went on the radio to assault both this preposterous notion and those who supported it. The idea quickly faded away, but the opposition to basketball persists in some quarters.

Dave understands Jennie's concerns. In fact, he shares them. He was a bush village schoolteacher for twenty-one years before he ever thought of becoming a coach. No one cares more about these kids and their future than he does. What he can't understand, he says, is why Jennie and the people in town who share her anti-basketball sentiments refuse to believe that this game, far from being at odds with the school's educational mission, is actually essential to it. Doc, the principal, certainly sees it that way. Doc's told Dave flat out that this school, even this village, would just about shrivel up and blow away without basketball. Dacho Alexander, who, thank god, says Dave, is a member of the committee, is no great fan of basketball. Dacho played when he was a student here back in the late 1980s, but he'll tell you himself that, quite frankly, he sucked—as did the team. Still, Dacho points out that this is just about the only program for kids in this town—not just in the school but in the entire village—that produces close to the results that it promises.

It's tough for Dave to make that argument himself, seeing as how he's the coach and a white man to boot. Never mind the nearly thirty years he's spent living in the bush. Never mind that he's married to a Native, that he has Native children. He's still considered an outsider by some of the people in Fort Yukon—especially those who don't care much for basketball.

But the facts speak for themselves. Forget the results on the court, says Dave. Look at the big picture. He took over this basketball team

seven winters ago with one purpose in mind: to build decent, respon-
sible adults out of these boys, to use the carrot of basketball to keep
them in school, and to teach them some tools for success that they might
take and apply to the rest of their lives.

How can you measure the results of something like that? Well, Dave
suggests, you can start with raw numbers. Consider the fact that the
current graduation rate at the Fort Yukon School is 37 percent. That's
roughly one out of three kids who finishes high school in this village.
That figure is about average for the 150 or so bush village schools across
Alaska. Since Dave began coaching in 1997, he's had thirty-nine boys
play for him who should have graduated by now. Thirty-seven have
done so. Thirty-seven out of thirty-nine. You don't have to be a high
school graduate, he says, to see that beats the hell out of 37 percent.

As for the money that's spent on the sport, Dave—and Doc, too—
points out that the state gives each rural school in Alaska a bonus "foun-
dation" amount of $4,100 per year for each enrolled student. That's
$4,100 per student beyond the basic statewide school budget allocation.
Last year the Fort Yukon School spent $20,000 on its basketball
program—the same as it plans to spend this year. Again, it doesn't take
a genius to see that if five kids—boys or girls—stay in school because
of this game, the program has paid for itself in terms of state money.
And there's no question, says Dave, that at least five of the twenty-one
kids currently in the program—boys and girls—would have dropped or
flunked out by now if not for basketball.

Sure, Dave understands it's more complex than that. He knows there's
far more for both sides—those who support the basketball program and
those opposed to it—to consider than just a couple of simple statistics
like these. But those numbers are not a bad place to begin.

Jennie's not interested in any of this. Dave can see that. She's looking
for any reason she can possibly find to eliminate what she considers a
wasteful, trivial game. As for Buzzy, the issue is more personal. For him,
this is about Dave as much as it's about anything else. Dave understands
this, too. And he feels terrible about it.

It happened two seasons ago, during a home stand against Nulato.
Shane Kelly, Buzzy's son, was the team's sixth man at the time, the first

sub off the bench. What Shane did best was shoot threes. Dave knew he could shoot them even better if he learned to step closer to the arc before pulling the trigger, rather than firing from a foot or two beyond it, which was his habit. It's simple common sense, Dave would tell Shane. That one step can mean a difference of fifteen to twenty shooting percentage points over the course of a season. That's what Dave tried to get Shane to understand. Every day in practice, he'd take Shane aside, urge him to catch the pass, take one dribble toward the line, then shoot, rather than turning and launching the thing right away.

So came the game against Nulato. This was Ryan's senior year, the 23-1 team, the best team Dave had coached up to that point, the best team the village had ever seen. With every win, the excitement in town grew, as did the expectations and the pressure on Dave. He'd never been one to feel pressure, and he'd certainly never been one to pass pressure on to his players. He hated coaches like that when he was a kid. The screamers. The little generals. The Bobby Knights of the world. "Good grief," he thought to himself whenever he'd see those guys go into their rages, "it's only a game, for crying out loud." He'd never dream of behaving like that.

Which is why it came as a shock when he put Shane in against Nulato that night, watched him break free on the wing a couple of steps beyond the three-point line, receive a pass with nobody near him, and, rather than take that one step in and then stroke it, he turned and flung the thing up from beyond NBA range. As the shot banged off the rim, Dave flew out of his seat, bellowing across the floor.

"Same mistake *again*?" he screamed. "I'll kill you, Shane. I'll *kill* you!!!"

You could have heard a pin drop. The entire gym, standing room only, went dead silent. At least that's how it felt to Dave. Nobody'd ever seen him do something like that. And that's not something anyone does to a kid in this culture, especially not a white man. You don't shame a child in public, not like that. Take him aside later, maybe. Dress him down then, one on one. But not in front of the entire village. And certainly not in front of his father.

Dave was mortified. He couldn't believe he'd exploded like that. He apologized to Shane and the team immediately after the game. He tried apologizing to Buzzy, but Buzzy would have none of it. Buzzy was furious. And he stayed furious.

The incident hung like a cloud over Dave for the rest of the season. He'd crossed a line he told himself he would never cross. That's what the winning had done to him. He'd become one of those guys, those chest beaters. So he decided it was time to step down, to quit. Diane was relieved. She'd seen what the pressure was doing to him. Until then the coaching had been a pleasure for Dave, a sheer joy. His blood pressure actually went *down* during the season. He loved being with the kids. It gave him a chance to be a kid again himself. The hour-and-a-half practices every night, the road trips, the banter, the teasing, the meals and motels, the sheer adrenaline rush of the games, the heat and the roar of the crowd banging the bleachers, the blur of the action, the whistle-burst dance of the referees, the beauty when it all came together, when those five boys on the floor purred like a finely tuned engine—it was everything Dave had imagined it might be when he first decided to do this.

Becoming a coach was the last thing he'd dreamed of when he was a kid back in the seacoast town of Blue Hill, near Bar Harbor, Maine. At five foot nine he wasn't much of a basketball player. Baseball was his game, though he was no more than an average infielder through Little League and high school. "Liked sports, didn't like coaches," is how he puts it. His dad was a plumber, his mom a schoolteacher. E. B. White grew up not far from the Bridges' house. White's grandson was a classmate of Dave's. One of Dave's daughters has a copy of *Charlotte's Web* inscribed by White.

The Blue Hill phone book was dotted with names like Rockefeller, Roosevelt, Goodyear, all of whom kept summer homes there on the rocky, wave-caressed coast. "They called them 'cottages,'" recalls Dave. "Twelve-bedroom cottages. All we knew was they were worth a buck to us because we could cut their grass and tend their gardens."

He worked summers in the fields, raking berries and digging potatoes alongside Natives from Canada, migrant laborers from tribes like the Passamaquoddy, the Penobscot and the Micmac. "Our town was lily white, but I learned early on that these were people just like us. We all bent over and sweated just the same."

Like just about every other college-bound kid in his high school, Dave went to the University of Maine. Like his mother, he studied to be a teacher. But his timing was terrible. It was the post-Vietnam era. Everyone was becoming a teacher. When he graduated in 1976, there were no jobs at all. If he was going to be poor, he figured, he might as well be poor someplace more interesting than Maine. When a friend told him of plans to drive up to Alaska that October, Dave decided to join him.

Which is how he arrived in Dillingham, on the state's southern coast. That's where he found his first airport job, unloading cargo. He moonlighted as well, as a substitute teacher. Before long he was teaching full-time in an Eskimo village called Togiak, not far from Dillingham. One teaching job led to another, one village led to the next, and basketball soon became an integral part of Dave's life—pickup ball with the Natives. "I was told there was a fair amount of prejudice against whites in the villages, especially among the kids, who had pretty big chips on their shoulders. Playing ball with them broke down a lot of those barriers. And besides, there wasn't much else for a single guy living by himself to do."

By the time he got to Fort Yukon in 1984, Dave was married with two daughters, but the marriage was just about finished. His wife, who was Gwich'in, was alcoholic, and her drinking was not getting better. They divorced in 1985, leaving Dave as a single dad with a three- and a six-year-old. He had no time for anything but teaching and taking care of his girls. Like everyone else in the village, he watched the Fort Yukon boys play on weekends during the winter, and it bugged him that the teams never did better. "I saw so many tremendous athletes pass through here, but the coaches kept coming and going, one after the other, mostly teachers. They'd do it a year and then be gone. There was no tradition, no continuity."

After he married Diane in 1994 and retired from teaching two years after that, Dave decided to try his hand at establishing that continuity and maybe building some of that tradition. His approach then, as it is now, was less about Xs and Os—he's the first to admit he's no Dean Smith—and more about shaping an attitude among his players, an attitude he hoped would carry over into the classroom and into the rest of their lives.

His expectations were not high that first season. "I figured we might win three games." It looked like they might win fewer than that after the first home stand, when one of the Fort Yukon players got up off the bench during the third quarter and walked past Dave toward the locker room. "I thought he was going to the bathroom." When the kid came back five minutes later, he was carrying an armful of pizza from the concession stand. "Not just one slice," says Dave. "He had enough for everyone." At the next practice Dave told the boys the team had a new rule. No pizza on the bench.

He coached the girls' team that year as well. "Something I'll never do again," he says. "*Never*." First of all, he had only five girls on the team. "I had to call at least one time-out a quarter just to give them a rest." Worse was what the girls would talk about during those time-outs. "We'd be in a close game," recalls Dave, "and I'd think, 'Boy, we're finally going to *win* one.' I'd bend down to talk strategy, and they'd be complaining about how someone on the other team smells. Or they'd be asking each other how their hair looks. Or should they go back out with their jersey tucked or untucked. We'd finally break the huddle, and they'd look at me and ask, 'What are we *doing?*'"

One of his starters developed a chronic backache midway through that season. She was constantly complaining but refused to let Dave take her to the doctor. He finally found out why when she revealed during the Regional Tournament that she was pregnant. They finished that tournament with four players. They finished that season with one win.

The boys won nine games that first year—six more than Dave had expected. The next year they won the Regional for the first time since 1980. They've never looked back. The continuity Dave set out to provide was just what they needed. With home lives and classrooms disrupted by the constant comings and goings of unstable parents and itinerant teachers, the boys on Dave's basketball teams found something they could depend on in that gym. They knew that not only would the game be there, but Old Dave would be there as well, with his tired one-liners, his diagrams of that half-court trap defense he's so in love with, and his conditioning drills, running them day after day after day.

Dave's boys came to rely as well—as did the entire village—on the fact that come every March they'd be headed to Anchorage, one of just eight teams in all of Alaska qualified for the elite State Class 1A Tournament. It was heady stuff. It was great. But something built up with all those wins, all those Regional titles, all those trips down to State. Diane could see it even if Dave couldn't. She saw him becoming more serious, year after year. He began bringing the game home with him, spending more time talking and worrying about it than he ever had before. She could see it was becoming a burden, just like the teaching had become toward the end of his time in the classroom, which is why he'd finally decided to retire from that.

Dave had always loved the classroom, loved watching that moment when the light turned on in the kids' heads, when they suddenly understood something, when they *got* it. He loved teaching them science and English and history and math. Back in Chalkyitsik, he loved taking them out every spring to go 'ratting, the whole class, boys and girls, tromping through the snowmelt and mud to check the traps in the muskrat mounds out by the ponds, bringing the carcasses back to the school, where the kids would skin them, hang the pelts from a wire strung across the classroom and eat the meat right there, roasted over the little propane stove kept in the school's little kitchen. The tails were the best part. The parents would call when their children got home from school with those baggies of meat, and they'd ask Dave where the tails went.

Dave adored the kids. It was the other teachers who drove him batty. Always bitching, complaining. He'd eat his lunch by himself in his classroom just to avoid the teachers' lounge with its gossip, its politics, the constant griping about the principal. "There's no way those people don't carry that negative vibe into their classrooms," he'd think, "no way it doesn't rub off on the kids."

That's one thing Dave loved about Diane from the first time he met her—the fact that she wasn't like that at all. She'd already been teaching longer than just about anyone at the school when Dave first arrived in the mid-1980s, and she never complained about anything. She was born and raised here, the fifth of her parents' twelve children, the steadiest of all of them, one of the steadiest people in the entire village.

Dave could see from the get-go that Diane was one of those people who holds a town like this together in the face of so much that threatens to tear it apart. He'd seen people like this in every village he'd lived in—the ones who step up to the plate, who fill in the cracks, pick up the loose ends, do what's needed with no questions asked. In the bush, in a place like Fort Yukon, there is no nursing home, no halfway house, no orphanage, no battered women's shelter, no beds for the homeless. Fort Yukon is lucky to have that little clinic, with its three physician's assistants and two EMTs, and a dentist who flies up from Fairbanks one day a week, and a doctor who flies in one day every month. There's a drug and alcohol counseling center as well, housed in a trailer near the police station. But in terms of the kinds of social service facilities most communities in America take for granted, that's about it. It's up to the villagers themselves to step in and take care of the rest.

And they do.

People like Charlotte Fleener—"Big Mama," they call her—who's been a surrogate mother to the Shewfelt boys while raising her own kids and working her job as dispatcher for the village police, and coaching the girls' basketball team when no one else would do it.

There's Charlotte's husband, Craig, who could easily have taken his master's degree to find some high-paying job in the city, but instead has dug in here, serving his people as director of the Fort Yukon–based Council of Athabascan Tribal Governments.

There's Georgie Engler—Chris Engler's mom—who's so much more than simply Doc's secretary at the school. Georgie's hands are on just about every event in the village, from the Spring Carnival to the Christmas bazaar to the cakewalks they stage at halftime of every home game.

There's Dacho Alexander, whose dad, Clarence, was Fort Yukon's chief in the 1980s and '90s, and whose mom, Ginny, ran an alternative school in her cabin for years. Her students liked to call themselves the "Alter-Natives." Dacho and his sisters and brothers, including his kid brother Sam, who graduated from West Point two years ago and just returned from combat in Iraq this past summer, are like the Kennedys of Fort Yukon—leaders, worldly and wise, with their share of personal hardships as well as success.

There's Evelyn James—Wes's and Bruce's mother—who, in this town with no public library, has built one, book by book, in her home, including a section on Fort Yukon history as complete as any university's.

There are the McCarty sisters—Aaron Carroll's cousin Deb, who runs the clinic; his cousin Laurie, who's on staff there as well; and his cousin Diana, who works at the airport with her boyfriend, Jay Cadzow. They're a team, these three women, eternal teenagers at heart, serving as sister-confessors to half the girls in the village and as surrogate aunties to half of the boys.

There are Earl and Cheryl Cadzow, Josh's aunt and uncle, with whom Josh is living this winter. Earl, with his passion for trapping and dogs, runs the village's Mushers' Association and pushes his passion for hockey as well, building an ice rink behind his house, coaching the village's bantam league team till the rink collapsed two winters ago under the weight of a heavy spring snow. And Cheryl, who, besides teaching at the school and running her café at night and raising her son and two daughters and taking night classes for her master's degree, and coaching the girls' basketball team, has served one stint herself as the village's chief—the only woman chief Fort Yukon has ever had.

These are the people of Gwich'yaa Zhee—the Native name for Fort Yukon, meaning "house on the Flats." These are the people the outside world doesn't see. The bureaucrats and government officials who fly in for a meeting and fly back out as soon as they can have no conception these people exist. The magazine writers and newspaper reporters who come seeking a sensational headline—about a murder, a rape, a bad accident—find what they're looking for and leave without meeting the Fleeners or Cadzows or Englers. The wealthy white hunters and fishermen and nature lovers passing through on their way into or out of the wilderness see only the surface of this village, the squalor and sadness that seems to envelop this community, and they go back to the world and confirm that "Fort Yuk" deserves its nickname.

Dave knew what he'd see when he first came here. More than half the homes without electricity. Most without plumbing. "Honey buckets" filled with raw human waste sitting open and stinking on living room floors. Sewage dumped into the river in summer and onto the ice in winter. Garbage dumped outside front doors, in yards, on the roads, everywhere. Grocery prices twice as high as the prices in Fairbanks, which are already steep. Fresh produce almost unheard of eight months of the year. Canned and processed and sugar-soaked food spiking the villagers' rates of diabetes and hyperglycemia. Liquor taking care of the rest. Whiskey-fueled knifings and shootings and beatings. Rape and incest. Horrific collisions of snowmachines. Hunting mishaps. Drownings. House fires. Suicides. There wasn't a person in Fort Yukon untouched by the nightmarish death of a loved one.

But with all that, Dave could see that this was—and still is—a community, in the deepest, fullest sense of that word. There is no such thing as a stranger among people who live in a village like this. Henry Flitt, who was born in Fort Yukon just after World War II and has been cleaning the school's floors since 1973, took a trip once to Chicago when he was a young man. He never felt so alone in his life, he says. "Millions of people," he says, sighing and shaking his head, "and it was like I was all by myself." Dave knows just what Henry means, the way humans live in those cities and suburbs, not knowing the names of their next-door neighbors, never seeing their sisters or brothers or parents because their families are scattered all over the country. They hire strangers to take care of their kids. They hire strangers to tend to their mothers and fathers. Everyone's in a hurry, frantically rushing from one day to the next. Dave has to laugh when people wonder how in the world he can live in a place like Fort Yukon. How in the world, he asks them, can *they* live in places like *that*? That's what he'd like to know. People say they feel sorry for anyone who has to live up here. Hell, counters Dave, the people of Fort Yukon should feel sorry for *them*. For all of their problems, he says, the villagers still have each other, in a way that's been lost in most of this country. If anyone in Fort Yukon drops the ball or falls through the cracks, someone else is there to catch them, to pick up the pieces. Someone like the Fleeners, the Cadzows, the Englers, the Alexanders, the McCartys. Someone like Diane.

And, yes, someone like Dave. This is why he came to Alaska back in 1976, beyond merely a taste for adventure. He wanted to find a life that meant something, a place to connect with, people with whom he could make a difference, no matter how small. Money, status, all those hollow rewards of the rat race, they meant nothing to him. Here in Fort Yukon he found what he was looking for. Home. Family. Neighbors. A place to raise his children, his flowers, his bees. A place where—and he knows this sounds trite, but it's true—he could contribute, give back to the community what it was giving to him. He did it first through the teaching and then through the basketball.

Which is what he found himself wrestling with, agonizing over, after that blowup with Buzzy. Dave had not gotten into coaching to become the kind of asshole he'd played for back in high school in Maine. He didn't need that, and neither did these kids. So at the end of that season—last season—he quit. He submitted his resignation and turned to his garden. The truth was it felt good—the relief, the lifting of all of that pressure. Sure, it was going to be hard sitting up in the bleachers, a mere spectator watching someone else coach his boys. But that's life, a tradeoff with every decision you make.

Come fall—last fall—no one had stepped forward to take over the team. None of the teachers at the school were interested. As for the men in the village, there are always plenty of them—mostly ex-players—who consider themselves better coaches than the guy sitting down there on the bench, whoever that guy might be. But when the time comes to actually step up and try becoming that guy, most of Fort Yukon's men realize it's just too much work, it takes too much time. They realize how much more this job requires than simply coaching the basketball games. The thought of having to show up for practice every weeknight from November through March is enough in itself to discourage most of them. The pay—two thousand dollars for a season—is next to nothing. Dave spends more than that just to hire someone to cover for him at the airport when he's on the road with the team. Then there are the nuts and bolts of actually ushering a dozen or so boys through a season of road trips: the flying, driving, feeding, clothing, nursing, entertaining, tutoring, disciplining, watchdogging and essentially parenting that is required to coach a team of bush village teenagers through a season of basketball. Not to mention the phone calls and faxes to other teams' coaches, to school administrators, to referees, to motels and rental van companies, to the airlines and even the damn National Weather Service, making constant adjustments to the vagaries of the Arctic conditions, to the sudden shifts in the weather that can turn the simplest trip into a logistical nightmare. Dave would love to see one of those guys up in the bleachers, the ones who are constantly dumping on the way that he coaches—the Paul Shewfelts and Willie Fields of the world—he'd love to see them actually try doing this job.

But none of them stepped forward last autumn. Freezeup arrived and still the team had no coach. The boys had assumed all summer that Dave was bluffing, that there was no way he'd actually quit. But when the deadline approached and he hadn't applied, they realized he meant it. They begged him to reconsider. Half the village called and asked him to come back. But Dave hadn't made this decision lightly, and he was not about to change it just like that. He was hoping someone, anyone half decent, would apply for the job. But nobody did. Finally, the day before the deadline, with the team facing the prospect that there might be no season because they might have no coach, a group of the boys, led by Matt and John, came to the house and sat down with Diane and pleaded with her to talk to Dave. Which she did. And he finally said okay, he'd do it.

What he didn't say, to anyone but Diane, was that he was never going to be drawn to the dark side again. He was never going to lose that perspective, never going to lose sight of what he was doing this for.

And look what happened next. A team with no expectations, a team everyone thought would stink up the gym, a team with no starters back from the season before, went all the way to the state finals, further than any team Dave had ever coached. Was there a lesson in that? Who knows? But now, with yet another season beginning, Buzzy and Jennie are here to remind Dave that nothing comes easy, that there's always something unforeseen just around the next corner, and the best you can do is prepare.

Which he's doing right now, for tonight, while Diane sews those gloves, and Gavin stares at his MTV, and Mickey takes his midday nap back there in the bathroom.

SEVEN

Scrimmage

SATURDAY NIGHT MID-DECEMBER. Thirty-two-below. Dave's van is parked outside the gym door as he lugs cases of soda, candy, hot dogs, chips and half-gallon cans of nacho cheese sauce into the court-side concession booth. Georgie and Diane set up the snacks while Cheryl Cadzow tosses a couple of balls out on the floor. As always, the girls will scrimmage a team of the town's women tonight before the boys take the floor against the men.

That's if enough girls show up, which right now is in doubt. Ruby and Amanda are out there warming up, along with Cheryl's daughter, Mandy, but that's it. Mandy's the girls' leader this year, no question. She's got a swagger to her. She's tough. The boys call her "Mandy-Man," and it's easy to see why. When Earl was coaching the kids' hockey team, they used to show up at the rink down in Fairbanks for a game, and the other team would see Mandy strapping on her pads and wonder what the hell a girl was doing out there on the ice. Then the game would begin and Mandy would throw a full-body check, crushing one of those boys into the boards, and they wouldn't wonder what she was doing out there anymore.

It's two dollars a head for the villagers to watch their kids play tonight. All proceeds, including concessions, go toward the teams' season expenses. Right now there are only a dozen or so small children scrambling over the bleachers, playing tag, climbing on Doc, grabbing at his ball cap. More adults will show up as the evening wears on, but kids always outnumber the parents at these preseason scrimmages. "It's a cheap babysitting service," says Dave, grabbing a dry mop to begin sweeping the floor. "Drop 'em off here, pick them up three hours later, all for two bucks? You can't beat it."

Three more girls on the team wander in a few minutes before game time, including Gina Shewfelt. Gina's back from Mount Edgecumbe, moved in with Jack and Matt. She's glad to be home. She missed her big brothers. And Matt's glad she's here. Now he's got someone to help with the laundry and cooking and picking up around the house.

The girls' game begins, with Dave running the clock and Cody Cadzow on the whistle. Cody's an eighth grader, a gym rat, just like the big guys. He's going to be a player, says Dave. He's got that swagger, just like his cousin Mandy. Cody will referee both games this evening, and he won't back down from anyone. It's tougher calling these games than playing in them, says Dave. Especially for a thirteen-year-old. The women are easygoing, but the men will get in the face of whoever's blowing the whistle. They'll dispute every call. They'll curse. But Cody can handle it. Cody's a tough kid.

By halftime the crowd is beginning to swell. About sixty people are here, including Fort Yukon's number one fan, Trader Dan. He's lived in the village for going on three decades now, but only a handful of people in town know that his last name is Teague. He's always been Trader Dan, period, for as long as anyone can remember. No one could tell you how old he is either. The fact is, he's not sure himself. He was born near El Paso either seventy-six or seventy-seven years ago, he says. "I'm not sure which. See, Mexicans count their age from the time of conception, not birth. At least the old-timers do."

Dan's mother was Mexican. He was raised among her relatives after his father, a U.S. border patrolman, died when he was eight . . . or nine. "That's me," he says, with a chuckle, "a half-breed, like everyone else around here."

He's sitting, as always, in the bleachers' front row. That gives him room to spread out a little, try to get comfortable. It's hard, what with the emphysema, the diabetes, the enlarged prostate and the sixty or so extra pounds he's carrying that his doctor would love to see him get rid of. He's got an appointment with an optometrist—who's monitoring his glaucoma—down in Fairbanks next month timed with the team's opening road game in Healy. Dan always schedules his personal and business trips to coincide with the basketball team's schedule. He figures it costs him about a thousand dollars a trip to watch the boys play, once you add up the airfare, the lodging, the meals and the expense of getting around for a few days—renting a car and whatnot. So he always tries to kill a few birds with one stone: take care of business, catch up with old friends, visit the doctor or dentist. When he's gone, he usually gets Justin James's kid brother, Barney, to mind the store. Barney's small for a seventh grader, hardly tall enough to see over the counter. It's funny when strangers stop in to buy something. They think the store's empty until they see the top of a ball cap moving around back there behind the register.

Trader Dan is a classic "end of the roader"—the kind of grizzled life-long wayfarer who winds up in a place like Alaska, in an outpost like Fort Yukon. He grew up picking produce alongside his cousins in Mexico, spent some time in an orphanage in California, took to the road as a teenager in the early 1940s, riding flatcars and freight trains throughout the far West, joined the army as World War II was just winding down, "bucked rivets" as a steelworker after leaving the service, did a few years of college, taught high school, learned welding, got married, had three kids and was drawn to Alaska in the early 1970s to work on the pipeline. "I won't lie to you," he says. "It was the money. You could make twenty dollars an hour washing *dishes* up here back then."

One thing led to another, and in the spring of 1980, after his wife passed away, with his kids grown and gone, an old army buddy talked him into coming up to Fort Yukon. The friend was in the riverboat business. "Next thing I knew," says Dan, "I was in that business too."

He worked the route from Circle to Fort Yukon, piloting tugboats, pushing freight barges loaded with fuel, supplies, furniture, trucks and automobiles through the baffling tangle of muddy channels, sloughs, oxbow lakes, spits and constantly shifting sandbars that comprise the vast Yukon River in summer. The Fort Yukon that Trader Dan recalls from that time is the same one Dave Bridges discovered when he first arrived here.

"It was pretty wild," says Dan. "Pretty rough. Reminded me of a border town back when I was a kid in Texas. Everyone bellying up to a bar and getting in a fight, and the next day they're all picking cotton together. Well, there was no bar here, but there was liquor everywhere, and they were cutting wood instead of picking cotton, but other than that everything else was just about the same. You had a killing every three or four months around here back then. I don't think we've had a killing now for four years or so."

He shifts his position, wheezing with the effort of moving his legs. He's got a loose pair of sweatpants on, sneakers, no socks. His beard could use trimming, but he's not in a hurry about that. When he goes down to Fairbanks, he makes sure to clean up, he says, "for the ladies." Here, it's not so important.

"Some people might have gone running the other direction as soon as they saw this place," he continues, "but I felt real comfortable. I hadn't had a home in a long, long time. That's what it felt like to me, like I'd finally come home."

That was twenty-five years ago. Dan opened his little store in 1983, put a gas pump out front a year later and has been a fixture in Fort Yukon ever since. The first thing outsiders ask about when they step into his place are the framed photos of past Eagles basketball teams nailed to the wall behind his cash register. He's only too happy to tell them about each one.

"I don't think I've ever been happier in my life than I am sitting in a gym watching these boys play," he says. "They do so much with so little. I just love that."

He hikes up his sweatpants, tugs down his T-shirt so it covers his belly.

"You've got to understand," he says, "there's a personal connection for me, for everyone here. We've known these kids since they were babies. Most of them sat on my lap when I used to do Santa Claus at Christmas. I know what some of these kids have been through, what some of their families have been through."

Cody's whistle blows as the ball bounces out of bounds, right into Dan's hands. He fumbles it, regains control and tosses it back onto the court.

"Watching these boys go down-country and play those bigger schools," he continues, "it's like David and Goliath. It's like that movie *Hoosiers,* only better. That was a little too polished for my taste, a little too Hollywood. I prefer the real thing."

The girls' game is winding down now. The bleachers are filling up, and the boys have begun arriving, sauntering into the gym in groups of two and three.

"*Look* at them," says Dan, watching Aaron and Wade and Tim Fields walk past. "Those are dynamic young men. You can't see it around town when they're all bundled up, but you watch them out on that basketball court, and you realize the potential for *greatness* in those boys."

The girls' game ends, the men start warming up at one end of the court, and Dave hands over the game clock to one of the kids in the stands. He grabs a trash can on wheels and begins pushing it from one end of the court to the other, picking up litter before the boys' game begins. Dan nods as the coach pushes past with the barrel.

"David was one of the first people I got to know when I moved up here," he says. "I had no idea he knew a *thing* about basketball. I still don't know where he gets his knowledge. But he knows what he's doing."

The bleachers are almost filled now, with adults as well as children. Wes and Bruce James's mom, Evelyn, is here, as are the McCarty sisters, all three of them. Dacho Alexander and his baby daughter, Da'achrai, are seated down by the boys. Earl Cadzow is squeezed into the top row, along with his brother Jay. A couple of bodies away is Jack Shewfelt, watching his son John warm up with the men while Matt shoots around with the boys. Ryan's not here, and the men's team misses him. They've got only seven players tonight, including Anthony Shewfelt and his dad, Paul, of all people. It's been years since Paul Shewfelt suited up for one of these games. Some of the crowd is tittering, watching him out there with his outdated headband, throwing up those archaic left-handed hooks.

Tim Fields's dad, Willie, ducks his head into the gym for a minute, then leaves. He's been a hard one for Dave to figure out. In some ways there's no one in town who's earned more respect than Willie Fields. He fought as a marine in Vietnam—actually fought, didn't just sit on a ship offshore from the action like some of the other vets in the village. He's a master musician as well, a fixture at the annual Fiddlers' Festival down in Fairbanks. It was Willie who helped organize the live music fund-raiser staged last month at the radio station for his brother Brewster—Matt's uncle—who has cancer.

But for all his good works, Willie's got a dark side, a temper that can flare in an instant, an anger that surges up from inside at the drop of a hat. For some reason, it seems to surge whenever basketball is mentioned. For some reason, Willie Fields just can't stomach the way Dave Bridges runs this basketball team. Whenever Paul Shewfelt broadcasts the games, it's Willie who handles the feed at the radio station. The two of them will critique Dave's coaching right there on the air, right in the midst of the game, talking about what Dave's doing wrong and why the team's not doing better—and Willie can't even see the game; he's in the studio, depending on Paul's meandering descriptions and his own distaste for Dave. It's not as if Willie should have problems with how his son Tim is treated. Tim Fields is one of Dave's starters, a fixture at power forward, the team's only true big man besides Aaron. Whatever the reason, Willie Fields, while a fan of Fort Yukon basketball, is no fan of Dave Bridges. And he's not sticking around to watch tonight's scrimmage.

The men's team will be counting on Anthony Shewfelt tonight, along with Ryan's sidekick Simon and one of the school's all-time scorers, Jeremy Peter. A year older than Ryan, Jeremy was a pure shooter, probably the best Dave's ever had. "He had ice water in his veins," says Dave. "End of the game, clock's ticking down, three-two-one, you want him to have the ball in his hands." It was Jeremy's streak shooting—one night he hit five three-point shots in one quarter—that inspired Dave's "hot hand" rule. It's simple, explains Dave. If a player hits a couple of threes, Dave stands up and hollers, "Hot hand!" That's an instruction to the other four teammates to get the ball to that shooter the next trip up the court, no matter what.

"He's got to at least touch it," says Dave. "If he decides not to shoot, that's up to him. But that's got to be his decision, not anyone else's.

"I remember what it felt like to be in the zone," he continues. "You just couldn't *wait* to get back up the floor and feel that ball in your hands again. But there always seemed to be players who'd come up the court the next time who would not give it to you. When they finally did, the feeling had disappeared. And you're like, 'What's wrong with you? I wanted it *then*, not *now*.' 'Hot hand' makes sure you get the ball *now*."

The last of the boys—Johnny Adams and Chris Engler—arrive a couple minutes before game time. Johnny is one of Dave's wild cards, a mystery. He's the quietest kid on the team, but he dresses the loudest. While most of the boys favor the standard skate-and-surf T-shirts and sweatshirts and ball caps from Billabong, Hurley and Fox, Johnny prefers the hip-hop street gangsta look, with color-coordinated velour sweatsuits accented by gaudy medallions and faux-gold-carat jewelry draped around his neck. His teammates dog him about the bling, but Johnny just smiles. Never says a word. He's the same way on the court, where Dave calls him the "silent assassin." Johnny's got the quickest, most accurate outside shot on the team, besides Matt's, and he's only a sophomore. At a slim five-eleven he's one of the team's tallest players, and his long, lanky arms make him play even taller. He's developed a smooth, silky drive over the summer, to go with his jumper. His offensive potential is almost limitless, says Dave, but Johnny tends to disappear on defense. Worse, he tends to do the same thing in class. Last year, like Wade's, Johnny's grades dropped so badly the second semester that he was only eligible for home games. This year, he's hovering right on that 2.0 fault line.

Chris Engler's got no such concerns. Georgie would kill him if his grades fell that low. Chris is a junior, one of the team's mainstays, but frankly, confides Dave, he hasn't fulfilled his potential. Chris has other interests besides basketball. His snowmachine, for one. He's always tinkering with that engine, taking it apart and putting it back together. Beyond that, there's the cabin he's spent the past eight months building for himself, behind his family's house. He's done it all alone, from cutting and hewing and shaping the logs, to laying the flooring and fitting the windows, to setting the rafters and roof, to the caulking. It's pretty impressive, says Dave, seeing a boy that age with the initiative and commitment to build himself an honest-to-god house; you've got to respect that so much, he says. But all the time and effort Chris has put into that cabin has taken away from his game. Dave can count on Chris for defensive quickness—he'll get his share of minutes this season based purely on that. But offensively, Chris's skills just haven't developed the way they should have after two years on this team. His shooting is sketchy, and he spends too much time horsing around with that useless between-the-legs dribble. They all do. It's that "And 1" nonsense they watch on ESPN and MTV, says Dave. That crazy hip-hop street ball. Half those moves, like that jive juke-step Chris likes to do before putting the ball on the floor, are illegal. The refs will call traveling every time. Dave tells the kids that, but they keep doing it, especially Chris.

They're all out there now, warming up while the sound system plays one of Chris's mixed CDs—Slipknot, Limp Bizkit, Eminem. The boys know every lump, every dead spot on this old, uneven floor. They've played on far worse. In Tanana, for example, there's a bulge near one of the foul lines so large you could actually trip over it. Nulato is almost as bad, with its court made from warped four-by-eight sheets of painted plywood. A couple of years ago the boys played on a floor down in Palmer that was made of linoleum tiles. They played once on a carpeted court, at a small Christian school in Fairbanks. They've seen every imaginable kind of backboard, from fan-shaped to rectangular, some made of metal, a few made out of wood. They played once in the village of Cantwell, high up in the Alaska Range, on wooden backboards so dead you could throw a line drive at them, hard as you pleased, and the ball would just die, drop straight down through the hoop. The strangest court his boys ever played on, says Dave, was a couple years back, on a trip to Anchorage. They stopped on the way for a game against a brand-new private academy, which Dave had scheduled at the last minute. When they stepped into the gym, they couldn't believe it. The court was so short there was no room for a three-point line. The ceiling was so low you couldn't shoot from any farther out than the foul line without risking hitting the lights. Dave instructed his boys to shoot nothing but layups that night—which, it turned out, they would have done anyway against this team. They were so atrociously bad that Dave was embarrassed for them. He never would have scheduled that game if he had known how inept this team was. Dave's boys feasted on their guards, turning steal after steal into breakaway layups. Dave called off the press early, cleared his bench, did all he could to hold the score down, but his kids still broke a hundred easy, which Dave hates to have happen. He hates to even give the appearance of running it up on somebody. He remembers how it felt the first season he coached, watching some of those teams run up the score on Fort Yukon.

The buzzer sounds, time for the game to begin. Dave sends out what would be his starting five if the season began tonight: Matt, Josh and Justin at guards, Aaron and Tim Fields inside. His instructions are simple. Work the 1-2-2 half-court trap. Justin up top, in the "1" position. Matt and Josh on the sides. Aaron and Tim down low. Dave reminds Justin to steer the ball handler toward the sidelines, where Matt and Josh will be waiting just past half-court. This is what Dave teaches every day in practice. That's where the payoffs happen, he preaches, where the sidelines and half-court stripe meet. That's where you spring the first trap, in those two corners. Don't let them get the ball to the middle, he tells his boys over and over again. Let them get the ball to the middle, and there's no place to trap. Let them get the ball to the middle, and they've got options, openings, choices. Let them get the ball to the middle, and you're dead. There's no principle more fundamental to the defense Dave teaches—and the offense as well—than this one simple rule: Squeeze your opponents to the sidelines when they've got the ball; push the ball up the middle when it's yours.

A lot of the people in town didn't know what to make of the way Dave coaches when he first took over the program. They were used to run-and-gun basketball, wide-open shootouts with scores in the 80s, sometimes even higher. When Dave took over, the scores abruptly dropped to the 50s and 40s. It wasn't as much fun to watch—unless you appreciated defense—but Fort Yukon's teams suddenly started winning more often. A lot more often. Some of the grumblers—Paul, Jack, Willie Fields—don't like Dave's focus on defense. They want to see offensive plays—sets and formations like they had back when they were playing this game. Dave doesn't bother with any of that. His boys run hardly any offensive sets at all. They count on their defense to dictate the tempo, to create scoring opportunities: turnovers, steals, fast breaks, and layups. Other than a handful of out-of-bounds plays, Dave's approach to offense is improvisational, free-wheeling—lots of ball movement, keep the defense shifting, lots of picking and cutting away from the ball, keep the floor spread, don't bunch up on one another, get the ball in to the post players—Aaron or Tim—up high or down low, give them a chance to turn, hit a cutter, drive, take a short ten- or twelve-footer themselves or kick it back out to one of the guards for a three.

Basic stuff. Dave believes in keeping it simple. He watches so many coaches micromanage their players, yelling out to their kids what to do every time up the court. It kills him, watching that. He can understand pro coaches doing it, even college. But kids at this level? Kids up here in the bush? They get a coach doing that, and they turn hesitant. Tentative. They play scared. They're afraid they might screw up, make a mistake, not run a play right and wind up on the bench. They're not running free, which is what Dave believes kids like this should be doing. Those are the words he uses—"running free." He sees those overcoached kids walk the ball up the court, the point guard holding up a finger or two, calling some play out loud, his eyes darting over toward his coach, everything so controlled, so methodical, and Dave and his boys just start licking their lips. They start drooling. It's lambs for the slaughter, as far as they're concerned. It's like waving raw meat in front of a pack of wolves.

Dave works hard in practice on technique, on individual skills: shooting, passing, screening, rebounding. And he teaches general concepts and principles: court vision, awareness, spacing, flow. He's got a short list of rules he recites like commandments, over and over and over again.

Who's the most dangerous man on the floor? Dave asks this question at least once every practice. The answer is the man who just passed the ball. Don't take your eyes off him on defense, he warns. And look ... im on offense. Everyone seems to forget about the man who just ... the ball. He's the one who will sting you every time, says Dave. ... on inbounds plays.

Scrimmage

Hands up on defense? Bullshit, says Dave. He watches teams play zone that traditional way, five guys staring at the ball with their arms high in the air, and it drives him nuts. Keep your arms *out*, not up, he preaches. The game's played down *here*, not up there. And quit staring at the ball. Look around you, talk to each other, be aware of what's going on behind you, to the sides. Know where the opposing players are cutting, where they're moving. Realize where your own weak spots are at any instant. If you're doing nothing on defense but staring at the guy with the ball, Dave tell his boys, you're as useless as tits on a bull moose.

And when you've got someone trapped, never slap down at the ball. Slap *up*, Dave preaches. You slap down, and it's almost guaranteed the ref will whistle you for a foul, he says. Slap up, and the ref will let it go. Maybe it's because the ref can't see as well when the hand's coming from below. Who knows? But this is another Fort Yukon mantra: Slap up, not down.

To Dave, beyond everything else, basketball is all about tempo and pace. It's about dictating the speed at which the game is played. It's about forcing the action. It's about pushing the other team out of their comfort zone, upsetting their rhythm, making them do things they don't want to do, that they're not used to doing. If a player likes to go to his right, Dave's kids make him go left. A team likes to walk the ball up the floor? There will be no walking against Fort Yukon, not with those guards swarming like a nest of angry hornets. To Dave, the game boils down to which team is able to impose its will on the other. This is why conditioning is paramount in his preparations. This is why he runs his boys every day till they're ready to vomit. They're naturally fast. What Dave wants to make sure of is that they're as fast in the fourth quarter as they were in the first. Because there's no letting up. This is what Dave Bridges's Fort Yukon teams are known for—their relentlessness. They keep pushing and pushing and pushing the action. They give you no time to rest, to regroup, catch your breath, settle down. Attack, attack, attack, on defense and offense. That's Fort Yukon's game plan, every game, no matter who they are playing or where.

That's the game plan tonight.

ien are all shooters, all scorers—all except Paul. They've got just
ch quickness as the boys, with Simon and even Anthony, who's
tively fast. Anthony doesn't look like much, with his thick eyeglasses
his roundish, overweight body. But he's got game. His jump shot is
impact—quick and deadly. And he's surprisingly effective driving to the
oop, using his body to shield the defender and draw fouls. He didn't
make honorable mention All-State for nothing. The fact is, his less-than-
impressive appearance is actually an asset. People tend to underestimate
him. By the time they realize this guy's a player, it's often too late.

Not so with Jeremy. From the moment he steps onto the floor, he
commands attention. The first shot he takes when he starts warming up
is always from well beyond the three-point line. And he usually nails it.
His form is near flawless. But he's put on a lot of weight since finishing
school three years ago. Most of the weight's come from drinking. Dave's
been more than a little disappointed to watch Jeremy slip into the routine
followed by so many men in the village: He works the odd job here and
there, parties as often as possible and, come wintertime, hangs around
the gym waiting for a pickup game to develop. He lives for these Friday
and Saturday nights in December, when he gets to play in front of a
crowd, like the old days.

From the opening tap, the pace of the game is frantic, frenetic. Both
teams are pushing the action, playing the way Dave has taught them.
Simon knows what to do against the boys' traps. He and Daniel Thomas,
who graduated four years ago and has a good steady job now as a heavy
equipment operator, run a nice little two-man game getting the ball up
the floor, staying away from the sidelines, avoiding the traps, knifing
across half-court and finding Jeremy and Anthony and the older guy,
Billy Adams, open on the wings for good looks at three-pointers. Adams's
shot is an odd one, kind of a heave off the shoulder, arcing high like a
mortar, almost scraping the ceiling. But it's deadly accurate. By the time
the first quarter's over, he's hit three of them. By halftime he's got four,
and the men are leading by three.

Dave's not concerned with the score. He wants to see how his boys
work together. Josh and Justin, for instance. They need to step up and
take charge on offense, which they're not doing right now. They're

holding back, reluctant to finish a play—take the shot, drive to the hoop. And it's because of Matt. Everyone on the team defers to Matt. He's the unquestioned leader, the only senior besides Josh, and Josh is a rookie. Matt is the established star, and he knows it. He's not loud or obnoxious, like Ryan, but he's every bit as cocky. That edge Dave talks about comes out in the way Matt carries himself on the court. He's got that cool kind of arrogance, the studied nonchalance of a player who's not going to let you see him sweat, who never looks like he's trying too hard. Which is all fine with Dave. But what's not fine is the other players' assumption that it's Matt who's supposed to take the big shot, it's Matt who's supposed to make the play when they need it, it's Matt who's supposed to be the first option. They're all looking to Matt every time before doing something themselves.

Justin, for instance, can shoot the lights out in practice. There's no reason he shouldn't be good for at least a couple of three-pointers a game. But he won't pull the trigger when an actual game begins, even if he's wide-open. It's as if he thinks that's not his place, that the shooter is supposed to be Matt. As for Josh, he's shown a nice knack for taking the ball to the hole, penetrating the defense. Dave didn't expect him to have that ability, considering his lack of experience. But when he gets there, he doesn't quite know how to finish. Instead of taking it all the way to the basket and getting the layup or drawing a foul, Josh gives it up, dishes it off to one of his teammates—typically Matt—who's often in nowhere near as good a position to score as Josh is himself.

Of course Matt's happy to have the ball coming to him. He's gotten quite used to being the star. He's even shown some resentment when one of his teammates tries taking the spotlight. During one game last season, Shane Kelly got off to a hot start, nailing shot after shot. The other team called a time-out, and Matt came to the bench grumbling about Shane "going Kobe on us." Kobe Bryant, the L.A. Lakers star. Dave couldn't believe it. He stared daggers at Matt and said, "I'm glad *somebody* is. Otherwise we'd have nothing right now."

Something Matt's doing tonight, and he's been doing it all this preseason, is throwing these crazy three-quarter-court bounce passes he picked up over the summer. He'll spot Justin or Josh or Derek or Wade streaking downcourt, and rather than leading them with a simple over-head toss, he'll try threading the needle with a long bounce pass, with a little sideways spin added for extra effect, and it looks fantastic when it works, the ball zipping between three or four defenders on its way to the target. But more often than not it goes awry, glancing off someone's body or simply flying out of bounds. It's hot-dogging, that kind of pass. It's showboating, pure and simple. But Dave's not going to jump up and get in Matt's face about it. For one thing, he doesn't want to kill Matt's creative instincts, which are so strong. Matt's got that knack all the great ones have for rising to the occasion and making a mind-blowing play when it's most needed. That kind of big-play ability goes hand in hand with making mistakes. No risk, no reward, that's how Dave sees it. Matt may throw that long bounce pass into the bleachers three times in the first half of a game, but come the fourth quarter, the game's final minute, the score tied, a teammate breaking open on a transition steal, he will nail that same pass, put it right in his teammate's hands, right in stride, for the winning bucket. You don't want to kill that kind of instinct in a kid, says Dave. But you don't want it to get out of hand, either. He's watched Matt throw that pass away four times tonight in the first half alone. This is something he'll talk to Matt about later, alone.

Dave likes what he's seeing from some of the others, especially Derek. The kid's got such a sweet stroke, and he's shown it tonight, gathering himself as he receives a pass, squaring up before the ball even arrives, his feet settled under him so he's ready to shoot as soon as it gets there. He's banging the boards as well, pushing back against the men's elbows and shoves, which you wouldn't expect, watching his shy, gentle off-court demeanor.

Aaron's shown Dave something new as well, using his left hand, which he never did last year, and using the glass as well, banking in a couple of eight- to ten-footers from the sides. Dave's been drilling the boys this preseason on using their weak hand and on using the glass, and it's clear Aaron's been listening. He's also fine-tuned his timing on blocked shots. Last year he picked up far too many fouls on clumsy blocked shot attempts. Tonight, he's swatted four of the men's shots into the wall and one into the bleachers, drawing a roar from the crowd.

Halftime Georgie and Cheryl run out onto the court and set up a cakewalk. A couple dozen kids and adults pay a dollar apiece to circle several homemade cakes and platters of cookies arranged on the floor, while a scratchy recording of Christmas carols plays on the sound system. The winner is the one standing on the right number when the music stops. All proceeds go to the team. Matt and Josh are out there, eyeballing a three-layer cake with blue icing. Zach's out there, too. Dave loves it. How often would you see something like this at a high school game in Detroit or L.A., he wonders. How many teenage boys and girls— ballplayers, no less—would get out there and march around to corny music like that, with no care or concern about not being cool. It's just one more thing to love, says Dave, about life in a village.

The second half starts, and Dave's up off the bench now, directing a nonstop stream of patter and one-liners at his own players, at the men, at the fans sitting behind him, who delight in the show.

"Step *up*, Justin!"

"Come on, Chris, you're *waltzing*. This ain't no two-step. This is a *fast* dance."

"No, Matthew, not to the side. To the *middle!*"

"Simon, you're all *over* him. You've never been that close to a *woman* in your life!"

"Push it. Push it. *Push it!*"

"You coulda *caught* that pass twenty pounds ago, Jeremy."

"*There* you go, Wes."

"Jiminy, will somebody give me a *post?*"

"Zach, you're not *helping* him by standing there waving your arm and hooting like a wounded goose."

"Stay *with* it, Wade! Don't relax when he backs away."

"Come on, Matt, you can get a better shot than *that*."

"I *like* it, Josh. Way to take it in!"

"I'd elbow you, *too*, Daniel, if you had your arms wrapped around me like that."

"Can we make some foul shots tonight, guys? Please? Pretty please?"

"Come on, John, clean it up. He ain't been slapped like that since the last time he tried to kiss a *girl!*"

By the end of the third quarter, the men are beginning to fade. They're breathing hard now, sucking air during time-outs, bent over and gripping their shorts, grabbing at water bottles. Dave's got fourteen boys on his bench, and he's using them all, cycling them in and out in waves. The men, though, for all their fatigue, keep hanging in. Daniel Thomas makes a couple of steals and nice passes for layups. Anthony keeps drawing fouls. Even Paul banks in a three-pointer. The score stays close, and the game's getting rougher. The men are shoving and grabbing to make up for what they've lost with their legs and their lungs. Cody's not blowing his whistle nearly enough to please Dave, but the crowd's into it. They came to see action, and they're getting it.

Half a minute to go, and the boys are up by a point. Daniel pushes the ball past midcourt, turns at the top of the key, flips it to Anthony in full stride down the left side. Everyone in the gym sees what's coming next.

Aaron's waiting.

He rises, so much higher than squat little Anthony.

But Anthony's savvy. He twists in midair, turns his back to Aaron, extends his right arm and flips the ball back over his shoulder, just over Aaron's outstretched arm.

The shot misses.

But the whistle blows.

Aaron screws up his face, but there's no complaint. He knows he bumped Anthony with the body.

Two shots.

Anthony hits both free throws, putting the men ahead by a point.

Fifteen seconds to go. The boys push the ball up the floor.

Twelve seconds. Justin gets the ball to Matt on the right wing, beyond the three-point line. The floor's spread.

Aaron flashes to the low post, planting himself at the base of the key on Matt's side, two men behind him, both helpless as Aaron spreads his legs and arms and looks for the ball.

Five seconds.

Dave points to the post. Everyone in the gym is waiting for Matt to dump the ball in to Aaron.

Matt keeps it.

He goes between his legs twice, right to left, left to right, rocking his body, staring down Simon.

Two seconds.

Matt jukes left, leans right and launches a rainbow from just beyond the arc.

It's long.

The ball bangs off the back of the rim as the buzzer sounds.

The men win.

Matt turns, expressionless. He mouths the word "fuck," but that's it.

Within minutes the gym's nearly empty, everyone headed back home or out to a party.

Diane and Georgie pack up the concessions. Dave makes one last pass with the trash barrel. He's thinking about that final shot, about Matt's choice to go for the win himself. Matt's done it before. Two years ago, he put Fort Yukon in the State Tournament with a buzzer-beating, end-of-the-game three from the corner against Mat-Su Christian. "Matt's Miracle Moment," people called it. They still talk about that one. Matt was only a sophomore, but even then he was fearless.

The problem is, Aaron was three feet from the basket, wide-open with both defenders sealed off. You couldn't ask for better position. And with plenty of time. Matt knew it. But he blew it off, and that bothers Dave.

If there's any top-dog nonsense going on here, Dave intends to nip it in the bud. There's nothing a quick talk with Matt shouldn't take care of. He's a good kid; he's not selfish. Dave sees it every day in practice, how Matt takes care of the others, particularly Wes, how he feeds Wes the ball, makes sure the freshman gets his share of shots.

No, most of what happened here, Dave's sure, is the father-and-brothers thing, Matt seizing the moment with his dad in the stands and John on defense and Ryan's shadow hovering over it all. The fact is, and Dave understands this, it's a deep, complex game whenever these boys face their uncles and cousins and brothers and friends in front of their families and neighbors, the whole village. The undercurrents of pride, honor, challenge, and respect run deep on both sides, on all sides.

It's far more than simply the boys testing themselves against men. That's natural, any time, any place, the rites and rituals of coming-of-age. What's different here, what amplifies everything, enlarging it far beyond the bounds of the basketball court, is the men's need to establish themselves, to say "This is who I am" in the face of having all that they are stripped away from them—their language, their culture, their history, their pride. With so little ground left to stand on, they stand here, on the court, all of them, the men and the boys, with the whole village watching.

Dave knows this, and so do the kids on his team. They all understand it's a whole different game, with more at stake in one sense, and less in another, when they go up against other boys like themselves, from other villages, boys who at this very moment are wrapping up their own Saturday night scrimmages in their own snowbanked gyms against their own fathers and brothers and uncles and cousins, all getting set for the season that starts in less than five weeks.

There are things to take care of, but overall Dave likes what he sees. This team is deep. God, but they're deep. There's no telling what might happen between now and March. Cripes, there's no telling what might happen between now and next week. But Dave does know one thing for certain: It's going to be one hell of a ride, no matter which way it goes.

PART TWO
The Season

EIGHT

New Year

MINTO HAS CANCELED its season.

The call came Friday afternoon, the first Friday of the new year—three days ago. Minto's principal was on the line to tell Doc his school won't have a team this year. Not enough eligible players. Doc immediately dialed Dave at the airport. Dave couldn't say he was surprised. He'd already tracked down Minto's schedule, knowing this might happen. Now he asked Doc to begin calling the coaches and principals of the schools on that list, hoping two of them might want to fill their own Minto dates as badly as Fort Yukon does.

Dave has to chuckle. The big 4A schools in Anchorage and Fairbanks don't have to deal with this nonsense. They're already one month into their season down there, while the 1A schools have yet to begin. West Anchorage High, ranked first in the state in this morning's newspaper, has already played twelve games. Bartlett, another Anchorage power-house, is ranked fourth with a 3–6 record, but those six losses have come at holiday tournaments down in Washington and clear across the country in South Carolina. This week Bartlett will be on the road again, at a round-robin in Missouri. They've got the top-rated senior point guard in the United States, according to all the recruiting services, which is why they've been invited to these big-name, big-dollar events. The guard's name is Mario Chalmers. A black kid. He's already signed with Kansas. He spent the past summer crisscrossing the Lower 48, playing ball with an all-star AAU team and wowing the scouts at high-profile camps from Las Vegas to Teaneck, New Jersey. Everyone's gone gaga over the kid from Alaska—Arizona, North Carolina, Wake Forest,

Georgia Tech, they all recruited him hard. He's six-foot-two, with a thirty-eight-inch vertical leap.

Six-two in Fort Yukon makes you the center, like Aaron. Six-two at Bartlett makes you a point guard. That's the biggest difference, right there, between 1A and 4A basketball in Alaska. Dave's always said most of his boys could play at the 2A level, some even at 3A. But they're simply too small to play with the big 4A kids. The idea of Josh, all five-foot-five and 135 pounds of him, squaring up against a thoroughbred like Chalmers ... well, Josh has got all the guts in the world, but he wouldn't have a prayer. At five-foot-whatever, most Native boys wouldn't stand a chance against the dozens of big black and white kids trying out for basketball at schools of that size.

But there are only twenty-one 4A schools in the state, ranging in size from Sitka High, with its 455 students, to Dimond, in Anchorage, with over 2,300 kids. There are twenty-eight 3A schools, with between one hundred and four hundred students. There are thirty-four 2As, with enrollments of fifty to a hundred.

And then there are the 115 1A schools registered this season with Alaska's high school athletic association, each with fifty or fewer students. That's more than five times the number of 4A schools in the state. It's more than the other three classifications combined. Almost every one of these small schools is Native. Almost all are in off-road communities, among the vast array of villages that dot the Arctic and sub-Arctic expanses of the state. Not all are able to field teams each season—fifty-nine have submitted rosters this year—but all are rabid about the game. Where the highway ends in Alaska, bush basketball— village ball—Native ball—1A ball—begins.

It's beginning this week, in those fifty-nine village schools, and every one of them is aiming at the same thing: that trip to Anchorage in March. The State Tourney is always a spectacle, a three-day gathering of tribes come to gorge themselves on basketball—eight games a day, boys' teams and girls'—and to feast on reunions with far-flung relatives and friends. They take over the city, which is only too happy to have them, a couple of thousand Natives with cash in their pockets, booking motels, buying meals at restaurants, spending their money on shopping sprees that some have saved up for all year. It's like an indigenous carnival. The only event that exceeds it is the annual meeting of the Alaska Federation of Natives, a quasi-political convention that takes place in Anchorage each fall.

This is Dave's goal every year—to get through the Regional and make it to State. He prepares by playing the toughest regular-season schedule he can draw up. He's always got at least half a dozen 2A teams on the list, sometimes even a 3A school or two. There's nothing sweeter than beating those big boys, especially on their own floor. Dave will never forget a couple of years ago, when Fort Yukon played Howard Luke, a 3A academy down in Fairbanks. Howard Luke had gotten serious about building a basketball program. The school had hired an ambitious coach, recruited a bunch of ballplayers from throughout the region. The team's front line ran six-three, six-two, with a six-one point guard. The coach was straight out of central casting: a black guy, dapper, shaved head, dressed to the nines in a crisp three-piece suit, with cufflinks, silk tie, matching silk handkerchief in the coat pocket, Italian shoes buffed so fine the gym lights gleamed off them. He came out before the game, glad-handing the refs like a politician. Then there was Dave, looking like he just tumbled out of the dryer, in his sneakers and jeans and rumpled button-up shirt. And there were his kids, warming up at the visitors' end, only one of them taller than six feet.

So the game started, and Fort Yukon simply devoured the Howard Luke guards, turning steal after steal into layups. By the end of the first quarter their coach had lost the jacket. By halftime he'd torn off the vest and the tie. He was all over his kids, all over the referees, but there was nothing he could do. At one point, after yet another trap-induced turnover, one of the Howard Luke players yelled, "Come *on*, guys. Can't you see how fucking *small* they are??!!"

That was a keeper, that line. Dave and his boys loved it.

They'll be meeting some higher-tiered schools this season, with 3A Susitna Valley and Hooper Bay and host Nenana signed up for the Little NIT, along with 2A Tok. They'll see 2A Galena and Skagway and Ninilchik at the Tok tournament, where they'll also have a possible rematch with 1A defending state champion Wainwright, the team Fort Yukon lost to in the state finals last year. Late this month they'll travel

down the Kenai Peninsula to that Russian village, Nikolaevsk, with its
2A team anchored by the six-foot-five center who tore Fort Yukon apart
last year, the huge kid with the beard. Cook Inlet Academy, a perennial
2A juggernaut, will be at the Nikolaevsk tournament as well. On the
way down to that event, the Fort Yukon kids will stop for a night in
Houston, outside Anchorage, to play that well-to-do suburb's 3A team.

Right now, though, Dave's mind is on the season opener, three days
from now, when he and his boys will fly to Fairbanks, then drive down
to Healy to play host Tri-Valley High that night in its annual kickoff
tournament. Tri-Valley is a 2A school. Lathrop and North Pole—two
Fairbanks 4A schools—will be there as well with their jayvee teams,
which Fort Yukon will play on Friday and Saturday. Dave always points
out to his kids that those 4A schools' junior varsity squads are next
season's varsity, so there's no shame in playing them, and there's immense
achievement in beating them. It doesn't happen often. Fort Yukon has
taken down far more 3A varsity teams in its history than it has 4A
jayvees.

Those Lathrop and North Pole games will have special meaning for
Derek and Zach, and for Aaron as well. Derek and Zach attended North
Pole last year. As for Aaron, when he transferred to Fort Yukon year
before last, it was from Lathrop. There's a saying in Fort Yukon about
village kids who move to Fairbanks and get swallowed up in those big
city schools. They call it "lost in Lathrop." Aaron was indeed lost among
Lathrop's 1,500 kids. As quiet as he is, the way he keeps to himself, he
was almost invisible there. He would never have dreamed of trying out
for basketball, and he probably wouldn't have made the team if he did.
The best move Aaron's mother ever made, as far as Dave is concerned,
was sending him back to Fort Yukon to live with his aunt, Diana
McCarty, and Diana's boyfriend, Jay Cadzow.

As for Derek and Zach, their dad saw the same thing happening to
them at North Pole. Among the thousand or so students there, Jerry
Carroll's boys were anonymous, nothing more than two Native faces in
a sea of white kids. In Fort Yukon everyone knows who they are. And
everyone wants to see how they'll do on the court, how they'll compare
to their father—the legend, the star. That's why Jerry sent them up in

September to live with their aunt Louie. Louie used to be a cop in the village. She knows how to keep two teenage boys in line.

Dave can bring only eleven players on this weekend's trip down to Healy. Their chartered plane, as always, will be one of Frontier Airlines' "Big Black Birds," as the boys call them—a nineteen-seat Beech twin prop. The girls will need six seats for their team—one girl is ineligible—plus one seat for Cheryl. That leaves Dave and eleven of his boys. He's already decided which of his team will stay behind. Wade hurt his back over Christmas break—strained it pulling his snowmachine out of a drift while ice-fishing upriver at a spot called Twentymile. So he's out. Kyle's got a sprained wrist, from slipping on the front steps of his cabin. He's out, as well. Which leaves one of the two freshmen. Wes didn't miss a practice over the holiday, while Zach went home to Fairbanks with Derek over the break. So Dave's decided Zach will miss this trip, too.

They wander into the gym, one by one. Both Tims—Tim Fields and Tim Woods—are limping with blisters. Matt's got a nasty bruise on his left calf; he was chainsawing a stack of Ginny Alexander's firewood over Christmas when Ginny's dog came out of nowhere, tore right through Matt's favorite pair of jeans, its teeth sinking into Matt's leg. Ginny felt awful about it, has no idea why her dog went ballistic.

Josh comes in, begins peeling off his coat and snowpants. Dave lifts his head, sniffs and grimaces.

"Are those your pants?" he asks.

"Why?" says Josh. "Do they smell like dog?"

Dave just looks at him.

"Those pants are *not* going with us on any road trips," he says.

Doc comes in, a sheaf of papers clutched in his hand. He drops down with a sigh onto the bleachers' front row. He looks exhausted. He's been on the phone all day, trying to fill those two Minto dates. It looks like he's got it worked out. Mat-Su Christian says its team will be happy to fly up in early February, as long as Fort Yukon is paying. Anderson High, from down near Healy, is willing to do the same thing next week. That gives Fort Yukon four home series this season—eight games. Their other fourteen regular-season games will all be on the road.

Wade saunters in with his hood pulled, as always, far over his head.

When he takes off the jacket, Dave sees he's got a bruised eye the color of plums. Wade mumbles when Dave asks him about it. All Dave can draw out of him is that Wade got into some kind of scrape over the weekend with some of the older guys in the village, in somebody's cabin. Dave doesn't need to know the details. He doesn't want to know.

"The walking wounded," he says as he lugs two black canvas bags over to the bleachers. The bags are filled with Fort Yukon's uniforms, folded neatly in sets and ready to hand out.

Doc's here to share some good news with the boys: All fourteen passed their first-semester eligibility requirements. Even Wade. That's what the papers in Doc's hands are about.

Dave shushes the kids quiet as Doc walks out onto the court and begins speaking.

"Well, boys," he says, "y'all made it—some by the width of this here piece of paper."

The kids grin, glance at one another.

"Now we still got some things we need to work on," he continues. "Like *hats*. There'll be no more wearin' ball caps in class, period. That's just common courtesy. You know that. And no profanity, either. We're cracking down on this, I'm tellin' you.

"Do this for me, fellas," he says. "I'm fixin' to spend a lot of money on you."

He fishes something out of his coat pocket. An athletic shoe catalog. He's marked several pages for the boys to choose from. Doc's treating the kids—the girls and the boys—by buying them each a brand-new pair of shoes, on his dime. They pass around the catalog, deciding which style they want, while Dave lays out the uniforms, in numerical order, in neat stacks on the bleachers. The boys decide on the Nike Shox Elevate. A hundred bucks a pop. That's twenty-one hundred dollars out of Doc's pocket, which he's happy to spend. He loves this. He loves being part of it all.

"The little kids in this town are gonna all know your numbers," Doc says, nodding toward the blue-and-white jerseys. "They're gonna know every *one* of your numbers by the end of next week."

Dave motions the boys over, stands back and lets them select their uniforms. The two seniors, Matt and Josh, get to go first. They'll be the cocaptains this season, Dave's decided.

Matt picks number 33, the same number Ryan and John wore before him. Three years ago, the number 33 jersey went missing. It cost Dave one hundred dollars to buy a replacement. He's still got scouts down in Fairbanks keeping an eye out for someone wearing it in a men's rec league game. No one would be foolish enough to wear it here in Fort Yukon. "I can't *wait* to see that jersey show up," he says.

Josh wants number 12, the number his dad Clifton wore back when he played for Fort Yukon. Josh gives Clifton grief every time they pull out an old photo of him wearing those tight early 1970s basketball shorts. "Nut huggers," Josh calls them. He wants his dad's number badly, but there's no number 12, so he picks 22.

The others then charge in, grabbing jerseys and warm-ups, trying them on, trading around till they've each finally got what they want.

Dave runs the boys hard this evening, and the next night as well. Meanwhile, he's watching the weather. And he's worried. The temperature's dropping, from eighteen-below on Monday evening, to the negative twenties on Tuesday, to minus-thirty-two on Wednesday morning, the day before the team's supposed to fly out. The state forbids schools to fly when it's colder than forty-below. It's too dangerous. Typical winter concerns such as airframe icing and blowing snow are normally not a problem for pilots in Interior Alaska, with its windless dry climate. But at forty-below the fuel or oil in the planes' engines can thicken, congeal or even freeze, especially if the slightest bit of condensation is allowed to occur. The tiniest bubble of moisture in a fuel line can mean disaster at Arctic temperatures. This is the primary reason 1A teams wait so long to begin their seasons. They want to get past winter's most severe stretch, typically from mid-December to mid-January, when temperatures in a place like Fort Yukon can plummet as low as the minus-sixties.

Back when the boys' parents were children, they'd routinely see seventy-below, but it hasn't gotten that cold here in years. The villagers just shake their heads when they see Ted Stevens, Alaska's pro-oil senator, step in front of Congress and the press like he did just last month and proclaim that global warming is a myth, that burning fossil fuels has no effect on the earth's climate. The villagers in Fort Yukon see the effects every winter. They see it in the later freezeups and earlier breakups of the ice on the rivers. They see it in the permafrost, which is getting just a little bit softer every year. They see it in the behavioral changes of the plants and the animals in the woods all around them. Sure, fifty- or sixty-below is plenty cold, they say, but you ought to feel seventy. They felt it all the time when they were kids, but not anymore. The Arctic is melting, no question, they say. Anyone who lives up here will tell you so. "Uncle Ted," as Stevens's oil and fishing industry patrons like to call him, doesn't live up here.

By Wednesday night, the temperature has dropped to minus-forty- seven. The TV news—the national news—reports that the Eskimo village of Kaktovik, up on the Arctic Ocean, near Prudhoe Bay, two hundred miles north of Fort Yukon, has been hit by a hurricane-force blizzard, pushing the wind chill to sixty-below and knocking out the town's elec- trical and water supplies. Blowing snow and winds have shut down Kaktovik's airstrip, making it impossible for rescue teams to fly in. A caravan of bulldozers and tundra vehicles has set out overland from the oil-supply town of Deadhorse, one hundred miles away, crossing a moon- scape of snowdrifts and ice to bring food, fuel and emergency supplies to the three hundred people of Kaktovik, most of whom are huddled in that village's little public works shop, the only structure in the commu- nity that has any heat.

In Fort Yukon, there's not a hint of a blizzard. The sky is clear—dark and dead calm. Contrary to the natural order of things in more southerly climes, where the temperature drops at higher altitudes, it's much warmer up there in the Arctic sky than it is down here on the ground. It's called an "inversion," this mix of warm upper elevations and cold ground. It tends to perpetuate itself. As long as the skies remain clear, any warmth at ground level rises, causing the ground temperature to plunge even lower. In Fairbanks, which is set in a bowl surrounded by low-lying hills, the neighborhoods built on those hills often have temperatures ten degrees warmer than the city they look down upon. The only relief from an inversion comes in the form of cloud cover. When clouds move in, the warm air on the ground is cushioned and stays there. But there are no clouds in sight this evening. Nor are there any the next morning, Thursday—game day. When Dave awakes, it's to a thermometer reading of fifty-three below zero.

By the time he gets to the airport, it's warmed up two degrees. The team was supposed to fly out at ten thirty this morning, but there's no way that's happening now. Dave's hoping against hope that they might get out late this afternoon. That would give them just enough time to load up the van and make it to Healy for the tip-off at seven thirty P.M.

The kids are all packed. Their bags are piled in the school's home ec room. They're going to classes, but no one's even pretending there's any teaching going on today. Everyone's waiting on the half-hourly updates from the airport.

Dave's phone is ringing off the hook, parents and villagers calling to see if the team has left yet. Trader Dan called this morning from Fairbanks. He flew down yesterday, checked into a motel, wants to know if the boys are still coming.

By lunchtime the temperature's still stuck at minus-fifty-one. Kyle Joseph's grandmother, Freda, the school's bilingual teacher, has turned impromptu cook, fixing a couple dozen grilled cheese sandwiches in the school kitchen for Dave's boys and Cheryl's girls. The kids are antsy, ducking their heads into the office every fifteen minutes to ask Georgie if she's heard anything.

Only once in the seven years he's been coaching has Dave had a road trip weathered out. That was to Tok, four years ago. By one o'clock it looks like this might be the second.

By two it's decided. The temperature's still in the minus-fifties. No way can they fly out. Dave sends word up to Doc, who breaks it to the kids.

The season won't start for another week.

NINE

Opener

AT LAST, IT'S game time.

The Anderson teams are here. They flew in this afternoon and were driven by van to the vo-tech center—Dacho's shop—where they'll bunk for the night. One member of their girls' team didn't make the trip. She was afraid to fly in an airplane that small, says their coach.

The refs are here as well. They flew up in a six-seat Navajo, were met at the airport by Georgie, who drove them over to the school, where they stored their gear—sleeping bags, shaving kits, DVDs for passing the time—in the Xerox room next to Doc's office. That will be their home for the next two days. All meals, for both the visiting teams and the refs, will be served in the cafeteria by women volunteers from the village.

Neither the Anderson teams nor the referees realized that the man in the fur hat pulling their bags off those planes was the Fort Yukon coach. Dave has had teams come to the village, stay for two days, and leave without knowing that was him up at the airstrip loading and unloading their stuff.

It's been a week since the Healy trip was canceled. That cold snap settled in for the following four days, dropping to minus-sixty Monday morning. It's thirty-five-below right now, Thursday night, as both sides of Third Street are lined with parked trucks and snowmachines, the villagers stomping the snow off their boots as they climb the gym's lighted front steps for the first game of the season.

Dave's already given the boys his standard home-opener speech. There are going to be 200 people out there tonight, he's told them, and 199 of them believe they can coach this team better than he can.

"You have to operate as a unit," he said, "and to do that you have to pay attention to me. Not to your dad. Not to your mom. To *me!*

"People are going to be yelling out to you on every play, telling you what you should do, screaming at you to shoot, pass, follow your shot, whatever. If any one of you acknowledges the crowd in the slightest, you're going to see someone standing at the scorer's table in about five seconds, getting ready to check in for you.

"The hardest thing about playing at home," he continued, "is winning the second game. You know why? Because after you win that first one, everyone's slapping you on the back and congratulating you. Your parents, their friends, everyone. You go over to somebody's place, and they're all celebrating, telling you how great you are. That takes about half an hour. Then they start telling you how great *they* were, and that takes about three hours. You wind up staying out till two, three in the morning, and you're completely exhausted the next day.

"They mean well, boys. Cut their veins, and they bleed Eagle blue. They think giving you that cold one and bending your ear about yourselves and about them is a good thing. But you've got to avoid it. Just don't do it."

From what Dave has heard, Fort Yukon should get that first win tonight, no problem. The Anderson boys' team has already played three games and lost them all. It didn't used to be that way. Not long ago, the Grizzlies were an Interior dynasty. They won six 2A Regional titles in the 1990s, finished second in the state in 1999, all under a coach named Rick Harris. Harris won more than four hundred games at Anderson before retiring in 2000. That's twenty twenty-win seasons. That's continuity. It wasn't just Harris's departure that started the downward spiral, though that certainly didn't help. What killed the program was downsizing at nearby Clear Air Force Base. Almost all 350 people who live in Anderson, just off the highway, eighty miles south of Fairbanks, work in some way or another at that base. When the Air Force began cutting jobs there at the turn of the decade, people began moving out, and the flow of military families upon which the school—and the basketball team—depended abruptly dried up. Anderson is still classified a 2A school, but it's now smaller than Fort Yukon, with only twenty-three high school kids.

Sixteen of them—boys and girls—are here tonight, and they're all white. The Anderson teams have always been white kids. In the past they could count on a couple of families to give them some height and some strong shooters. There were the Paul boys, a whole line of them, who ran six-six, six-five, year in and year out. And there were the Harrises, one Harris after another, all of them deadly from three-point range. But they're gone now. There's not a Paul or a Harris on this year's Anderson roster. The tallest kid on their squad is a six-footer, and frankly, watching him walk into the gym with his teammates, the Fort Yukon boys don't think he looks like much.

They're watching Mandy and company dismantle the hapless Anderson girls. The third quarter has just ended, with the score 41–8, Fort Yukon. The gym is packed, including Jack and his pals sitting in what they like to call the "wet" section, beside the boys' locker room door. Every now and then one of them slips into the bathroom, pulls out a flask, pours some rum or whiskey into the Coke he's bought at the concession stand, then returns to the bleachers.

Paul's perched at his table at midcourt, chattering into his radio headset. "Come on down," he urges his listeners. "There's still room."

It doesn't look like there's room. The bleachers are jammed. The folding chairs lining the walls behind each backboard are all taken. The boys have grabbed seats under the Fort Yukon basket, exhorting the girls and munching on popcorn and chips. Wes is finishing a soft pretzel lathered with cheese when Dave comes over and motions them all to the locker room. Time to suit up.

The locker room reeks of something called Axe, a body spray the boys swear by. Dave's seen the ads on TV, unspeakably gorgeous women throwing themselves at men who wear Axe. The boys apparently believe it. They're constantly perfuming themselves—before leaving for school, before going to bed, and here, in the locker room, before taking the court. Dave can't quite figure out why in the world they need to freshen up now, but he doesn't bother asking.

A head pokes in the door, tells Dave there's two minutes left.

He gathers the boys in a circle. There's not much to say at this point, nothing they haven't gone over a thousand times in the past six weeks of practice.

"I don't want them to have a chance to *breathe*," he says.

He pauses, studies the boys' faces.

"I want to step on 'em and I want to step on 'em *fast*," he says. "If I see you walking the ball up the floor, you're coming out."

With that, he drops his head, clasps his hands behind his waist and closes his eyes. The boys drop their heads as well.

"Heavenly Father," he intones, "watch over these boys. Keep them safe and sound, Lord. Make them fast, strong and true. Let their spirits be light, and let their feet have the wings of eagles. In Jesus' name, amen."

"Amen," answer the boys.

Dave leaves the room as Josh and Matt gather their teammates into a tight huddle, all fourteen boys bending into one another, pushing their heads together, draping their arms over each other's shoulders.

"What *time* is it?" shouts Matt.

"Game time!" the others yell.

"What *time* is it?"

"Game time!"

"What *time* is it?"

"Game time!"

"Who are we?"

"Eagles!"

"Who are we?"

"Eagles!"

"Who are we?"

"Eagles!!!"

"What're we gonna do?"

"Kick some ass!"

"What're we gonna do?"

"Kick some ass!"

"What're we gonna do?"

"Kick some ASS!!!"

With that, they hit the door, bursting into the heat and the roar of the gym, the crowd rising as one, a gauntlet of the village's children lining the way to the court as the boys pass between them, Josh leading the way with the team's one warm-up ball. "Get Psycho," by Disturbed, blasts out of the sound system.

The Anderson boys are already on the floor, in their purple and gold warm-ups, nicknames inscribed on the back of each one. "A-Bomb." "Wild Child." "Oh Baby." They make a point not to look at the Fort Yukon players as Josh and his teammates circle the floor and begin shooting layups.

The referees, both servicemen stationed at Fort Wainwright in Fairbanks, stand by the scorer's table chatting with Doc. One, a burly black staff sergeant named Jesse Myles, spins the game ball in his hands. His partner, a wiry white sergeant named Stanley Arnold, fiddles with the sound system, punches up a number by the rapper Jay-Z and breaks into a spontaneous dance, hip-hopping out onto the floor as the music thumps from the speakers and the crowd explodes with delight.

"Stan the *maaaan*," Doc crows into his handheld microphone as the music shuts off and the teams move to their benches for pregame introductions. Doc loves this part of the evening, stepping out to midcourt, welcoming everyone, introducing each player on each team, one by one, as they sprint to the other team's bench and shake hands with the opposing coach. It's a ritual that never gets old, not for Doc, or for Dave, or for the kids.

"And now," intones Doc, introducing the last player, "let's get ready to *rumble*."

It's no contest.

Anderson wins the opening tip, then watches helplessly as Josh, Matt and Justin swarm over their guards like mosquitoes. Three minutes in, the score is 14–2. By the end of the first quarter, Aaron has six blocked shots. Fort Yukon has eleven steals. The score is 19–6, and Dave goes to the bench.

Second quarter, Johnny comes in and hits three long three-pointers, along with a sweet double-pump drive. Wade is a bullet, stripping the

Anderson guards four straight times up the floor, zipping the other way for uncontested layups. Halftime it's 57–10. Johnny leads all scorers with fourteen points. Wade's next with thirteen, all in the second quarter. Everyone but the freshmen have already checked into the game.

There's not much for Dave to say. He's already called off the traps, pulled his boys back.

"There's no way they can catch us," he tells the kids as they sprawl on the locker room floor and benches, sucking on bottles of water and Gatorade. "We don't need to humiliate them."

With that, he sends them back out. The second half is more of the same. Anderson's boys are a beat slower, a full step behind the Fort Yukon players. The crowd shows compassion, cheering each Anderson score. Midway through the third quarter, at 65–14, Wes enters the game, his first appearance in a Fort Yukon uniform. The villagers make note, standing and whistling and stomping their feet. Halfway through the fourth quarter, the score 75–26, Zach makes his debut to the same appreciative ovation.

It takes Zach precisely two trips up the court to get his hands on the ball. When he does, it takes him no time at all to turn and launch it, a leaner from beyond the top of the key that finds nothing but net.

The gym detonates. The wet section goes nuts, howling and high-fiving one another, toasting the birth of yet another Carroll stud.

Zach backpedals, a grin on his face as he adjusts his eyeglasses.

Dave drops his head in his hands. This is all he needs—Zach being encouraged to shoot.

"I am cursed," he says.

Sure enough, the next time Zach touches the ball, he fires it. And the next. With 1:20 to go, he takes his fourth shot in three minutes, nailing a floater from the right side for his second score of the game.

"It's the GENES!" someone shouts, and the place cracks up.

The final is 86–28. Johnny is high man with sixteen, more than his total for all of last season. Four others are in double figures, including Derek with eleven and Matt with ten. Aaron just misses with nine, to go with eleven blocked shots and at least that many rebounds. Again, there's not much Dave can say.

"Go home, get some rest," he tells the boys as they peel off their uniforms and change into their street clothes.

Most of them do.

Jack and a half dozen friends make their way across the road to his cabin, each of them grabbing a log or two from the woodpile outside the front door before going in. They dump the wood by the stove, stoke the flames, break out some whiskey and light up a couple of joints. Jack holds court, taking a chair in the center of the hot, stuffy room, snorting about the "bogus" team the boys just beat. Matt and a friend stick their heads in the front door for a second, then take off into the night.

Next morning, Georgie has to beat back the kids as they clamor for a copy of the *Fairbanks News-Miner*—the sports section. A highlight each day in the village is the late-morning arrival of those bundles of papers at the AC, at Trader Dan's, and here, at the school. The villagers devour the news, especially during basketball season, especially when Fort Yukon has played. First thing Dave does when a game ends, at home or on the road, is find a phone and call in the score to the *News-Miner*'s sports desk. The night editors know him by now. Sometimes they'll hold off their late-evening deadline to fit in the Fort Yukon score. Dave can't understand why every village coach in the state doesn't do the same thing. It means so much to the townspeople to see their kids' names in print, to see their village's name in some section of the paper besides the bush crime report.

Dave particularly enjoyed calling in this one. Ten of his kids scored, five in double figures. Only one of them—Matt—has a name any other coach in the region will even recognize. It's going to drive those coaches nuts, Dave is sure, trying to figure out from the box score what Fort Yukon's got this year.

Today's game will be played in the afternoon, to allow the Anderson teams to fly home tonight. A handwritten sign posted on the school's front door announces that classes will be dismissed early today because of the one P.M. start. The Anderson kids, along with the refs, enjoyed a buffet breakfast this morning, complete with a skillet of fried moose meat, which some of them actually tried. They then walked across the

TEN

The Road

LUNCHTIME MONDAY. DAVE'S at his desk at the airport, picking at a bowl of microwaved noodles and staring blankly at the wall. Georgie just called from the school with the grades. Seven of Dave's boys are flunking Brian Rozell's class.

Seven.

Dave knew there was something up with that class. Rozell was absent last week, had a substitute taking his place. Dave heard that some of his boys were blowing off the sub, ignoring the daily assignments left behind by Rozell. But he had no idea it was this bad. Seven? That's half the team, including two starters—Tim Fields and Justin. Including the team's high scorer after the first two games, Johnny. And including—no surprise here—Wade.

So much for depth. Now Dave's got to rethink his entire approach to this week's trip, the longest road trip they'll be taking this season: four games in four days at three different schools. Fouls will now be a big issue, not good for a team that plays as aggressively as Fort Yukon. Derek and Chris will now suddenly be starters, and Dave has no idea how they'll respond. The two backups he'll have on the bench will be Wes, the untested freshman, and Tim Woods, whose spirit is willing, but whose skills, frankly, are sketchy. Dave's worked with Tim for two years on getting some air under that flat line-drive shot of his, but Tim insists on firing it like a laser at the basket. It's a shock to everyone, including Tim, when one of his shots actually goes in.

It's a shame they're going to be so undermanned against what promise to be some of the tougher teams on this season's schedule: Houston,

Nikolaevsk, and a possible matchup with Cook Inlet Academy. But what bothers Dave more than the basketball is the fact that half his boys are going to miss the highlight journey of this season. Every year he tries to schedule one excursion to some place the kids have never been, give them a chance to see a part of Alaska they may never get to the rest of their lives. These trips are the cherry on each season's sundae. In years past they've flown to Galena, some 350 miles west, and to Nulato, almost 400 miles away. Three years ago they went north to Anaktuvuk Pass, a village of "mountain Eskimos," as they call themselves, high up in the Brooks Range, on the North Slope. That was a rough weekend. Dave's boys beat Anaktuvuk twice, winning the second game by one point on a buzzer beater by Jeremy. The home crowd wasn't happy. The scorekeeper spit on Jeremy, and the boys had a hard time sleeping that night, what with the snowballs some Anaktuvuk kids were flinging at the windows of the classroom in which Fort Yukon was staying.

Dave's been especially excited about this season's trip. It will be the longest any of his teams have ever made—300 miles of flying, from here to Fairbanks and back, with 1,200 more miles of driving, from Fairbanks up and over the towering Alaska Range, down into Anchorage and beyond, along the coast of the Kenai Peninsula to Nikolaevsk—and back. That's a total of 1,500 miles—the distance from Boston to New Orleans. It's going to be an epic journey. And half the boys are going to miss it, as well as two of the girls.

This is what Dave tells them at practice that evening. He's surprisingly upbeat, frank, matter-of-fact. First off, he says, they have no right to be angry with Mr. Rozell.

"Did you think he was never going to come back?" he says, shaking his head as the boys sprawl on the bleachers. They're downbeat, sheepish, watching Dave walk back and forth.

"You've got nobody to be pissed off at except for yourselves," he goes on, twirling his whistle around his finger.

"This isn't the biggest *basketball* trip of the year that you're missing," he says. "The NIT means more than this in terms of the games themselves. But this trip is going to be a once-in-a-lifetime experience, and I'm sorry that some of you are going to miss it."

He draws a deep breath.

"For those of you staying behind, your problem will be keeping in shape while we're gone, not losing your edge. You'll have to do that on your own."

Another breath.

"As for those who are going, I know it's not cold out like last week, but you've still got to wear your heavy-weather gear: your Carhartts, coats, scarves, warm hats. That's not my call. It's state regulations."

Josh pipes up from the back row.

"But it's only about zero out there right now," he says.

Dave stops pacing.

"Did you hear what I just said? Do I have to repeat it? I don't like to chew my cabbage twice."

With that he whistles them down on the baseline. There'll be nothing but gassers tonight. He's going to run them till they drop, partly for punishment and partly because the seven boys making this trip are going to need their lungs and their legs more than ever.

Wednesday morning brings clear skies, minus-eleven degrees. Twelve kids—seven boys and five girls—trudge through the icy darkness of the airstrip to board the nine-thirty Frontier flight to Fairbanks, along with Cheryl and Dave. And one bag of basketballs. And two metal first-aid boxes. And twelve personal travel bags crammed with clothing and uniforms, pencils and textbooks, Discmans and DVDs, toothpaste and brushes and washcloths and towels and plenty of Axe.

It's a thirty-five-minute flight, a trip the boys have taken so often it seems like a cab ride. The cluster of twinkling lights that is Fort Yukon recedes as the Big Black Bird bends south over the moonlit Flats toward the faint glow of dawn above the White Mountains. The kids hardly have time to fall asleep before the plane begins its descent into Fairbanks.

They all know the drill. Dave and Cheryl fetch the rental vans, one for the boys, one for the girls. From here on they travel like two separate teams. They have different itineraries, different timetables, sometimes even different routes to the same destination. They have different schedules once they arrive at the schools where they'll play. They eat separately, hang out for the most part on their own, have little to do with each other except to watch each other play. There's no animosity. They're simply two autonomous units.

The boys stuff their gear in the back of the van. Seniors get first pick of seats—typically all the way to the rear, where they can take turns lying atop the luggage to sleep. Then it's off to have breakfast at THE NORTHERNMOST DENNY'S IN THE WORLD, as the ice-crusted sign outside the restaurant proclaims.

There was no Denny's in Fairbanks when the boys' parents were kids. There was no Sam's Club or Wendy's or Home Depot or any of the suburban sprawl that has spread to those hillsides surrounding the city over the course of the past thirty years. Downtown still retains just a touch of the frontier rawness that defined Fairbanks in the old gold-rush days, with a couple of log cabins still standing. A string of neon-lit bars—the Elbow Room, the Trapper's Tavern—still do a brisk business on Two Street, alongside the city's main tourist attraction, its Ice Museum.

Josh's dad, Clifton, drives up in his pickup, comes in and joins the team at their table.

"Where's the rest of you?" he asks. He can't believe half the boys missed this trip for not doing their homework. "Why didn't you help them?" he says, helping himself to Chris's unfinished pancakes.

Clifton's been working in Fairbanks for close to five years now, super-vising construction for the Native regional housing authority. He's not wild about living here. He hates having to box up his dogs and strap his sled on the back of his truck and drive half an hour just to find some open woods or a frozen river on which he can let his teams run. He misses Fort Yukon, misses hunting and trapping with his brothers, Earl and Jay. Clifton's the only man from Fort Yukon ever to enter the Iditarod. He failed to finish but did the village proud just by trying. He and his wife, Janet—they were in the same class all the way from kinder-garten through graduation at the Fort Yukon School—and their four kids go back to the village quite often, for holidays during the school year and to fish salmon come summer. They've still got their house down toward the river, which they rent out to teachers. Clifton intends to move back as soon as their two youngest boys are finished with school.

It was because of school that he and Janet decided to leave Fort Yukon for Fairbanks, to give their kids the chance for a better education. Janet herself will be getting her master's degree soon. But they miss their hometown, and so do their children.

Clifton regales the boys with a couple of stories from his playing days. He reminds Dave that Josh will have to skip the championship game of next week's NIT, should the team make it that far. Josh is entered in the Junior Yukon Quest dog race, which will be run that same weekend here in Fairbanks.

Next week is light-years from Dave's mind at the moment. He's got four games in the next four days to think about, beginning with tonight's matchup against . . . Anderson. This one was already on the schedule before Anderson stepped in to fill Minto's spot last week. Dave would rather not be playing against Anderson yet again, but at least it will give Derek and Chris a chance to work with the starting five, in preparation for the tougher tests of the coming three days.

Clifton warns the boys about being overconfident tonight. Then it's time to leave—Clifton back to his job and the boys back to the van. Dave dials in a classics station on the radio. It's playing ZZ Top, one of his favorites. Tim Woods reaches over and punches the dial to something by Nirvana. Then the rapper Fabolous. Then the death metal group Slayer. Then Dave says, "Enough," and switches it back to the classics.

They make a quick stop at Aaron's mom's house, to pick up the new PlayStation he just got for Christmas. Then it's on to the mall to let the boys do some shopping: a pair of Vans shoes for Derek, some headphones for Wes, a hat and a smoothie for Aaron, and a DVD copy of *Friday Night Lights*, which Chris buys for them all to watch tonight after the game. Finally, they stop at the massive Fred Meyer superstore, where Dave stocks up on provisions—including a couple of hot pizzas for lunch on the road—and Matt buys a stick of blue greasepaint, which he and Chris use to draw flames and write the numbers of each player and the words FORT YUKON CREW on the van's windows.

It takes a while to herd the boys out of the store and into the van. "Two come out, one goes back in," says Dave, shaking his head. "It's like trying to nail Jell-O to a wall."

Finally, after a head count, they pull out.

And now it begins.

Dave senses it every time he takes his boys on the road. As soon as they roll onto the snowplowed George Parks Highway and up into the white, wintry hills of the Tanana Valley State Forest, a feeling settles over the van, a sense of exhalation, of relief. They're his now, these boys. All the tension they live with in the village—in their homes, at the school, in the simple fact that they are adolescents, awash in the same stew of desire, confusion, hope and collusion that comes with coming of age anywhere—all that pressure seems to dissipate, to vanish like the exhaust puffing out from the back of the van as Dave punches it south.

They can just see Denali in the distance ahead, the tips of its peaks rimmed by the apricot glow of the vanishing midafternoon sun. An icy haze hangs over the valley to both sides as they follow the ridgeline along Goldstream Creek, past Sawmill Island, down over the ice-locked Tanana River and into Nenana, where they'll be playing next week. Dave pops a lemon drop into his mouth—he always keeps a bag of hard candy at hand on these drives—as the van shoots past the riverside village's cluster of cabins and houses and the little school where the NIT is played every year. "Our name has never gone up on that board," Dave says, referring to the list of NIT champions inscribed on the wall of Nenana's gymnasium. "I'd like to see it go up there before I retire."

The road flattens now, paralleling the snowswept tracks of the Alaska Railroad as the sun sets and night falls and the glow of a lone street-light by the side of the highway appears in the distance, marking the turnoff for Clear Air Force Base and the village of Anderson.

It's close to five when Dave pulls the van into the Anderson school parking lot. Cheryl and the girls are not far behind. The school's principal meets Dave and the boys at the door and shows them to the classroom where they'll be spending the night. His name is Fred Deussing. He's sixty-two, a single dad with two sons, twelve and four. He's slim, balding, upbeat and unabashed about his desire to meet a woman—"a younger woman," he says—to share his life with him and help take care of his boys. He's been married three times: once for nineteen years back in Pennsylvania, once for thirteen after he moved to Alaska, and once for thirty days, to a woman from Seattle he met through the Internet while running the school in the village of Noatak, up in the state's remote Northwest Arctic Borough. "That was a big mistake," he says of the last one. "I like to say I've had two strikes and a foul tip." This is his first year here at Anderson, and he intends to stay. He loves the little community, loves the family feel of the school. All he needs to make everything perfect is a wife. He's got four grown children from his first marriage, as well as his two young sons, and he's not ruling out having more. "Why stop now?" he says, leaving Dave and the boys to settle into their room.

They don't waste any time. Desks are pushed to the side, sleeping bags are laid on the carpeted floor—Dave's, as always, is beside the room's door—Aaron's PlayStation is plugged into the classroom's TV, and Matt and Tim Woods pop in an NBA video game.

A few Anderson fans have already begun trickling into the gym for the girls' game, which starts in about half an hour. This school is smaller than Fort Yukon's, but the gym is twice as large, with ten rows of bleachers on each side and a waxed, gleaming hardwood floor. Championship banners from the glory years of the 1990s hang on one wall.

But those years seem long gone now. Only a dozen or so people are in the bleachers when the girls tip off. Again, Cheryl's girls have little trouble with Anderson. By the time the boys come out to warm up, fewer than forty fans dot the stands. The squeak of the players' shoes and the bouncing of basketballs echoes in the near-empty gymnasium.

"Where the hell is everybody?" says Dave, setting up his first-aid boxes and a case of bottled water by his seat on the bench. "You live in Anderson. It's Wednesday night. What *else* is there to do?"

He knows the answer. He's seen the same thing happening in all the villages, where the advent of cable television, of the Internet, of video games and DVD movies has drawn people away from the community events they all used to attend. Dave knows this sounds somewhat simplistic, but it's true: There's nothing wrong with sitting at home by a warm fire and reading or whittling or listening to the radio, but if that's all there is to do night after night through a long Arctic winter, then you'll jump at any opportunity to get out among others, anything at all, from a potlatch, to a children's play at the school, to, yes, a basketball game. Given all these new technological options, however, it becomes easier to simply stay home. As big as basketball still is in Fort Yukon, not as many villagers come to the games as they used to. Here in Anderson, where the teams' recent mediocrity hasn't helped matters, attendance has dropped to almost nothing.

Nearly a fourth of the people in the bleachers tonight are Fort Yukon fans, including Chris's mom, Georgie, and a few of her brothers—Chris's uncles, the Solomon boys. Of course, Trader Dan is here, too. He and Georgie and the others do what they can to make some noise as the starters pull off their warm-ups and take the floor for the opening tip. There is no radio broadcast of this evening's game. Paul is back in Fort Yukon. He couldn't afford to make this trip but vows he'll be in Nenana to do the NIT next week. There will be no broadcast of tomorrow night's game at Houston either. But the Fort Yukon radio station has made arrangements for an Anchorage-area freelance broadcaster to drive down to Nikolaevsk this weekend and do the play-by-play of the boys' and girls' games there.

Dave tried his best back in the classroom to get his boys focused, to get them to take tonight's game seriously. He gave the same spiel he always does about the home court being worth ten points to the host team. He warned them that playing a team like this three times in one week is dangerous, that Anderson is now used to what Fort Yukon does, that they've gained confidence.

And he's right. The first four times up the floor, Anderson breaks Fort Yukon's traps with ease, getting the ball to the middle and finding one of their forwards for open looks at the basket. Anderson gets off four shots in the game's first two minutes—they didn't get off four shots in the entire first quarter of last week's opener.

Meanwhile, Fort Yukon looks tight. Their first three trips up the court result in two turnovers and an air ball by Derek. Midway through the first quarter the score is tied, 4–4. Dave sits back, just watching. He isn't happy, but he's not upset either. A burst by Fort Yukon—a Derek ten-footer, a turnaround flip from the foul line by Aaron, and a Josh layup after a steal—makes the score 10–4. But Anderson responds with a run of their own, helped by Matt throwing a behind-the-back pass out of bounds on a two-on-one break, Josh fumbling the ball on an open layup, and Aaron launching an air ball of his own on an open three-pointer.

The score at the end of the first quarter is an astonishing 12–12 tie.

The boys flop into their seats, sucking on water bottles, their blue road jerseys soaked with sweat as Dave hunches down in front of them. He's calm, as calm as if he's sitting out in his yard watching his bees. No temper. No tirade.

"Your shot selection has to be better," he says.

He looks over at Josh.

"Charging into a zone doesn't make any sense."

He looks over at Derek, who already has two fouls.

"Do you understand?"

They nod, toss the bottles away and return to the floor.

The traps begin working. Matt and Josh begin feeding on steals. Chris hits two free throws for his first points of the season, bringing the Solomon contingent to their feet. Halftime, Fort Yukon has pulled away to a ten-point lead, 29–19. The third quarter is like a layup drill for Josh, who strips the Anderson guards time after time.

"That's just what his dad used to do," says Dave, leaning back and enjoying the show. "*Zip*, the ball's gone. You don't even see it happening, it's so quick."

Josh's eleven third-quarter points, along with eight from Chris, fuel a 15–0 Fort Yukon run for a 52–25 lead. They coast through the final eight minutes to win 66–40. The only downside is Matt's left ankle, which he twisted in the third quarter. They'll have to find a brace somewhere on the drive down to Houston tomorrow.

"Hey," Dave tells them as they undress in the tiny visitors' locker room, "we won by twenty-six tonight on somebody else's court. With seven players. That's not bad, not bad at all."

With that, the boys shower and dress, hang their sweat-soaked uniforms around the classroom to dry overnight, and stroll down to the cafeteria for a late dinner of burritos and fruit. Fred Deussing joins them, chatting with the kids as if they are guests in his home. Dave finds a phone, calls in the score to the paper. High scorer tonight was Josh with twenty-three—the team's third high man in three games. Then it's back to the classroom, where Chris cues up the movie, the boys slip into their sleeping bags and Dave shuts off the lights. By the time the opening credits have rolled, Dave's already out cold.

Next morning, six thirty, he's the first one up, carrying his towel and shaving kit down the pitch-dark school hallway to the locker room, where he showers and dresses. By seven he's roused the boys. By eight, they've put on their clothes and had breakfast, again with the principal—hot cakes and sausages, along with vitamins provided by Dave. Then it's out to the van, where they load their bags in the twenty-four-below-zero darkness as the Anderson students begin arriving for school. Eight fifteen, the van pulls out, its headlights cutting through a wispy ice fog that's settled over the highway.

The boys have all gone back to sleep by the time they roll past Healy, a half hour down the road from Anderson. The lights of the little town's coal plant cast a pink glow through the fog. It was here, back in the spring of 1992, that a young hitchhiker named Chris McCandless—a kid not much older than the boys in this van—was dropped off and walked into Denali National Park, intending to live off the land through the following winter. His decomposed remains were found four months later in an abandoned school bus just off a trail some twenty-five miles west of here, in the shadow of Mount McKinley.

The boys all know that story. Everyone in Alaska knows it. Most were furious when a book called *Into the Wild* was published, recounting the story of McCandless's young life and what might have led him to this kind of death. They felt it romanticized this kid, who to them was an idiot—the same kind of idiot who's been coming up to Alaska forever, all the way back to the gold-rush days. They have nothing against dreamers up here. Alaska is a lodestone for dreams. All frontiers are. But like all frontiers, it can kill you as well. What galls the hell out of the people who live here, the ones who understand and appreciate how hard it is to survive in a place like this—not in the climate-controlled comfort of cities like Anchorage or Fairbanks, but in the real Alaska, in the bush—what the locals resent is the lack of respect shown by these backpackers and hippies and seekers-of-truth who have no idea what they're in for in roadless Alaska and don't take the time or the trouble to find out.

Dave sees them all the time, passing through the Fort Yukon airport on their way into the wild. Some stop in the village and actually stay for a time. Others move straight on into the backcountry. Most arrive in the summer. Some are never seen again. A stack of next-of-kin forms is kept at the airport, which the state requires anyone venturing into the bush beyond Fort Yukon to fill out. Dave's watched all kinds of people fill out those forms. He's met Vietnam vets "looking for their sanity," as he puts it. He's seen the "fruit and nuts" people, as he calls them— the ones from the communes—looking to get back to nature, which really drives him up the wall. "Most of them come from cities or suburbs," he says. "They've never lived like this. People who grew up in this kind of world don't romanticize it like that. I was raised without running water back in Maine. We didn't get plumbing till I was in eighth grade. People would ask us if we had running water, and we'd say, 'Yeah, when we spill it.' You're happy to have running water when you've lived without it. You're not going to go out of your way *not* to have it."

There are some aspiring bush rats who come up and actually make it out there. People like Heimo Korth, a Wisconsin native who passed through Fort Yukon thirty years ago on his way deeper into the woods. He built a cabin two hundred miles north of the village, taught himself how to trap, met and married a Native woman and raised a family out there in the honest-to-god wilderness. Heimo and his wife, Edna, and their two daughters keep a home in the village, just across the road from Dave's house, where they come and spend time in the summer. The people in Fort Yukon respect Heimo. They love him—him and his wife and his girls. They consider them part of the community.

But for every back-to-the-lander who actually makes it in the trackless wilderness, for every Heimo, there are a dozen Chris McCandlesses, who are too ignorant, or arrogant, or both, to realize what they're up against.

The boys are reading *Into the Wild* right now, in Mr. Rozell's class.

They've got paperback copies of the book in their backpacks, along with the rest of their homework. They'll pull out the books later—Dave will make sure of that—but as the van passes Healy, they're sleeping, all seven of them.

The road begins climbing from here, up into the snowblown peaks and passes of the Alaska Range. Landslide warning signs begin to appear. The occasional tractor-trailer shoots past, its headlights piercing the midwinter darkness. Other than that, the highway is empty, a ghost road. Denali National Park is closed until spring, when the tourist traffic—the RVs and double-deck buses that typically clog this road in warm weather—will take over again.

By the time they reach the mountainside truck stop at Cantwell, the midway point between Fairbanks and Anchorage, the sun has begun rising. Denali—Mount McKinley—is right there before them, its south face glowing orange in the morning light. The boys pile out, still half sleeping, to use the bathroom, buy some snacks, stretch their legs. Two ink-black ravens are perched atop the gas pumps, squawking wildly at each other as the icy wind whips their feathers. An old Gwich'in proverb says when ravens squabble, the weather will be cold and windy. They must squabble all the time here in Cantwell, in winter.

Now the highway descends, dropping into the Mat-Su Valley. The radio is on, crowded with stations. Dave punches the button till he finds a Led Zeppelin song. The boys gaze wordlessly out the windows at the white landscape, perking up when a moose warning sign appears. Chris makes a crack about Wade wishing he was here with his rifle. Wade's by far the best hunter among them.

Talkeetna. Trapper Creek. Kashwitna. Clusters of houses begin to appear in the woods. The land flattens out. The highway is now busy with traffic, coming and going from Wasilla or Palmer or one of the other exurbs near Anchorage. They're into the world now—convenience stores, fast-food restaurants, fireworks outlets. Soon a sign for the town of Houston appears. Three hundred miles from Fairbanks, right on the nose. It's high noon. A bank clock flashes the temperature. Thirty-three-above—fifty-seven degrees warmer than it was when they left Anderson this morning. The boys haven't felt air this warm since September. They strip to their T-shirts as Dave pulls into a Subway for lunch.

They've got several hours to kill. After lunch, Dave drives on to Wasilla, ten miles down the road, finds a Fred Meyer, hunkers down at the Starbucks inside with a cup of coffee and a book while the boys cruise the store looking at girls—mostly clerks and cashiers, since everyone else is in school. Matt finds a brace for his ankle. Tim Woods goes back to the van and works on some math. The bright sun beats down on the asphalt parking lot, turning the plowed snow to puddles.

Five o'clock, they head back to Houston, pulling up to a massive— by Fort Yukon standards—modern school building, tucked back in the woods off the highway, all brick and stone, beige and burgundy, geometrically angled, with a parking lot large enough to hold every vehicle in Fort Yukon. Inside the front doors, a trophy case touts Houston's 1991 3A state champion basketball team. But hockey is king here. The school has won three of the past four Alaska state hockey titles.

It's a busy place late on this Thursday afternoon. A couple of teachers jog past in sweatsuits, getting their workout inside the school's halls. Packs of kids—all white kids, no Natives—lounge around lockers, cell phones pressed to their ears, skipping downstairs from the school's second floor, the girls giggling and gossiping and shooting sideways glances at the seven Indian boys standing outside the main office.

Inside, Dave waits until one of the staff looks up from her ringing phone and asks if she can help him. He says he's looking for the AD— the athletic director. She points at a young guy in a shirt and tie, busy like everyone else in this room. He hardly looks up when Dave introduces himself.

"I talked to you on the phone," Dave says.

"Yeah, you probably did," says the guy, scribbling notes on a pad of paper. He's got a phone to one ear. A couple of kids hover over his desk, waiting to ask for something. He motions a colleague over, asks the man to show Dave and his team to the room where they'll be spending the night, then gets back to the phone.

The man leads the way to the gym. It's immense, like the inside of an industrial warehouse. Pale cinderblock walls rise to a ceiling that's three stories high. The bleachers pull out and roll back with the push of a button. Music—the Eurythmics' "Sweet Dreams" at the moment—blasts out of a stadium-quality sound system. A scrimmage game has just ended, between Houston's jayvee girls' team and the school's "C" boys' team. It's hard for the Fort Yukon kids to believe a school has enough bodies for a "B" team, much less a "C" team.

The man unlocks a door at one end of the floor. It opens to a stale windowless room with nothing inside but rubber mats on the floor. It's the wrestling practice room—Fort Yukon's home for the night.

The boys stake out their spots, toss their bags on the mats and stroll back out to watch their girls play. It's a strange sight, seeing eighteen Houston girls warming up at one end of the floor while Cheryl's five kids shoot layups at the other end. A dozen or so Houston students are scattered throughout the bleachers, most watching out of curiosity more than anything else, while they wait for their rides home.

"Fort Yukon?" one girl says to a friend sitting beside her. "Where is that?"

"It's by the border," the friend answers.

"What border?"

"I don't know."

"Is it in Alaska?"

"I don't know. All I know is it's by the border."

The Houston girls wash over Fort Yukon from the opening tip, wearing out Cheryl's kids with wave after wave of fresh substitutes. Mandy and Ruby and the others play their hearts out, but they lose by a dozen, 53–41.

By the time the boys take the floor for their warm-ups, there are maybe a hundred fans in the bleachers. This is not a big game for Houston. It's scheduled as a jayvee game, but the Houston coaches are treating it like a varsity scrimmage, mixing their best players in with the jayvees. They're not too much bigger than the Fort Yukon boys, but there are twice as many of them. They've got a squadron of four coaches on the bench, all wearing matching red-and-black Houston Hawks polo shirts. Dave walks over and shakes their hands, wearing his Red Sox ball cap, untucked pinstriped oxford cloth shirt, and jeans.

Just before the opening buzzer, he takes off the cap and tucks in the shirt.

Houston comes out crisp and well-schooled, starting their varsity five. They're hardly bothered by Fort Yukon's traps. They've got a half-court trap of their own, which they spring for a couple of steals and a quick 7–2 lead.

Matt's up to his tricks again, trying those high-risk five-star passes when a basic two-star would do. By the end of the first quarter he's already thrown the ball away three times. Houston leads 13–8.

Second quarter, Houston sends in some of its jayvees. A flurry by Fort Yukon—two putbacks by Aaron sandwiched around a steal and a layup by Matt—ties the game at 15. Houston calls time-out, puts its best players back out on the floor. Dave's boys are upbeat, but they've got a problem. Matt and Josh each have two fouls. There's no one on the bench but Wes and Tim. Sure enough, with 3:10 left in the half and Fort Yukon ahead, 19–17, Matt picks up his third.

Dave springs from his seat, motions Matt over. Normally, Matt would be out of the game. But this isn't normal. For all intents and purposes, Dave's got five players tonight.

"Matt," he says, "should I leave you in?"

Naturally, Matt says yes. And of course, one minute later, he picks up his fourth foul. Now Dave has to take him out.

"Fuck," says Matt, flinging a towel on the floor, "I didn't *touch* him."

"I don't want to hear it," says Dave, motioning Tim to check in. "That was the right call."

"Fuck. Fuck. Fuck."

Houston closes the half with a 5–0 run for a 22–19 lead.

The boys collapse on the wrestling room mats, breathing hard, slugging down swallows of water. Dave's worried about those fouls, but he's pleased with the score.

"We're doing fine," he says. "They've got twenty-two points. That's some pretty good defense on our part.

"Matt, you're going back in. Just be careful.

"Derek, we're going to need more shots out of you. I want you popping out on that wing. If they come out on you, I want Josh to post down."

The boys screw up their faces and look at Dave like he's crazy. Josh? Posting down? He's the tiniest guy on the floor.

"I don't care about your size, Josh," Dave says, reading their minds. "You're too *quick* for anyone on their team."

Josh flashes a bring-it-on smile.

He scores early to open the quarter, on a spin-move inside. But Houston is brutalizing Fort Yukon on the boards. The Eagles miss Tim Fields terribly. Aaron and Derek are doing their best, but Houston has six front-line players who are wearing them down. Midway through the quarter Derek is belted in the face. He comes to the sideline, blood spewing from his nose. Dave sends Tim Woods in while Derek presses a wet towel to his face and leaves for the bathroom. He returns in two minutes and checks back in, as the assault continues. Aaron's beginning to foul. With 1:14 left in the third quarter, he picks up his fourth.

"Coach," says the scorekeeper, "that's four."

"I know," says Dave, leaning back in his seat, his hands clasped behind his head. "What am I gonna do? His backup is in Fort Yukon trying to get his *grades* up."

Everyone at the scorer's table cracks up.

The third quarter ends 36–31, Houston.

They're coming at Aaron now. He weathers three Houston drives in a row, drawing two charges and swatting one shot into the wall. But Fort Yukon is having trouble scoring. With five players essentially going the whole way, and the pace so intense, they're worn out. It shows in their shooting. Matt's taken six three-pointers and missed every one. Derek's taken six as well, hitting just one. Dave could have predicted this. When the legs start wearing out, the shots start getting wobbly.

Still, they hang close. With 2:40 left, Aaron somehow steals an offensive rebound over a Houston forward's shoulder and is fouled on the putback attempt. He drops in both free throws to trim Houston's lead to four, 42–38.

Dave's into it now. He's up off the bench, barking instructions, pointing directions, dropping down to his knees, slapping the floor.

Houston scores.

Fort Yukon misses, and Houston rebounds with 1:48 left and a six-point cushion.

One of the Houston coaches flashes a signal. His guards move into a weave, flipping the ball to one another out near half-court. They have no intention of shooting. They're happy to eat up the clock.

Josh, Matt, Derek and Aaron each have four fouls. The only Fort Yukon player who has one to give is Chris.

"Chris!" Dave yells. "Foul him!"

They're at the far end of the floor. The crowd is screaming. Chris doesn't hear him.

"*Chris!!*" Dave hollers again. "*Foul him!!*"

Houston continues its weave. Chris still can't hear him. The Fort Yukon players are going for steals, but no one's stopping the clock. Dave is beside himself, trying to get Chris's attention. By the time Chris looks over, realizes what's going on and bear-hugs one of the Houston guards, seventy seconds have gone by. There are only thirty-eight seconds left in the game.

It's too late.

The final is 50–38, Houston.

The Fort Yukon kids file into the wrestling room, fall to the mats. Dave's as sweat-soaked as they are. But he's not upset. Nor are they. They're disappointed, but not upset.

"Hey," Dave says, wiping some moisture off his glasses, "nothing to be ashamed of. This was a good experience for us, a good experience to play with those fouls. We didn't execute well at the end, and that's my fault. I hadn't anticipated that situation and hadn't prepared you for it."

He wants to make sure Chris does not feel the brunt of this.

He pauses, studies the boys' faces. He's not sure what exactly they're feeling.

"Do you understand that that was their varsity you just played?" he says.

Aaron's face pops up from the towel in which it's been buried. He played his heart out tonight, was the team's leading scorer, the fourth high man in four games.

"That was their *varsity*?" he says. "And us, with seven players?"

Matt breaks into a grin.

"Fuckin' 3A varsity," he says.

Josh nods, slaps his knee and turns to the matter at hand.

"Let's go *eat*," he says.

ELEVEN

The Russians

"**L**ET'S GO EAT."

Dave loves it. Except for a few head cases like Ryan, this is the way most of the boys he's coached approach the game. They give every ounce they've got when they're out there on the court, but after the game, they don't dwell on it. Aaron's face was buried in that towel not from emotion but from sheer exhaustion. They don't get too low when they lose. They don't get too high when they win. What's next? What now? That's what they want to know. They're the same way in their personal lives. Most of the people in Fort Yukon are. They can't afford to get too emotional in the day-to-day tumult and upheavals too many of them face in their homes, in their families, among the pressures, public and private, that envelop their tribe. Life throws too much at them up here to get too caught up in the moment. Triumph or tragedy, a good day or bad, you deal with it and move on. Otherwise, you simply could not survive.

Dave loves how the boys moved on last night. They went out to eat down the road, in Wasilla, at a restaurant with a neon lobster out front. The menu listed no dinner entrée for less than $13.95. Dave's budget per player, per meal, is ten dollars.

"What do we order then?" asked Josh.

"Look at the *lunch* menu," said Dave, flipping to the back page—burgers and sandwiches.

"I've never had lobster," mused Wes, gazing out at the sign.

"You're not having it tonight either," said Dave.

When they got back to the school, a staff member assigned to spend the night in the building while Fort Yukon was there opened the front doors and let them in. It was ten P.M., an hour before their nightly on-the-road curfew of eleven. Tim, slow to gather his gear, was the last one in.

"Where'd everybody go?" he asked, seeing the empty wrestling room.

"They found the weight room," said Dave.

"Cool," said Tim, bouncing out the door.

Within minutes the boys, and the girls too, were back out on the basketball court, shouting, laughing, playing a match-the-shot game called "knockout," their glee echoing throughout the empty gymnasium, throughout the dark vacant halls of the building. Dave came out and joined them, all of them having a blast. They would have stayed up for hours if Dave hadn't clapped his hands at eleven, pointed them toward their sleeping bags, passed out Tylenol to everyone and flipped off the lights.

"I'm not *tired*," Josh's voice piped up in the darkness.

The room burst out laughing. With that, lying in their bags, in the dark, the boys launched into a group discussion of—at Tim's suggestion—"the scariest movie ever made."

"*The Grudge*," offered Tim. "That freaked me out."

"*Leprechaun*, me boy," came Matt's voice, in a dead-on Irish brogue.

"*White Noise*," said Chris.

"Ew, I gotta see that," said Tim.

Soon they were talking about tomorrow's drive, about those Russians and what it will be like to see where they live.

"I drink *vodka*," came Matt's voice again, this time dead-on as Arnold Schwarzenegger.

The kids cracked up again, especially Wes. Wes has been devouring this, all of it, since the moment they boarded that plane back in Fort Yukon. Dave loves watching freshmen like Wes, traveling with the team for the first time, wide-eyed, almost giddy, awash in the whirl of it all. If Dave got nothing else out of coaching than this, it would be enough.

They had to get up early this morning, six thirty, to be out of the building by seven, when the Houston students start arriving for school. There is no breakfast for the Fort Yukon kids here, just as there was no dinner last night. There's no principal sitting down and chatting with them, the way Fred Deussing did at Anderson. There's too much going on. It's doubtful the Houston principal, whoever he or she is, even knows Fort Yukon was here.

Dave understands. A place like this rarely puts up a visiting team for the night in its school. This is not a village. People here—the students, the teachers, the staff—live miles away from the school. They have busy lives. No one's walking anyone over to a radio station to interview them on the air. There are no volunteer parents to come feed these kids. It's not feasible. The school would have to pay someone to do that, just like they had to pay a staff member last night to come stay in the building and make sure things were secure. There are legal liabilities to worry about, for god's sake. In the villages, the townspeople consider themselves hosts. It's personal for them when other ball teams visit. They take care of the kids, all of the kids, not just those from their village. It's a cultural thing. Call it a Gwich'in thing. Or a Yupik thing. Or an Inuit thing. Here, in a setting like this, in suburbia, it's different. It's simply not personal. Dave understands.

His boys don't mind. It's doubtful they've even thought about any of this. That's something else Dave loves about coaching these kids. They never complain. They take whatever comes, adjust to it, make the most of it, enjoy it. "We're sleeping on the cement floor of a church basement tonight? Cool." "We're staying in one motel room, fourteen of us? I got dibs on the chair in the corner." "There's only three ice cream sandwiches left in that box we just bought, and there's four of us haven't had one? Give mine to Wes." Dave knows these boys are fully capable of bitching and moaning with the best of them, like any teenagers. But when they get out on the road like this, they're so good at pulling together, going with the flow. It's an adventure for them, all of it.

Like leaving Houston this morning. It's pitch-dark outside, eighteen degrees, as the boys make their way to the van. A half moon hangs over the trees. A line of headlights snakes up the drive from the highway. Mercedes, Lexuses, SUVs with the stereos pounding, pull into the lot or up to the curb. Girls with long straightened hair and short skirts and bare midriffs emerge in groups of two and three, clutching their books, hurrying out of the cold into the warm brightness of the school building. The Fort Yukon boys stand transfixed.

"Dave," says Matt, his eyes glued to a tall, leggy blonde, "can we stay here for a couple of days?"

A half hour later they're at a McDonald's for breakfast. An hour after that, they've done Fred Meyer again, stocked up on snacks for their stay in Nikolaevsk, and they're back on the road, rolling south through Wasilla, past Palmer, then down toward Anchorage. The sun rises over the white saw-toothed peaks of the Chugach Mountains as the van zips past the city limits of Anchorage, on down to the waters of Turnagain Arm. The inlet is famous for its strong tidal shifts, like the Bay of Fundy's. But this time of year it's frozen near solid, its brown turgid waters locked in large chunks of ice.

They turn east now, up along the Arm toward the blue frozen walls of Portage Glacier, the most visited tourist attraction in Alaska. Most of the boys have been here, with their families, or through school. But none of them, not even Dave, have been farther south, where they're headed right now, down onto the Kenai Peninsula.

They're beyond the inlet now, bending back due west, cutting through the Kenai's flat forests. They stop for lunch at a crossroads called Soldotna. Dave finds a phone and calls back to Fort Yukon, to talk with Diane and to check in with Doc, see how the rest of the team's doing. They're getting along, Doc tells him. They've been coming to practice each night, and most of them have been staying after school, getting their grades back up. It's thirty-seven-below in Fort Yukon right now, says Doc. He can't believe it when Dave tells him the temperature down here is twenty-above.

Josh gets on the phone, talking to Wade and Justin, who have picked up at the other end, in the school office.

"Hey, you guys are missing out," he tells them. "We saw about fifty girls with skirts on this morning. White girls. Blondes. Dave said there's plenty of room in the van."

He grins at the others.

"Kissed?"

He looks over at Matt.

"Yeah, he's been kissed twice."

"What's that?" he says.

"Yeah, we played their varsity team."

He looks over at Aaron and Derek, covers the mouthpiece with one hand.

"They had, what, twelve players?" he asks them.

"Fifteen!" the others shout. "Fifteen or sixteen!"

Now it's back in the van and on to the coast, where they turn south again, the dark choppy waters of Cook Inlet on their right.

This is where the British explorer Captain James Cook got his first look at Alaska, sailing up this sound in the late 1700s, seeking the Northwest Passage, a trading route across the top of North America. The passage didn't exist, but Cook didn't know that. Turnagain Arm got its name from his frustration at having to constantly tack his ship to avoid running aground in those shallow shoals. He gave his own name to this much larger waterway.

Dave doesn't bother explaining all this to the boys. He says nothing of the oil drilling that's gone on down here since the late 1950s, of the bidding taking place right now for more offshore leases out there in the depths of the inlet, or of the wreck of the *Exxon Valdez* in 1989, the year half the boys on this team were born. Oil from that spill made its way here, to the forested beaches past which Dave is now steering the van.

He doesn't talk about any of this. The boys are transfixed, gazing out at the largest body of water some of them have ever seen. They've all squeezed to the right side of the van, gawking and pointing at the snowcapped volcanic peaks out there in the distance, across the inlet. Mount Redoubt. Mount Iliamna. Mount Augustine. The boys have no idea those volcanoes are active, that Code Yellows and Oranges were issued just this past month after small tremors alerted seismologists to the possibility of eruptions. Ash plumes and magma are spewing this very moment from Mount Veniaminof, southwest of here. Mount Redoubt, the big one the boys are all pointing at right now, nearly brought down a KLM passenger jet when it blew the same year as the *Exxon Valdez* spill. The ash from that eruption settled over the city of

Anchorage, falling like powdery snow. The volcanoes in this range erupt roughly every fifteen to twenty years, according to vulcanologists. Most of those cones last blew sometime during the 1980s, which means they're due for the next one any time now.

Dave could tell the boys all about this, but he'd rather have them just take in the splendor of that gorgeous water and those magnificent mountains. It's hard for him to keep his own eyes on the road.

By midafternoon they're passing coastal hamlets with names like Kalifonsky, and Kasilof, Clam Gulch and Ninilchik. The boys have all heard of Ninilchik. Its girls' basketball team has won the past five state 2A championships in a row. They're ranked number one again so far this season.

Just past Ninilchik one of the boys shouts, "Hey! Look on the left! On the left!"

There, by the white picket fence of a little log cabin, stands a cow moose the size of a small pickup truck.

"There's your lunch, guys," says Dave, not skipping a beat.

They're getting close now to a fishing village called Anchor Point. It's time to start looking for the turnoff to Nikolaevsk. Dave was warned by the Nikolaevsk coach when he gave Dave directions over the telephone that there won't be any signs for this town. It's not on most maps. Which is how the four full-bearded men who founded the village back in the summer of 1967 wanted it.

They called themselves "Old Believers." They still do. Their people have been running from religious persecution for more than three hundred years, first in Russia, where they broke away from the Russian Orthodox church in the mid-seventeenth century, when Peter the Great introduced reforms they considered heretical. They scattered to China, Turkey, Brazil and New Zealand after the Bolshevik Revolution. At the turn of the 1960s, a group of them settled in Oregon. Then, in the summer of 1967, the Summer of Love, those four men came here, to this forested patch of rainswept Alaskan land, to stay one step ahead of the immoral encroachments of this modern world.

They've grown to more than three hundred now, the villagers of Nikolaevsk. The women and girls all wear *talichkas* (long, floor-length dresses). And *kasinkas* (colorful head scarves). And *shaels* (bright patterned shawls made to cover their shoulders). The men and the boys dress in *rubakhas* (long-sleeved, ornately embroidered, loose-fitting collarless shirts), cinched at the waist by *paisoks* (braided cloth belts woven for each boy at birth to symbolize his lifelong ties with the church).

They have been compared to the Amish—simple, plain people devoted to hard, honest work and a strict, austere faith. The men fish, farm and raise livestock. The women garden and cook and keep house. The males do not shave. The females marry young, often before they are finished with high school. They speak both English and Russian—at home, in the school, and, as the Fort Yukon boys discovered last year, on the basketball court.

"We didn't know *what* they were saying," says Matt, helping Dave hunt for the turnoff. They had two guards, Matt says, who were as quick as any he's ever played against. They called out their plays in their native tongue, feeding the ball to their monster of a center, a huge six-foot-five kid with a beard. This was at last year's NIT, which Nikolaevsk won for the first time in the school's history. The big kid is back this season. The two guards are gone, but they're supposed to have another one—a left-hander—who's even better.

"There it is," says Josh, pointing at a narrow blacktop lane snaking off the main road, away from the water and into the woods. There is snow on the ground, but it's patchy. The road bends and winds over timbered ridges and down into stream-fed gullies, past small one-horse farms, a clapboard stable here, a log cabin there, wood-hulled fishing boats drydocked on cradles in yards. And then, quite suddenly, on a bare, nearly treeless plateau, a huddle of neat frame houses appears. And a dirt parking lot filled with cars and two buses. And a school.

Nikolaevsk.

At first glance it looks like any of the small fishing villages Dave and the boys just passed through on their drive down the coast. The church is a little different, adorned with those onion-shaped domes and ornate three-bar crosses. But the homes and the town's general store—Fefelov

Mercantile, Nikolaevsk's version of Fort Yukon's AC—and the Samovar Café don't look out of the ordinary, at least from the outside.

The same with the school. It appears much like Anderson's. About the same size. Low-slung. One story. Cozy. Much more modern than any other structure in town.

But once the boys step inside, they know they are in a different world.

The tournament has already started. Cheering and whistling can be heard from the gym, down the hall. Women and girls scurry past wearing *talichkas*, carrying platters of food, chattering in Russian. The men walking past have big bushy beards, every one of them. Most are dressed roughly, in fur hats and thick jackets and workpants weathered from the salt spray of fishing. The boys wear *rubakhas* with their jeans and Vans sneakers.

Dave leads his kids to a classroom with a FORT YUKON sign on the door. Every door in the hall is marked with a similar sign, for each of the three visiting schools' teams—boys' and girls'.

Dave's kids dump their gear and head straight for the gym.

There's a concession stand by the gymnasium door, where several Nikolaevsk women and girls are busily selling hot homemade *pelmeni* (pork dumplings). And *piroshki* (turnovers stuffed with ground beef and cheese). And blackberry and rhubarb *shangis* (fruit-slathered pastries).

Dave goes straight for the *shangis*, as does Aaron. The other boys screw up their faces at the weird Russian food, opting instead for something they recognize: pretzels and chips and corn dogs. Then they move into the gym.

The Cook Inlet girls are playing Mat-Su. The bleachers, just five rows on one side of the floor, are half filled. A beat-up sofa is incongruously mounted a few rows up in the stands, near midcourt. Dave and his boys wonder what's up with that.

The Cook Inlet boys will be playing the Mat-Su boys next. Then the Nikolaevsk girls will play the Fort Yukon girls, followed by tonight's highlight game, when the hometown boys take on Dave's team. There won't be a seat left by then.

It's like this at most tournaments—waiting, often for hours, until the time comes to play. Dave's boys are used to it. They're adept at passing the time, hanging out in the classroom where they'll be sleeping, doing their homework, playing video games, maybe watching a movie, roaming the halls, meeting kids from the other teams—especially the girls—even walking out into the village, if Dave lets them. And, of course, spending most of their time flopped in the bleachers, taking in the action.

That's where they are at the moment, watching the Cook Inlet girls polish off Mat-Su, and waiting to see what Cook Inlet's boys have got this year. Cook Inlet is undefeated at the moment, ranked number one in the state's 2A poll. The winner of this game will play the winner of Fort Yukon's game for the four-team tournament championship tomorrow afternoon.

The gym is new, built three years ago to replace the school's old one, which was so small there was no room for a center-court circle between the tops of the two keys. Visiting teams were simply given the ball to start each game. The $1.5 million it cost to build this facility came from a county bond referendum—a controversial vote for those area residents who resent the reclusiveness of these Russian expatriates. The money it costs to put on this tournament came from the oil company whose banner is draped on the wall across from the bleachers: ConocoPhillips. Dave would love to stage something like this in Fort Yukon, but finding a sponsor like that would be next to impossible, at least right now. Maybe when drilling begins in ANWR, he jokes. Or the drilling they're talking about doing right there in the Flats, around Fort Yukon. Dave would love to have a new gym, but he doesn't see that happening anytime soon.

The Mat-Su and Cook Inlet boys have come out for their warm-ups. Cook Inlet is big—nine kids six feet or taller, including two six-fours. They're cocky, laughing and joking as they look over at the much smaller Mat-Su squad.

Dave and the boys are taking it all in, sizing up the competition, when the big kid from Nikolaevsk, the center, walks up with a roll of raffle tickets in his hand.

"Fifty cents each," he says.

"For what?" asks Josh.

"If you win, you get to sit on the couch for a game," says the big kid, nodding toward the sofa behind them.

He introduces himself, sits down for a few minutes. His name is Anecta—Anecta Kalugin. He's as large as the boys recall from last season: six-foot-five, close to three hundred pounds. He's wearing a beige *rubakha* embroidered with delicate flowers around the neckline. His hair and his beard are the color of copper. He's much friendlier here than he seems on the court. That's his CD mix blasting out of the speakers: Dashboard Confessional, Kazzer, Matchbook Romance. Yes, he speaks Russian, he says, as well as English. His grandfather was one of those four men who founded this village. He's seventeen, the oldest child in his family. He will be the first to attend college when he enters the University of Alaska at Anchorage this fall. He has mixed feelings, he says, about leaving Nikolaevsk.

"I feel like I'm ready to start my life, sure," he says. "But I love the life I've led here."

The boys are listening, most of them. A couple make a point of not looking, fixing their eyes on the action out on the floor. Wes doesn't bother with any pretense. He stares at the huge Russian kid with undisguised awe.

"There's good things and bad about living here," Anecta continues. "Almost everybody is my family. Either they really are my family, cousins and such, or they're like family. You just feel like you belong."

The Fort Yukon boys can relate.

"But it's not fun to have to travel at least twenty miles to shop for anything, or to have to go two hundred miles to Anchorage to *really* shop," he says. "The same for finding a job."

Again, the Fort Yukon boys can relate.

There are only seventy-two kids in the entire school here, says Anecta. Little kids all the way up through high school. One or two of the players on the girls' team, he says, true to Old Believers' tradition, are already engaged to be married to young men in the village.

The Fort Yukon boys cannot relate.

The school used to have more students, says Anecta, but the village lost half its families when a rift occurred between two factions roughly twenty years ago. The more stringent Old Believers did not like the direction in which the village was moving. They felt the modern world was encroaching, even here. They did not approve, for instance, of basketball. When one of the village's elders returned from a visit to Russia wearing the black robes of an ordained Orthodox priest, open conflict broke out. The Old Believers had lived without priests for hundreds of years, ever since they first broke away from Peter the Great. The more traditional among them vowed to keep it that way. The village's church was set on fire. Houses were burned. Alaskan state troopers were called in. The firmer Old Believers finally moved out, down the coast, beyond Homer, beyond where the highway ends. They have lived down there ever since, in a wooded hamlet called Voznesenka.

"If you think this is isolated," says Anecta, "you should go down there."

With that, he excuses himself to go sell more tickets. Cook Inlet is already pulling away from Mat-Su, and it's only the first quarter. Chris and Derek go back to the classroom to get some homework done—geometry and science. Chris peppers Derek with questions about radioisotopes.

Out in the hallway, another Nikolaevsk ballplayer is passing the time. His name's Stepan Nikitenko. He's the guard the boys have heard about, the left-hander who's supposed to be able to shoot the lights out. He's more taciturn than his teammate Anecta. He's tougher, close to unfriendly. Unlike Anecta, he has no facial hair. He's also eight inches shorter, more Fort Yukon's size. Like Matt and Josh, Stepan and Anecta are Nikolaevsk's only two seniors. But unlike Anecta's, Stepan's roots in the village are frayed.

His family moved to Nikolaevsk when he was in fifth grade, he explains. They came from Khabarousk, a Siberian city of close to one million people. Neither he nor his parents spoke English when they first got here, he says. They knew nothing about fishing or farming. They were city people. But their city had become unbearably corrupt in the wake of the fall of the Soviet Union, he says. So they came to Alaska to begin a new life.

"It was hard," he says. "We had a bad family situation."

His parents separated not long after they arrived here, he says. His mother moved out. His father married a village widow. Stepan says he turned to basketball out of boredom more than anything else. And also for comfort.

"I didn't even know what basketball *was*," he recalls. "But there was nothing else to do. So I'd go out and shoot for four or five hours a day."

He was a starter on this team two years ago, but at the end of that season, with tightened immigration security checks in the wake of the 9/11 terrorist attacks, his father's papers were found to be out of order and the family was deported, sent back to Russia, to Khabarousk.

"It was awful," says Stepan. "People in Russia are so depressed. How could you not be depressed? Go to work, work hard, not a lot of money, can't buy food. It's terrible."

He kept playing ball there, he says, catching a bus each afternoon, riding halfway across the city to a decrepit gymnasium where a local university team practiced.

"It was a mess," he says. "The roof leaked. They had buckets on the floor to catch the water."

But the games were first-rate, he says. He's only five-nine, but he learned to hold his own against older, much taller players—six-foot-six and six-seven guards.

"They play European-style ball over there," he explains. "Even the big guys, the six-tens and six-elevens, don't post up. They like to move outside and jack up three-pointers. They're shooters, like all those Europeans in the NBA now. Like Dirk Nowitzki or Peja Stojakovic."

Stepan says the university would have offered him a schoolarship, but he didn't want to stay in Khabarousk. He was happy, he says, when his father was approved for permanent U.S. residency and the family returned here last summer. He's having a good season—"decent," he says—averaging a team-high twenty points a game so far. He's eager to play tonight's game, to go up against Fort Yukon. "Bring it on," he says.

It's six P.M. now. The Cook Inlet boys have demolished Mat-Su. It's time for the second girls' game of the day to begin. The guy from Anchorage, the radio announcer, is set up, plugged in, ready to broadcast the game back to Fort Yukon. The gym is nearly filled now, as the hometown Lady Warriors take the floor. Until the turn of the 1990s, the Nikolaevsk girls wore their *talichkas* on the court, with numbers sewn onto the fronts and backs of their dresses. Game balls would sometimes disappear beneath the long hemlines. Tonight they are wearing jerseys and shorts, just like the Fort Yukon girls.

And they're good. Their passes are crisp. Their point guard—one of the engaged girls Anecta mentioned—is a deft dribbler, clearly the team's leader. She sets up her teammates and scores when it's needed. The Fort Yukon girls make a game of it, but with only five players against Nikolaevsk's thirteen, they're overwhelmed. The final score, much to the delight of the whistling, cheering, foot-stomping hometown fans, is 46–31, Nikolaevsk.

Now, finally, it's time for the night's marquee game. Nikolaevsk comes out in their maroon and white warm-ups, Anecta and Stepan leading the way. Word has already spread among the spectators that half of Fort Yukon's team is not here. The Nikolaevsk fans wonder how that will affect the game, whether this skeleton squad of Indian boys will be able to make it a contest.

For some reason, the big man doesn't start for Nikolaevsk. Josh scores off the opening tip, then forces Stepan into a trap and a turnover. Chris comes up with the steal, feeding Matt for a layup. Aaron blocks a short jumper by Stepan, leading to another layup by Josh. Four minutes in, the score is 12–4, Fort Yukon, and Nikolaevsk calls time-out. The crowd is subdued, almost silent.

Anecta checks in, and the tide and the tone immediately turn. He looms in the key like a sequoia, forcing Fort Yukon to alter their shots. He lumbers from one end of the floor to the other, trailing the action when the pace is swift, but he's a dominant force when his teammates slow down and give him a chance to set up. He has a surprisingly delicate shot off the glass, he sets a pick like a mountain, and he's a nimble passer, dropping the ball on the mark to his cutting teammates.

The quarter ends 14–12, Nikolaevsk. A 10–0 run since the big man came in.

Dave is low-key, composed, as he gathers his boys on the bench. The one thing he's worried about right now are three fouls Aaron picked up in the first quarter. He's got to sit Aaron down, bring Tim Woods in and shift Derek to center, to battle the big man. This trip has already been a trial by fire for Derek, with the beating he took up in Houston. If Dave had his way, he'd be bringing Derek along more slowly, give him a chance to come in off the bench as a sub for Tim Fields. But Tim isn't here. Dave needs Derek right now, to lean against the big Russian.

Both teams come back out firing. Matt, Chris and Josh each hit short floaters, just over the reach of the big man. Stepan answers with three scores of his own, slicing in from the left side each time, stopping on a dime from ten feet or so, flicking in a feathery fallaway jumper. After the third one, Josh stops by the bench and asks Dave if they should go to a box-and-one, with Josh on Stepan. "Do it," says Dave.

Meanwhile, Derek is trying his best to bang with the big man. He's in pain, limping up the floor with a badly turned ankle. Again, with no bench, he has to play hurt.

With 3:40 left, Tim Woods stuns Dave—and himself—by hitting a line-drive bank shot to cut it to four. Stepan and Anecta close out the half with six points between them for a 34–26 halftime lead. Together, they have all but nine of Nikolaevsk's thirty-four points.

Dave's not unhappy with his boys' performance, not at all. Derek and Matt are playing injured, both with hurt ankles. Josh has got an ice pack on his right thigh, thanks to a knee from Stepan. Aaron and Josh have three fouls apiece. Dave could use some more bodies. "Boy," he says, sending his seven kids out to begin the second half, "it just steams me not having the rest of those guys here."

The hometown fans applaud Fort Yukon as they come out on the court. They know their basketball here, and they respect the effort of Dave's undermanned team. They're particularly delighted with Josh, the tiniest kid on the court. They love watching him jet from one end to the other, driving fearlessly into the midst of the Nikolaevsk defense, going right at Anecta like a bothersome gnat. The Mat-Su kids—both the boys and the girls—have adopted Fort Yukon, gathering behind the Eagles' bench, screaming and stomping the bleachers.

The teams take turns trading scores until Derek nails a long three to cut Nikolaevsk's lead to five with three minutes to go in the third. The game has become an all-out sprint, both teams streaking up and down the floor. Anecta is hardly a factor. The guards have taken over the game. The fans love it—the rush, the excitement, the heat. The quarter ends with Fort Yukon still trailing by seven.

This is it, Dave tells the boys. You've got at least one run left in you, he says, and seven points is nothing. Sure enough, Chris comes out, scores on a layup and is fouled. He hits the free throw, trimming the lead to four, 46–42. The Nikolaevsk fans—the men in their fur hats, the women in their *shaels*—are up on their feet, urging their team on.

Stepan responds with a six-footer, off a pick by Anecta.

Josh picks up his fourth foul on a reach with 6:30 to go. Dave drops to his knees on the call.

Anecta scores on a putback.

Chris gets the ball on the right side of the key, makes that jive little juke move, right out of the "And 1" playbook . . . and is whistled for a travel. He spins in disgust, rolling his eyes at the call.

"That's the *right* call!" snaps Dave. "We've gone *over* this in practice!"

Nikolaevsk scores again. Then again, on a coast-to-coast layup by Anecta, who looks like the Hulk pounding the ball the length of the floor as the Fort Yukon players peel away. The crowd goes ape. Even the refs are smiling, shaking their heads.

"Hey," Dave yells out, enjoying the play himself, "I'd get out of his way, *too*!"

Josh responds with a crowd-pleaser of his own, taking it right at Anecta, twisting in midair, turning his back to the basket as the big man rises, and flipping the ball blindly over both of their heads, finding nothing but net. Dave goes nuts over that one, like everyone else.

The final is 63–48, Nikolaevsk. Aaron is high man for Fort Yukon with eleven, followed by Josh with ten. Stepan went for twenty-five, followed by Anecta's twenty-three. Dave shakes the Russian kids' coach's hand, winks and says, "See you next time," meaning next week, when both teams will be at the NIT.

Then he goes back to the classroom, where the boys are scattered all over the floor, exhausted again.

"Good job," says Dave. "Two or three more guys rotating in off the bench would have made a world of difference."

He scans the room.

"Chris has given us good floor time. I appreciate it. Derek has gotten good floor time, too. He's found out you can get *hurt* out there."

The boys chuckle, glancing over at Derek.

"And Josh," Dave says, looking at his little floor leader, "has *emerged*."

He sends them all off to shower. Then they eat. Then it's out into the hallways, to mingle with the other teams' kids, except for Cook Inlet's. The Cook Inlet teams are both gone. They've chosen to drive home for the night rather than spend it here. They'll be back for the championship games tomorrow.

By eleven, the Mat-Su boys and girls are out in the gym with the Fort Yukon kids, playing "knockout" at one end of the floor and a mixed game of four-on-four at the other. Dave lets the curfew slide. His boys are having a wonderful time. They can sleep in tomorrow. They don't play till almost noon.

It comes quickly, though, game time the next morning. The first game tips off at ten, to a near-empty gym, with Dave and a couple of the boys camped on the sofa, cheering the Fort Yukon girls on. The rest of the boys are back in the classroom still sleeping, something the girls will give them grief about later.

Dave is in heaven, a hot cup of coffee in hand, firing off one-liners, to the delight of his kids and the handful of spectators in the stands.

"*Ride* her!" he yells out to Mandy. "Ride her like a rented *mule!*"

The boys crack up.

"*Turnovers!* Come on! It's Betty Crocker time. Lots of turnovers!"

His guys are eating it up, Dave at his corniest.

Meanwhile, they're debating the merits of the best-looking Mat-Su girls on the court.

"Number twenty-one," says Aaron.

Chris nods his head.

"I want number twenty-three," says Matt.

Cheryl's girls have no trouble with Mat-Su, pulling away in the second half for an easy win. Dave's mood is still playful, a little bit giddy, as he gathers his guys to take the court for the boys' third-place game, against Mat-Su.

"To the victors go the spoils," he says, leaning into their huddle. "We win, we get to take their women."

From the opening tip it's a blowout. Four minutes in, the score is 16–2, Fort Yukon. The only possible danger is fouls. Sure enough, Matt picks up two in the opening quarter, and Aaron gets three. The period ends 20–12, with Matt heating up for the first time this season. He's got twelve.

Derek takes over in the second, bringing the small crowd to its feet as he nails three three-pointers. Mat-Su responds with a box-and-one. "A box-and-one on *Derek*," says Dave. "Now that's something."

The Mat-Su kids are smiling, upbeat, even while taking a beating. They pat the Fort Yukon boys on the back after each foul. One of their forwards has a large cross tattooed on his right bicep, with PAID IN FULL lettered beneath it. They're committed young Christians, every one of them. When the teams break their huddles after time-outs, the Fort Yukon boys chant, "One, two, three, *Defense!*" while the Mat-Su boys chant, "One, two, three, *Jesus!*"

Halftime, Fort Yukon leads by sixteen. Midway through the third quarter, they're up by eighteen when Aaron and Matt each pick up their fourth foul, and the play starts getting sloppy.

Derek air-balls a twelve-footer, bringing Dave to his feet.

"Derek!" he hollers. "How about hitting the *rim* next time?"

Derek flashes a sheepish smile as he heads back up the court. Mat-Su closes the quarter with an eight-point run, then opens the fourth with another score to cut Fort Yukon's lead to eight.

Then Chris draws his fourth foul, giving Dave three players with four.

Mat-Su cuts it to seven with six minutes left. Suddenly, this has gotten serious.

"Patience!" Dave yells out. "Patience!"

He orders his boys into a stall, a triangle weave with the guards out near half-court. They eat a couple of minutes off the clock, with Derek and Josh both getting layups off Mat-Su lapses. The final is 57–49. Not a pretty win, but a win nonetheless. Matt is high man with eighteen points, followed by Derek with seventeen.

"All right," Dave says, back in the classroom again, "get your showers, get dressed. When these last two games are done, they'll have the awards ceremonies, then, *bang*, we're gone. Bags packed, room cleaned, out to the van, and we leave. We've got some traveling ahead of us."

The two games go quickly, both Cook Inlet teams winning by routs. Their boys are impressive, completely outclassing Anecta and Stepan and their teammates. Dave's guys are convinced they could play with those Cook Inlet kids if their whole team was here. But they won't get that chance, not today.

Four thirty, the awards are handed out. Third-place team trophies for both Fort Yukon teams. All-Tournament medals for Mandy and Gina, and for Josh and Matt.

With that, Dave moves toward the parking lot.

"*Hunchi! Hunchi!*," he says. Gwich'in for "Hurry! Hurry!"

By five, they're back out on the two-lane coast highway. Black storm clouds are gathering over the inlet. The radio's warning of northeast winds, forty to fifty knots, with seas to twelve feet, and freezing rain.

By five thirty, all seven boys are asleep as Dave pushes the van north, through the sleet, toward Fairbanks.

Toward home.

TWELVE

NIT

A FUEL TRUCK is parked in the Monday night darkness outside the Fort Yukon gym. Its engine is idling, the exhaust from its tailpipe tumbling down to the snow in the forty-eight-below-zero air. The driver is inside the building, with a large box of tools, trying to figure out why the gym has no heat.

The boys are gathered in the bleachers, bundled in their jackets and hats as if they're still outside. The temperature is well below freezing in here. They can see their own breath. There will be no practice this evening, but the team's still got some business to take care of.

They arrived home last night, the seven who made the trip. Doc drove the school bus over, met them at the airstrip, dropped each one of them off at their houses. Today he passed out those new Nike shoes to the players who traveled last week. The others will have to wait, Doc decided, till they pull their grades up. They'll find out tomorrow who's eligible for this week.

Dave's got his fur hat and coat on as he paces in front of the boys, a sheaf of papers in his gloved hands.

"How ya *doin'*?" he says, nodding to Wade.

"Good to *see* ya," he says, reaching out to shake Johnny's hand.

"Now *there's* a familiar face," he says, looking at Justin.

They squirm just a little, don't know if they're supposed to smile or what.

"We missed you last week, boys," he says. "That's why we called, to let you know we missed you. And to rub it in a little bit.

"I'm sorry *you* missed it," he continues. "We went to some places I have never been. I saw some things I've never seen, and I'm fifty-one years old. I've seen a lot."

He draws a deep breath, flips through the papers.

"Okay. Weather permitting, Thursday we travel to Nenana."

The NIT pairings are set. Eight teams will be there, Dave tells them. Two brackets of four. Hooper Bay, Tok, Nenana and Nikolaevsk will be in one bracket. Tri-Valley, Fort Yukon, Susitna Valley and . . . yes, yet again . . . Anderson will be in the other. Fort Yukon's first-round game will be against—who else? says Dave—Anderson.

The boys roll their eyes.

The nice thing, Dave continues, would be to win the first two games and meet Nikolaevsk in the finals, face them with a full team this time and maybe get some revenge.

"I'd like to see our name go up on that big board," he says again, for those who weren't there when they drove past Nenana last week.

With that, he sends them all home.

Matt walks across the road, back to his cabin. His dad's not there. Neither is Gina. She had a rough time yesterday, when both teams got to the Fairbanks airport to fly home. Their mom, Mary, showed up to give them both a hug. She had her current boyfriend with her, a nice enough guy as far as Matt's concerned. But Gina made kind of a scene, breaking down and crying. It's been harder on Gina, it seems, than it's been on Matt and Ryan and John, their parents not being together and all, and living in two separate towns like they do. But hey, Gina's a girl, figures Matt. Girls get emotional like that.

Matt misses his mom, too, of course. But it isn't as if they ever all lived together as one big happy family. His parents split up just after Gina was born. Matt was two at the time. His mom took both of them with her and moved to Fairbanks, where Matt lived until he was in the fourth grade. There was a funeral that winter in Fort Yukon for Matt's uncle and cousin, who were hit and killed by a truck while riding tandem on a snowmachine in the village. Matt remembers flying up for that burial. His mom left him and Gina with their dad when it was over. Matt's lived with Jack ever since, except for the nine months Jack went to jail for that Pierre Tremblay deal and Matt had to stay with the Hardys.

He checks the fridge, grabs something to eat, flips on the TV and flops on the sofa. His dad's already taped Matt's All-Tournament medal from Nikolaevsk on the wall, above the kitchen table, along with a couple of newspaper clippings. By the time the season's finished, that wall will be covered with clippings and maybe a couple more medals. Jack does the same thing every year. He's done it ever since Ryan first started playing.

Ritchie Carroll shows up and joins Matt on the sofa. Within a few minutes, there's a commotion outside the door, then it swings open and in bursts Jack, his arms full of firewood, ice fog rolling in behind him.

"It's fuck-ing *cold* out there!" he says, pushing the door shut and dumping the wood on the floor by the stove.

He claps the sawdust off his gloves, then removes them, tossing them on the sofa beside Matt.

"Listen to this," he says, standing in the middle of the room, an ear-to-ear grin on his face, his eyes dancing and wet. "I had the *weirdest* fucking dream last night. I dreamed I was sitting right there on that couch watching *Beavis and Butt-head*."

The boys burst into laughter, as does Jack.

"And then I was on *their* couch, sitting with Beavis and Butt-head, watching TV."

Ritchie and Matt are almost on the floor now. Jack walks over to the refrigerator, pulls out a can of Miller, pops it open and turns back toward the boys.

"Wood!!" he suddenly shouts. "Go!! Sell it!!!!!"

The boys stiffen, straighten, reach for their coats without questions.

"Move, move, *move!!!*" Jack continues. "I don't care what you get for it. Fucking *sell* it!"

They're already headed out the door. They know the drill. Jack gets home from the wood yard, the bed of his pickup loaded with ten-foot-length logs, and he may head right out and sell the load himself, or he may come home and get Matt to do it, tell him to go cruise the village, check out the woodpiles in the front yards, knock on the door of anyone whose supply looks low. This is the way all the wood Nazis in town do it. That's what Jack and his pals like to call themselves. Wood Nazis.

Jack draws himself half a glass of warm tap water, then fills it with whiskey. He pulls out a baggie of dope and a pipe, sits down at the table and lights up a bowl. He's forty, but he looks ten years younger, with his floppy brown hair and his big shit-eating grin. He's a happy guy most of the time. He's happy as hell to be a grandfather—John and Samantha's baby girl is over a month old now, as is Paul's new granddaughter. The two of them—Jack and Paul—have been crowing about being certified elders now, eligible for free lunches up at the tribal headquarters dining room. Not much gets Jack down, but he's not happy with the basketball team right now, not at all. That Nikolaevsk trip was a disaster, as far as he's concerned.

"I was fucking *pissed* at the ones who didn't go, and I told them so," he says. "Tim Fields came by when we had the game on the radio, and I told him to get *out*. I told him you're not coming in *here* to get warm."

Jack listened to both Nikolaevsk tournament games. So did Paul, who kept statistics, tracking each shot made and missed by each player. They got a kick out of the announcer assuming Mandy and her cousin Corrina were sisters, since they're both named Cadzow. The same with Aaron and Derek—the guy thought they were brothers, the Carroll boys.

Jack and Paul were none too happy with how the team played, but neither of them was as upset as Willie Fields. Willie handled the radio feed at the station, and he kept a shot chart, too. He's been stewing about how in god's name Matt and Josh were named to the All-Tournament team down there. Matt made four out of sixteen shots against Nikolaevsk, according to Willie's chart. Four out of sixteen! Never mind that he scored a game-high eighteen against Mat-Su. As for Josh, says Willie, he played just as shitty. "They got no *plays*!" That's what bugs Willie. He says it over and over. "How can they win if they got no *plays*?"

That's not what bothers Jack as much as the fact that this group of kids just doesn't seem to have it together. Sure, they beat Anderson by thirty or whatever it was. But they should have whipped a sorry-ass team like that by *fifty*, he says. And the way it sounded like they played against those Russians, well, if they play like that this weekend, says Jack, they're going to get their butts kicked.

Next afternoon, Tuesday, the first day of February, it's forty-below, and Dave is plenty worried. It went down to fifty last night, with more of the same predicted for the rest of the week. He's got Georgie on the phone at the school, asking her to check if Frontier can possibly fly the teams out a day early if there's a break in the weather. Doc's already called down to Nenana, seeing if the school can take in the Fort Yukon kids sooner than planned

It's been a slow day for Dave, what with the cold weather. He didn't see an airplane all morning. That gave him time to give the bathroom a good cleaning. It's something he normally does on the weekends—pulls out the disinfectant, gets down on his hands and knees, gives everything a good scrubbing. But during basketball season, with so many weekends spent traveling, he has to fit in things like this whenever he can.

One big change in both his and Diane's lives has been Gavin's moving out. It finally got to be simply too much, the constant eruptions, the strain and the tension for all of them. They'd do anything in the world for Gavin. They love him. But they realized, after yet another trip down to the clinic in Fairbanks, where the doctors met once again with Gavin, and he came back home and went right back to the explosions, both at school and at home, and he's getting bigger now, stronger, so his outbursts are more severe than ever—they realized they just can't deal with this anymore. So they sent Gavin back to live with his mother, on the other side of the village. He still comes by the house, still hangs out, watches TV, cadges a couple of dollars here and there from Dave to buy snacks at the AC, but the pressure is gone now, the time-bomb anxiety of living with Gavin's mood swings.

That night, with the gym warm again, Doc stops by to congratulate everyone. They're all eligible for this week. Same with the girls, which means four boys won't make this trip: Zach, Kyle, Tim Woods and Wes. Dave was going to bring Kyle, but he got in trouble at school yesterday. He was wrestling with another kid in class and broke a picture frame. So he's staying behind. Bruce will come in his place. Dave tells the ten who are making the trip to pack and prepare to possibly leave tomorrow.

It's fifty-three-below when Dave awakes the next morning. By lunchtime, it's up to the low forties. Doc's on alert at the school, waiting to pull the trigger as soon as the needle hits thirty-nine. He's got the kids' teachers scrambling to pull together their assignments for the rest of the week.

Meanwhile, Trader Dan is champing at the bit at his store. He wants to bring Justin's brother, Barney, along with him, reward the boy for working so hard every weekend. But Dan doesn't want to pay for two tickets, fly down to Fairbanks, and find out the team isn't coming after all, the way it happened three weeks ago with that Tri-Valley Tournament. He's got a motel room booked in Nenana. Paul has asked if he can stay with them, to save a few bucks. Dan told him, sure, if you're willing to sleep on the floor.

Three o'clock that afternoon, the temperature hits thirty-nine. Doc doesn't check it again. Six P.M., everyone arrives at the airport, ready to go. Dave's surprised to see Tim Woods there. Tim's mother, Gladys, has offered to buy Tim a ticket on another flight out, if that's okay with Dave. Tim really wants to make this trip, even if he probably won't play. Dave has to go through these little "soap operas," as he calls them, all the time, with players and parents chafing about who gets to go on each road trip and who has to stay home. But he hasn't had too many parents offer to pay out of pocket, the way Gladys is doing. She's willing to pay the $175 for Tim's round-trip ticket. Dave decides it's okay.

As soon as Dave gives Tim the nod, he's got Wes and Zach making the same request. Their parents are willing to pay to fly them down, too. As are Kyle's. The whole thing's getting out of hand now. The terminal is overflowing with players and parents and baggage. A Duke–Wake Forest game is blaring on the lobby TV, adding to the din. Dave doesn't have time to go through all this. Two planes are approaching this minute, a Warbelow's six-seater due in ten minutes, with Frontier's Big Black Bird close behind. Dave says fine, everyone can come. The four add-ons are in. They'll get on that Warbelow's as soon as it lands, with the others boarding the Bird.

Doc hands Dave a sack of protractors and rulers, courtesy of the boys' geometry teacher. Hugs and kisses from the parents, then it's out to the tarmac—twenty-one kids and two coaches. They don't typically leave on a night flight, but this isn't typical. Again, the boys are asleep as soon as the planes are airborne. Upon landing in Fairbanks, the first thing they do after loading the vans is stop at a Pizza Hut for dinner— a treat worth the trip in itself for most of the kids. Those frozen pizzas for sale at the AC or over at Cheryl's place taste like cardboard compared to this. The kids love it, all they can eat.

Then it's on to Nenana, where the school's been kept open for Fort Yukon's arrival. It's almost ten P.M. when they get there. A shroud of ice fog hangs over the river as the kids pull their bags from the vans. The boys are led to a carpeted classroom. Quotes from Tennyson, Browning and Lawrence adorn the blackboard. The desks have been shoved to the walls, chairs stacked high in a corner, but still, there's hardly room on the floor to fit fourteen sleeping bags—fifteen, counting Dave's. The room's baseboard heaters are turned on full blast. It's stifling. Wade cracks open a window to let in some fresh subzero air. By half past eleven, everyone is asleep.

Dave's up first in the morning, as usual. He showers and shaves in the gym locker room, then finds the teacher's lounge and a hot cup of coffee. It's early, not yet seven. There's no one here but a janitor, who's brought in the morning paper, the *News-Miner*. Dave opens it to the sports section. The season's first 1A state rankings are out, and there is Fort Yukon, ranked fourth. With one first-place vote. Dave can't believe it. He's never put stock in these rankings. The sportswriters who vote on the list—most of them downstate—have seen very few, if any, 1A teams play. Alaska's simply too damned big, the villages far too spread out and remote for anyone to keep track of. This early in the year, these rankings are based on nothing more than reputation and hearsay. The reporters poke around, call a few coaches and that's it. Even at the end of the regular season, as far as Dave is concerned, the rankings mean nothing. Look at Wainwright. They're ranked first this morning, naturally, as defending state champs. But who knows what they've got this year? Dave sees they've already lost two games, just like Fort Yukon. He has no idea who's beaten them. He has no idea who they've played. Wainwright is more than five hundred miles north of Fairbanks, for

Christ's sake. There are no reporters up there. The same with Emmonak, ranked number two, and Savoonga, ranked third. There are no reporters in any of the 115 bush villages that field Class 1A teams—including Fort Yukon.

But Dave knows back home they'll open this morning's paper and celebrate. Georgie will clip the article and post it in the school office for all the kids to look at. They'll pass it around down at the tribal headquarters. Jack will tape it up on his wall. Only the hard-core naysayers—Willie and Paul and the like—will ask why the team's not ranked higher, why they're not doing better.

By nine, the boys are up and have had breakfast. Dave gathers them back in the classroom, passes out the protractors and curls up with a paperback—a mystery—while the kids do their homework.

School's been called off today and tomorrow here in Nenana, because of the tournament. The other teams will begin arriving this morning, boys and girls, moving into their own classrooms, where they'll spend the next three nights. This is close to the biggest event of the year in Nenana. Only the village's annual Ice Classic is bigger. The Classic's been staged every spring here since 1919. The whole state looks forward to it. The Nenanans set out a striped metal tripod on the ice-locked Tanana River sometime in March, and people all over Alaska buy tickets predicting, to the day, the hour, and the minute, precisely when the ice will break up and the twenty-six-foot-tall tripod will begin to move, tripping a cable tied to a clock on the shore. Last year, more than one hundred thousand Alaskans paid for a guess. When the ice finally broke on April 24, stopping the clock at 2:16 P.M., six winners split the jackpot of $301,000.

Ice Classic is a big deal, but the Little NIT is bigger. It began in 1984 as a showcase for the state's smaller schools. Since then it's become a tradition, much like the State Tournament in Anchorage, an opportunity for far-flung Alaskans, most of them Natives, to come together, catch up on old friendships and watch some good high school basketball. The talk of the tournament this year are the 3A schools—Susitna Valley, and Hooper Bay, whose team is flying in from the far western coast, six hundred miles away. The defending champions, Nikolaevsk, are back, as is Tok. And then there's Fort Yukon, the only 1A team in the field. The host team, Nenana, looked strong until yesterday, when their best player was busted after the cops did a sweep of the school and found three bags of weed in his locker.

Matt's cousin Russell has been telling the boys all about it. Russell plays for Nenana. He lives here at the school, in a dorm built to house sixty-five students from around the state, almost all of them Native, almost all from the bush. They attend classes along with more than one hundred local Nenana kids. It's not as large a boarding school program as Mount Edgecumbe's, in Sitka. More than three hundred Native kids live and attend high school down there. Mount Edgecumbe is where most of the parents in Fort Yukon who can afford it, and bear it, send their kids for at least a couple of years. Dave's daughters went to Mount Edgecumbe. So did Dacho and all of his siblings. Mandy Cadzow's older sister is there right now. That's where Gina was before she transferred back home last semester. Almost every Native kid in Alaska who thinks about going to boarding school thinks of Mount Edgecumbe. But Nenana has a good, growing program. And it's got the advantage of being more than six hundred miles—half the width of the state—closer to the rest of Alaska than Sitka.

Russell's excited about his team's game tonight against Hooper Bay. He's excited about everything. He rubs some kids the wrong way with his nonstop chatter, but Matt enjoys him. Besides, he's family.

Russell says he hopes the Hooper Bay team gets here in time. He heard they had trouble catching the plane out of their village this morning. Half the Fort Yukon boys are listening to him. The others are packing their gear, getting set for the short drive down to Anderson, where they'll play tonight's opening-round game. If they lose, they'll be in the loser's bracket on the Nenana floor tomorrow morning. If they win, they'll be in one of the highlight semifinal games tomorrow night. The boys are counting on winning.

So, frankly, is Dave. He's not too concerned about Anderson, although you never know. He's more interested in watching Su-Valley play, to see what they've got. The Su-Valley–Tri-Valley game is already in the second quarter by the time Dave and the boys get to the Anderson gym.

Su-Valley is blowing Tri-Valley off the floor. A contingent of Fort Yukon fans is scattered throughout the half-filled bleachers. Josh's family. The McCarty sisters. Aaron's cousin and aunt. Trader Dan, of course, along with Barney. Georgie and a couple of her brothers. Jack's not here—he couldn't afford the trip. But Paul's made it. He's perched on the top row, headset at the ready, prepared to broadcast his first away game of the season. They're all talking about how cold it is back in Fort Yukon—negative-fifty-six this morning—and what a good call it was for the team to fly out yesterday. Barney's excited to be here. He slept in the motel room's closet last night, letting Paul have the floor while Dan slept on the bed. Everyone's joking about how that closet is the first bedroom Barney's had to himself since he was born.

Su-Valley looks good. They're tall, with a front line of six-four, six-three and six-two, all white kids from over the mountains, down toward Anchorage, on the highway. They've won this tournament once, back in 1994. The way they're carrying themselves tonight—laughing and goofing the way Cook Inlet did down at Nikolaevsk—they look like they're counting on winning it again this weekend. As soon as their game's over—a 64–18 final—they pack up and leave, head back to Nenana. Dave can't believe it. They're not even bothering to stay and scout which team they'll be playing tomorrow night. Must not matter to them, Dave figures. He makes a note to mention this to his boys later on.

It doesn't take long for Dave to see that his guys have come ready to play. Matt's dialed in, hitting two threes in the first quarter and one more in the second. He scores fourteen points in the game's first ten minutes. Even better, he's throwing strong, solid passes. He's playing smart, like the team leader Dave expects him to be.

Johnny seems ready as well, sinking two threes of his own and looking like he actually understands the defensive scheme. Josh and Justin, with Wade coming off the bench, are like lasers, vaporizing Anderson's guards. Halftime, the score is 47–18. It only gets worse in the second, even with Dave clearing his bench: Anderson scores just five points the entire half. The final is 81–23. All fourteen Fort Yukon boys get to play. All fourteen score, led by Matt's sixteen points. Dave's kind of glad Su-Valley left early. They have no idea what they're in for. If his kids bring their "A" game tomorrow night the way they brought it this evening, those Su-Valley boys will have no idea what hit them.

"Gentlemen," Dave tells his team as they pack up their bags, "Gwichyaa Zhee has arrived!"

It's late, close to eleven, by the time they get back to Nenana. The cafeteria is crowded with kids and coaches munching on pizza and fruit and juice, buzzing about the two games played here this evening. In the opener, Tok—as in "smoke"—came out and simply destroyed Nikolaevsk. The center for Tok, a monstrous Norwegian-American kid, completely outplayed the Russians' big man in the middle. At six-five and three hundred pounds, the Tok center is hard to miss. Just to make sure he stands out, he's got his hair gelled into a spiked saw-toothed Mohawk. He and his teammates led Nikolaevsk 22–6 at the end of the first quarter tonight and never looked back. The final was 71–50.

In the nightcap, Nenana edged Hooper Bay by a point, thanks to a couple of questionable calls in the game's final minute. No one's coming out and saying the refs helped out the home team, but the implication is there.

The Hooper Bay coaches and kids, all Yupiks, are exhausted, eating their pizza in silence. They were tired and hungry when they got here, says their coach, a soft-spoken fifty-some-year-old Native named Luke Tall. He does maintenance and repairs at the Hooper Bay school. His kids flew a long way today, arriving just in time to suit up. But that's no excuse, he says. They lost, and that's that. "You've got to take your medicine," he says. Which, in this case, means playing the Russians in the loser's bracket tomorrow.

Everyone's talking about a Su-Valley–Tok final. Which is fine with Dave. He likes seeing his team underestimated, forgotten, ignored.

He lets his boys stay up late, hanging out with the Hooper Bay kids, watching a slasher flick on one of the school's TVs. By one, everyone's back in the classroom, asleep.

Come morning, the temperature's pushing forty-below. Dave hopes it gets even colder. The Junior Quest dog race will have to be canceled if it gets too cold, which will give Dave back his starting point guard.

Josh's mom, Janet, is coming to fetch him this morning, drive him up to Fairbanks for the day to take care of the vet check, the food drops and everything else his dogs will need for the 170-mile event. Josh will be back for tonight's game but not for tomorrow's. Not unless it gets colder, which Josh, like Dave, hopes it does. He'd rather play ball.

The boys pass the day watching the other teams play. They get a kick out of the Hooper Bay girls chanting in Yupik as they cheer on their boys against Nikolaevsk.

"*Wanguta malruneng piurrtugut!*" they yell, over and over.

"What's that mean?" Tim Woods asks one of the girls.

"Now we want two points!" she answers.

Hooper Bay wins, sending the Russians into the dreaded eight A.M. Saturday morning seventh-place game.

Dave passes the time at what the tournament hosts call "Coaches' Row." It's a section of chairs set up at one end of the floor, under the backboard, where the coaches convene to take in the action while munching on a buffet spread prepared by the Nenana athletic director's wife. That buffet is one of the highlights of Dave's season. He's been talking about it since practice began in December.

On the opposite wall, at the far end of the court, is the big board, with the name of every NIT champion since 1984, boys' and girls', inscribed in block letters.

NORTHWAY. HOUSTON. TRI-VALLEY.
POINT HOPE. MCGRATH. TOK.
UNALASKA. NENANA. GLENNALLEN.
DELTA. SU-VALLEY. MINTO.
ANDERSON. COOK INLET. NINILCHIK.
SELDOVIA. WAINWRIGHT. NIKOLAEVSK.

The year 2005 has been freshly painted, with two blank spaces beside it, awaiting this year's winners.

Midafternoon, the Fort Yukon girls take the court. They beat Anderson last night in a close game, but this one they lose, to Tri-Valley. By the time the final horn sounds, the gym, which seats 350, is packed.

The Nenana pep band is rocking the crowd. Su-Valley's cheerleaders—the first cheerleaders Fort Yukon has seen this season—exhort the Rams as they take the floor in their crisp blue-and-gold warm-ups. Dave's still got his boys in the classroom, for last-minute instructions.

"They're ready to be had," he says.

"I want you to *drop* on them, drop on them hard and fast.

"If I'm not seeing what I want, I'm gonna sub and sub quickly, do you understand?"

With that, and the prayer, they head down the hall and out into the thundering din of the gym. The Su-Valley kids look over, smiling and pointing as the little Fort Yukon boys run through their layups. "Either this team is ripe for the picking," thinks Dave, "or they're really so good they don't need to be worried."

It doesn't take long to see that they're pretty damned good. The first four trips up the floor, Su-Valley's guards split Fort Yukon's traps for easy scores. Two minutes in, the score is 8–0, Su-Valley.

Paul is apoplectic, shouting the play-by-play into his headset behind the Fort Yukon bench. It's all he can do to keep from tearing off his equipment and running out on the court.

Three minutes in, Fort Yukon scores their first point, a foul shot by Matt.

Four minutes in, the score is 10–1, Su-Valley.

Dave doesn't panic. He doesn't call time-out. He hates to spend time-outs early. You never know when you'll need them at the end of the game. He sends Derek in, and Wade, too. Derek responds with an offensive rebound and putback. Matt hits a baseline jumper and free throw to make the score 14–6 at the end of the first quarter.

Dave gathers the kids by the bench, assures them they're doing fine, instructs Derek and Matt to isolate themselves on the right side of the floor, run a little two-man game against Su-Valley's guards.

It works like a charm. First, Matt finds Wade cutting backdoor from the far side and feeds him for a layup. Then Derek hits a long three after an inside-out pass from Matt. Then Wade strips a Su-Valley guard and jets the other way for a score. Just like that, it's 16–13, Su-Valley.

"Ball game," says Dave. He smiles, leans back in his seat. "We got a ball game."

Su-Valley calls time-out. They look a little unsettled.

"Keep it up," Dave tells his boys. "Don't let up."

The crowd loves it. This what they came for, a boxing match, two evenly matched teams trading punches.

Su-Valley emerges from the time-out intense, deliberate. They regain control, feeding their front line, stretching the lead to five points, then six points, then eight. Derek and Josh each pick up their third foul and have to sit down. Matt's keeping Fort Yukon in the game by himself, driving, drawing fouls, directing the defense, doing whatever he can to force the action.

Five seconds to go in the half, Su-Valley scores to make it 29–21.

Matt takes the inbounds pass, comes up the floor as if he's got all the time in the world.

Four seconds. He pushes the ball toward the right side, to half-court.

Three. He crosses back to the middle, splitting two Su-Valley guards.

Two. He pulls up at the top of the key, flanked by two more defenders.

One. He pump-fakes one player into the air, leans past the other and shoots.

The ball arches high toward the ceiling, nearly grazing the rafters.

The gym falls silent, every eye on the shot.

Zero. The halftime horn sounds.

Swish.

The ball splits the net, and the place goes berserk.

29–24, Su-Valley.

"Boys," Dave says, back in the classroom, "just keep playing our game. Do that, and you'll be in the finals tomorrow."

He tells Josh to check back in to open the second half. Josh responds on the first possession, with an up-and-under, double-pump drive for a score. Then he feeds Aaron inside for a layup. Another Josh dish to Aaron, who's fouled and makes one, and now the score's tied for the first time tonight, 29–29. An eight-point run for Fort Yukon.

Su-Valley comes right back with a seven-point run of their own. It's only midway through the third quarter, but the crowd has already come to a boil. They're up on their feet, stomping the grandstands. It's been a game of spurts by both teams, each answering a run by the other. Now, once again, it's Fort Yukon's turn.

Seven points down with four minutes left in the third, Wade starts the fire, slapping the ball from a Su-Valley guard's hands and scooting the other way for a layup, which he misses while being shoved from behind by the frustrated defender. He hurtles headlong into Coaches' Row.

The ref whistles a flagrant technical foul. Wade shoots two free throws, makes one. Matt steps in for two more, making them both. And now it's Fort Yukon's ball.

Dave sees Wade rubbing his head, looking groggy. He grabs Johnny, tells him to check into the game.

"For who?" Johnny asks.

"For the guy with the *headache*," shouts Dave, pushing Johnny toward the scorer's table.

Before Dave can sit back down, the ball's already inbounded, to Johnny, who bangs in a twelve-footer without even blinking.

"Bingo!" says Dave, clapping his hands. "Johnny Big Shot, right off the bench."

Su-Valley scores to go back up by four, but their players are livid. One of them clutches Matt's jersey as he comes up the court, and the ref blows the whistle. Another technical foul.

Matt hits one free throw, then, on the inbounds, he slides to the corner, gets a snap-pass from Justin and buries a three to tie it at 38 with 1:05 left in the quarter. When Aaron rattles in a twelve-footer the next trip up the floor, Fort Yukon has its first lead of the night, 40–38. Su-Valley tries holding the ball for the last forty seconds, but Justin knifes in front of a pass with eight seconds left, makes the steal and fires the ball ahead to Tim Fields, who just beats the third-quarter buzzer with a soft eight-foot jumper.

Speed over size. Dave's said it a million times. He'll take speed over size any day. Tonight is just such a test. Su-Valley is not slow, by any means. Fort Yukon is only a hair quicker, but that hair is making the difference right now. Whenever Su-Valley breaks through Fort Yukon's traps, they score, mostly inside. When they don't, however, Fort Yukon's bevy of guards—Josh, Justin, Matt and Wade—swarms the other way, feeding each other for layups or wide-open jumpers.

The fourth quarter goes just like that, back and forth, size against speed. With five minutes left, Su-Valley has pulled back ahead by four. Dave is crouched in front of his seat, imploring his boys to reach deep inside, find the juice for just one more run.

Josh locates Derek slicing through the lane, hits him for a layup that cuts it to two.

Su-Valley misses.

Aaron rebounds, hands the ball to Matt, who walks it up the floor. Two Su-Valley guards await him at the top of the key. Five feet before he gets there, he looks to one side as if to pass, then abruptly brings the ball back, squares and strokes the longest shot anyone's taken all night, an NBA-range three-pointer that grazes the rim on its way through the net.

The bleachers explode.

Dave shakes his head.

"Ice water," he says. "Absolute ice water."

Fort Yukon is back up by one.

Su-Valley misses, Derek is fouled on a drive and hits both free throws, banking one off the backboard.

"That's a brick that I *like*," hollers Dave, cracking up his own kids along with the crowd.

Another Su-Valley miss, and Derek is fouled again. He makes one, pushing the lead to four. The inside shots Su-Valley was hitting in the first half are rimming out now. They call time-out with two minutes to go.

"These guys are not used to playing at this speed," Dave tells his kids. "They can't shoot when they play fast. They can't pass when they play fast. I want you to keep playing *fast*."

They do. And Su-Valley can do nothing to stop them. Josh makes yet another steal for a layup. Matt sinks yet another three-pointer, bringing yet another ovation from the crowd.

"They're really *with* us, aren't they?" says Dave, looking up at the sea of faces behind him.

The last seconds tick away, with the crowd counting them down.

The final is 63–58, Fort Yukon.

The tournament's only 1A team has dropped a goliath.

The boys have to push their way through the backslaps and hugs as the spectators flood onto the court. It takes them a while to work their way back to the classroom. Dave finally gets them inside, shuts the door, draws a deep breath. He's soaking wet, grinning, just like the kids.

"This was a team win, guys," he says. "Right straight down the bench, this was a *team* win. You didn't panic. You came back. And you *finished*.

"I'm proud of you. Gwichyaa Zhee is proud of you.

"And Josh," he says, "now we're praying it's seventy-below tomorrow."

The boys dress, go back out and watch Tok take Nenana apart. So the championship is set, the Fort Yukon kids versus 10–1 Tok, tomorrow evening at eight.

But right now, it's still Friday night. After the crowd has gone home, including Josh with his mom, back to Fairbanks, the school's doors are locked and the hallways are filled with herds of wandering kids. The Su-Valley boys are in shock. They look sad, catatonic. As for Matt and his teammates, they're the center of attention, especially from the other schools' girls, especially Matt. He went for a tournament-high twenty-five points tonight, and he did it in style—the same way he's doing his thing right now, strolling the halls with that detached, don't-give-a-shit shuffle. He's got on his favorite bright-red Bulls jersey—number 23, Michael Jordan—with a crisp white windbreaker and white sweatpants to match, his eyes hidden behind a dark pair of wraparound shades, knockoff Oakleys that he swiped from the AC. "Five-finger discount," he says, chuckling.

They're styling, all of them, every kid from every one of the teams. It's like a parade out there in the halls, all of them dressed to the casual nines, the boys in their Ecko and Billabong kicks, the girls breaking out their tight T-shirts and jeans. Johnny, as always, is over the top, the height of hip-hop, in a chocolate-and-beige sweatsuit, with a pair of caramel-colored Lugz shoes on his feet, and a black-and-white Air Jordan ball cap cocked sideways on his head.

Again, Dave lets the curfew slide. He knows what this means to these kids. He remembers being that age himself.

It's forty-five-below when Dave awakes the next morning. Josh calls from Fairbanks during breakfast to tell him the race has been delayed. It's hour to hour, Josh says. The dogs, the drivers, the race officials—everyone's hanging around at the starting line, waiting to see when they might take off.

Midafternoon, the temperature's climbed into the thirties. Dave's heard nothing from Josh, so that's that. He and his boys watch the Fort Yukon girls lose the third-place game to Nikolaevsk. Matt cheers for the Russians, seeing as how he hit it off last night with their star guard, the one who's engaged. They had a nice conversation. She gave him her e-mail address, though what that might lead to Matt has no idea.

By the time Su-Valley beats Nenana for the boys' third-place trophy, the gym is jammed. Standing-room only. Close to four hundred people. The host school's girls' team takes the floor for their championship game and delights the home crowd by jumping all over Tri-Valley.

Halftime of that game, Dave leads his boys to the classroom, to dress and get ready. He's intense, more so than ever. There's nothing to match the State Tournament for drama and glory, but as far as the regular season goes, this is the biggest game Fort Yukon has ever played, at least since Dave started coaching. He reminds the boys that no 1A team has ever won this thing. If they do it tonight, the whole state will take notice.

They can hear the horn sounding, the cheers of the crowd as the girls' game winds down. Then the classroom door opens.

And in walks Josh, his basketball gear in hand.

"I wanted to race, boys," he says. "But I wanted this championship, too. Get our name up on that board."

He scratched just before the race started, he says. He talked his dad into it, promised him he'll run the Junior Iditarod next month. He told his dad there will be plenty of dog races in his future, but there's only one basketball game like tonight's. Clifton finally said okay, go ahead. The Quest officials were none too happy, with Josh and his team in the number one starting position. But so be it. He's here.

Dave doesn't skip a beat. He gets right into the game plan. Tok's always got an interesting mix of players, being the melting pot that it is, the "Gateway to Alaska," as its chamber of commerce calls it, a crossroads community of fifteen hundred or so people at the far eastern edge of the state, the first town drivers on the Alaska Highway come to after crossing the border from Canada.

"They'll be playing their two-three zone, as always," says Dave, "with Mongo in the middle."

The boys crack up. "Mongo." The big dude with the Mohawk. They love it.

"The key to this ball game," Dave continues, "is to make him work harder than he wants to, make him keep moving, get him tired. I want you to make him move *laterally*. Side to side. He's used to going up and down the court, north to south. I want you to make him go east to west."

The boys nod. They understand.

"If you drive," Dave says, "be prepared to dish off, which means I need a baseline cutter at all times."

More nods.

"As for their guards, I want you to make number twenty-one work every time he brings the ball upcourt. They like to play that half-court game, get it in to the big man. I want you to push twenty-one hard, wherever he goes. Bait him into playing our game, at our speed, not theirs."

Finally, Dave says he wants Tim Fields, not Aaron, to front the Tok center. Tim gives up half a foot to the giant, but that will leave Aaron free to roam and block shots by Tok's other four players.

"I know it takes both of you out of your comfort zones," Dave says, "but I think it's something we need to see if we can do. They won't expect it. If it goes to hell in a handbasket, we can always switch."

He motions them to stand, form the circle.

"You know how I talk about imposing our will, boys" he says. "Last night we kept pushing, and that team kept bending. They bent and bent and bent some more, until they finally broke. *That* is what I mean by imposing our will. Let's do it tonight."

With that, the heads bow, the eyes shut, and Dave prays, adding a phrase he has not used before.

"Lord, let them reach for a goal they have never attained."

The big board.

The grandstands erupt as Fort Yukon takes the floor. The Hooper Bay kids scream for the Eagles. So do the Russians. It seems the whole gym has adopted Dave's team, partly because they are underdogs, and partly because the Fort Yukon boys are all Native. Tok has one Native player on the floor—their point guard, 21. He and the big man are the keys to Tok's game.

Matt is the key to Fort Yukon's. They need him tonight, and he knows it.

He wastes no time answering the bell. Off the opening tip, he slides to the left wing and drops in a three-pointer. A travel by Tok, and Matt's open again in the same spot. He hits it again. One minute into the game, it's 6–0, Fort Yukon—6–0, Matt.

Tok scores to make it 6–2. Aaron answers with a short turnaround bank shot. Tim's working hard, fronting Tok's big man, denying him the ball, but Tok's other players pick up the slack. With 21 breaking the traps and feeding his teammates, the Wolverines go on an 8–0 run to lead 10–8.

A minute to go in the quarter, Fort Yukon is back ahead, 14–10, when Josh gets the ball in the right corner, in front of Coaches' Row. He likes to think of himself as a shooter, but he's not. His game is quickness—defense and driving and passing. He's developed a nice arsenal of inside moves: quick-release floaters, reverse layups, fingertip flips. But his outside shot is unsightly, a knuckleball that floats through the air with no spin at all.

He lets go of one now. It's high and wide to the right, so far off it nicks the side of the backboard . . . and glances into the basket.

The gym detonates. The coaches fall out of their chairs. Dave rolls his eyes. A bank shot from the corner? A three-pointer?

"Call that one next time," Dave yells, to the delight of the crowd.

The words are hardly out of his mouth before Josh and Matt strip a Tok guard and Josh streaks the other way for a layup. Five points in five seconds for the littlest man on the floor. The crowd goes ballistic. They enjoyed Josh last night, but now he's their darling.

Matt caps off the run with a heave from just past half-court as the buzzer goes off. The shot is not even close, but a Tok defender slams into him on the release.

The ref blows his whistle and holds out three fingers.

Three foul shots.

"I can't believe he did that," says Dave, watching the Tok kid holding his head.

The refs clear the court, and Matt steps to the line

Swish.

Swish,

Swish.

22–10, Fort Yukon.

They're on a roll, unlike any so far this season. A three and a two by Matt to open the second quarter make it nineteen straight points for the boys wearing blue. Tok finally hits a free throw for their first score in eight minutes, and the game settles into a back-and-forth rhythm. Matt, Wade, Justin and Josh continue forcing the action, maybe a little too much. The adrenaline's kicking in. Their passes are starting to sail out of bounds. They're losing control of their dribbles. They're driving into the lane, into the maw of Tok's center, and there's no one to dish off to. Nobody's cutting baseline. The big man is swatting away their forced inside shots like King Kong batting at biplanes. But Dave's not too upset. It's hard to ask his kids to dial it back when they're pushing the pace the way he's instructed. His biggest concern is three fouls each picked up by Aaron and Tim. Tok's big man takes advantage, dropping in seven second-period points to keep his team within reach. Halftime, Tok trails by fourteen, 37–23.

"Boys," Dave says, back in the classroom, "I know you've got family and friends in the stands, and they're excited, but *relax* just a little, okay?"

Matt gulps a bottle of water in three swallows. He's got sixteen points. Wade is still glowing from the insane, contorted, under-the-hoop, over-the-head, spin-reverse layup he threw past the arms of Tok's big man to close out the half. Coaches' Row is still buzzing about that one when Fort Yukon returns to the floor.

Dave has warned his team that Tok has a run of their own in them, and he's right. It comes now, with the start of the second half. Tok's point guard, 21, stays away from the sidelines, dribble-penetrating Fort Yukon's traps each time up the floor, feeding his front line for close-range shots. Aaron and Tim and Derek are overmatched when Tok gets the ball inside like that. Meanwhile, on defense, Tok doesn't give Matt room to breathe. And none of his teammates can pick up the slack. Three minutes into the half, Dave is forced to call time-out. It doesn't help. One minute later, Aaron picks up his fourth foul and has to come out. With 2:45 to go in the quarter, a short bank shot puts Tok ahead, 40–39.

A 17–2 run, just like that.

The crowd is beside itself, begging Fort Yukon to answer.

Dave sends in Johnny, hopes he can stop the bleeding. Johnny responds with a quick-trigger three from the left wing, sending the crowd into a frenzy.

The quarter ends 44–42, Eagles.

Dave once again tells his kids to relax, tells them they're pressing too hard on offense, that they're guiding their shots rather than simply letting them go. There's nothing wrong with their defense, he says. Tok might be breaking those traps right now, he tells them, but they're wearing down. 21's getting tired, he says. The big man's already worn out. Just keep squeezing on defense, he says. It's going to pay off.

And it does.

Momentum can be a mysterious thing. Fickle. Faithless. Flipping from one side to another, for no apparent reason at all.

It happens right now. The traps that weren't working throughout the third quarter abruptly start yielding turnovers again. On offense, Fort Yukon's shots begin falling.

A floater by Derek.

A free throw by Tim.

A steal and a layup by Josh.

A three-ball by Matt.

A jumper by Aaron.

With 4:05 left, Fort Yukon leads, 54–45.

Tok calls time-out, comes back on the floor, and brings the ball up, once again into a trap, right in front of Dave's seat. Their guard splits it this time, leaving Josh in his wake.

Or so it appears. What happens next, even Dave can't believe.

At what seems like warp speed, Josh gathers himself, flashes past Dave, past the Fort Yukon bench, catches Tok's guard from behind, passes him, plants himself in the guard's path and forces a travel by the stunned, confused player.

Dave's mouth hangs open. There's nothing to say. Josh had no right to make that play. He was beaten. Left behind. That Tok player was running full speed. And he isn't slow.

Imposing his will. That's what Josh just did. Of course it couldn't have happened if he weren't quicker than anyone else on the floor. But that play wasn't about quickness as much as it was about simply not quitting.

There's no quit in Josh, no quit in any of these kids. This is what Dave is beginning to see about this team. This is something no one can teach. It's what people mean when they talk about character, resiliency, guts, whatever you want to call it. It's what Dave's talking about when he tries to explain to people like his sister-in-law why this game is so important to these kids, why they'll learn things out there on that floor— about each other, about themselves—that will serve them for the rest of their lives.

The crowd understands what it's just seen, and gives Josh a standing ovation. The men on Coaches' Row are shaking their heads. They cannot believe this kid's never played high school ball before this season. When Dave told them that, they called him a liar. No way, they said.

There's 2:50 left. Fort Yukon's up, 56–47. Whatever hope Tok still has is extinguished when Matt pulls up near the right hash mark, beyond the arc, lets fly another NBA three and backpedals toward half-court, his flipped wrist held high in its follow-through position as the ball settles into the net.

"Warm up the bus!" someone shouts from the stands, and the place detonates.

Tok has no choice now but to foul. Their big man winds up near half-court, flailing his arms as he lumbers after Fort Yukon's guards. It looks like a cartoon, Gulliver chasing the Lilliputians.

Fifteen seconds to go. The crowd chants, "Eagle Power!" Dave works his way down the bench, shaking each of his boys' hands.

The final horn sounds. 65–54, Fort Yukon.

The boys are swarmed by their families, their fans. Clifton makes his way across the court, wearing his fur-trimmed canvas boots, puts his arm around his son's shoulder. Yes, he says, this was worth missing that race. He watches as Josh and Matt step up to receive their All-Tournament medals. Everyone roars as Matt is named MVP. Friends and family line up to snap photos as the boys pose with their first-place trophy.

Finally, back in the classroom, Dave has them alone.

"You guys gotta understand," he says, "it's *fun* watching you play basketball. Even the referees love watching you play.

"You came back tonight," he tells them. "*They* came back. And you weathered it. You showed your emotional strength. We may lose to Tok next time, on their floor. Who knows? But this is the one that matters. This is the one that goes up on the *board*."

With that, they shower and dress. They've got some basking to do. There's one last tradition here at the NIT, besides Coaches' Row, and the buffet, and the big board. There's always a Saturday night dance in the school's auditorium, with a deejay and a light show, for all sixteen teams.

It's just picking up steam when the Fort Yukon boys get there. The Nikolaevsk girls have been asking where they are. The Goo Goo Dolls thump from the sound system as the boys enter the darkened, strobe-lit room.

The last sight of Matt and Josh is the lights glinting off the All-Tourney medallions draped around each of their necks as they wade into the crowd.

THIRTEEN
Home Stand

MATT AND JOSH wore those medals all the way home the next day, all the way back to Fort Yukon. It was snowing when they arrived. The monthlong cold snap has finally broken, with temperatures climbing into the twenties-below. It seems everyone in the village is outside—walking, gunning their snowmachines, running their dogs, simply glad to be out of their cabins. There's more daylight now than Fort Yukon has seen since October—seven hours of it, the low-angled rays of the sun etching sharp shadows on the fresh-fallen snow, bathing the cabins in a liquid-orange glow.

The big news is there's a wolf loose in town. Earl Cadzow came across the fresh tracks a couple of days ago, down near his and Cheryl's place. He followed them across the river before losing them in the woods. The animal was back yesterday, bolder, its pawprints circling the yards of several homes. It's probably an old one, says Earl. That, or it's injured, couldn't keep up with the pack and veered off into the village, where it's easier to find food: garbage, dog pots, even the dogs themselves, if they're small enough. There's little worry that the wolf would attack anybody—wolves rarely go after humans—but Earl's keeping a gun in his pickup, just in case.

The villagers are abuzz with the boys' win in Nenana. A couple of hand-painted banners were draped on the front of the school this morning, greeting the kids as they arrived for their first-bell classes. It's been hard for Dave to get any work done, what with people stopping by the airport, one after the other, to congratulate him on the team's triumph. They're starting to talk of a state title. Dave had a couple of coaches come up after the Tok win and tell him how impressed they are with his team. One of the refs took him aside after the game and told him Fort Yukon is his pick now to go all the way.

That's all well and good, but Dave knows better than to think about Anchorage at the moment. There's too much that can happen between now and next month, both on and off the basketball court. There are bombshells he can't even imagine, waiting to go off around every corner.

One explodes the very next morning, Tuesday, with a phone call from Doc. The school board just held its monthly meeting, Doc tells Dave, and voted to cut the funding for basketball next season. Slice it down close to nothing. Kill it.

The news is still sinking in as Dave sits at the desk in his office, picking at a plate of dried salmon. The way the system has worked until now is the Yukon Flats School District receives a certain amount of money each year from the state to spend for student activities at all eight village schools in its region. This year, it got about one hundred thousand dollars. It has always divided the money proportionately, according to the number of students enrolled in each school. The tiny school in Stevens Village, for example, with its twelve kids, gets about one twelfth what Fort Yukon, with its 140-some students, receives. Those seven smaller district schools—Beaver, Circle, Central, Venetie, Arctic Village, Chalkyitsik, and Stevens Village—have always chafed at how little they get compared to Fort Yukon. The number of students at all seven of those schools combined is roughly equal to the number of kids at Fort Yukon. That means about fifty thousand dollars or so of that activity money goes to Fort Yukon. Close to half of that fifty thousand—roughly twenty thousand dollars—goes to the basketball program. The rest goes to the school's other activities, ranging from its Native dance group to its science fair contestants. From where Dave sits, it's not that much money—not with all the fund-raising Fort Yukon still has to do to put a basketball team on the floor. But to those other seven villages, it looks like a gold mine, and they've been fighting behind the scenes for years now to get more of it.

Yesterday, they finally got their way. The seven-member board voted to redistribute those funds, beginning next year, with each school getting a straight one-eighth share, regardless of size. Doc can't believe it. It's damn near insane, he says. This means Central, for example, with eight students in its school—eight kids, from kindergarten through twelfth grade—will get just as much money as Fort Yukon. That's more than a thousand dollars a kid, Doc points out. Hell, he says, they could pack their bags and take those eight kids on a trip to Disneyland if they wanted. Why not? Meanwhile, Fort Yukon will be left with about six thousand dollars to spend on its basketball teams. That's compared to the twenty thousand dollars they get right now. They're already doing all they can to make ends meet, asking the villagers to pitch in in so many ways, out of their own pockets. How much more can the people of Fort Yukon be asked to give?

Dave doesn't want to even imagine the backroom politics and personal power trips behind this decision. It's a waste of energy to think about all that. What needs to be done at this point is to deal with this, figure out the next step. That's what he and Doc talked about this morning. What are their options? The way they see it right now, they've got three choices. The school could withdraw from the district and become an independent entity, like Nenana, for example, which would allow it to receive its activity money straight from the state rather than having the money be filtered through a regional board. But that would be a big move, complex and risky, with ramifications far beyond just basketball. Their second option would be to get professional about fund-raising, move beyond cakewalks and bake sales and go after corporate sponsors, the way Nikolaevsk went after ConocoPhillips to underwrite its tournament. But there are no corporations in Fort Yukon. There are no oil companies here—at least not yet. The school would have to reach down into Fairbanks to find donors like that, which wouldn't be easy. A third option would be to have each boy or girl who plays basketball pay to cover the cost of participation. Pay to play. That's how the downstate schools that field football teams do it: Each athlete down there has to raise about $1,500 or so to buy pads and helmets and all the other equipment it takes to put a team on the field. Football is an expensive sport.

None of these options would be easy. There might be other solutions, but right now Dave doesn't have time to deal with it. He's got a ball team to coach. His boys have four games this week, beginning tomorrow night, when Allakaket flies in for a two-game stand, followed by Mat-Su's arrival Friday for two more. Dave will leave it to Doc to deal with this stuff. Worst case, this will be Fort Yukon's final basketball season, at least for a while. It happens all the time in other villages. For one reason or another, a program folds up and vanishes, disappears just like that. It's happened to state champion teams. Sure, it would be a tragedy if it happened here, says Dave. But if it happens, it happens. The villagers would deal with it and move on, just like they have to deal with everything else.

By Wednesday all of Fort Yukon has heard about the school board's decision. No one is sure how to respond. There's talk of arranging a town meeting, but frankly, there are more pressing matters to deal with at the moment than saving the basketball team. The newspaper this morning featured a front-page story on the city of Fairbanks's designs to annex Fort Yukon, absorbing it into the Fairbanks North Star Borough by extending the borough's boundaries north over the mountains, across the Flats to the village. The plan is transparent to the people of Fort Yukon. A government study released just last month announced that geologists believe close to six trillion cubic feet of recoverable natural gas lies under the land surrounding Fort Yukon—Native land. That's nearly as much gas as the fields down at Cook Inlet have produced over the past thirty years. It's funny, say some of the villagers, how Fairbanks has never given a damn about Fort Yukon, and suddenly they're eager to make the village part of their city. Less funny is the fact that the Doyon Corporation, in the name of the Tribe, is negotiating at this moment with the U.S. Fish and Wildlife Service to approve a "swap," as both parties are benignly calling it, of that gas-rich Native land for federal land elsewhere in the region. Senator Stevens—Uncle Ted—has wholeheartedly endorsed the deal.

Adlai Alexander, an EMT at the clinic, who played ball with Earl Cadzow on those first Fort Yukon basketball teams back in the 1970s and is now the village's chief, is outraged over these plans. So is the rest of the Tribal Council. They're trying to fight back, trying to organize the Gwich'in people here in Fort Yukon and throughout the region to block this deal. They've called for a summit meeting of tribal leaders from throughout the Interior next month here in the village. They're passing out informational flyers that proclaim, "Keep Native Lands in Native Hands!"

With all this going on, the future of Fort Yukon's basketball team is on the back burner, at least for the time being.

The boys are aware of the news—the school board's decision, the annexation, the land swap—as they drift into the locker room to dress for Wednesday night's game against Allakaket. Dave has warned them against a letdown after their win at the NIT. He's urged them to stay focused, to resist the distractions of being back home. He has no idea how they're going to play tonight. This will be their first test this season against a team of Natives like themselves. It will be their first game against a 1A rival, one of the teams they'll have to beat at the Regionals in order to make it to State. Allakaket has been up and down in recent years. Their school, like their village, is about half the size of Fort Yukon's. Last season, with only four boys on its team, Allakaket had to fill out its squad with two girls. When they came up against Fort Yukon, Dave's guys refused to guard Allakaket's girls. It was only after one of the girls scored ten points to keep her team close that Davis Carroll bit the bullet and stepped up to stop her. Some of the boys still mock him for that.

Allakaket looks ragged in warm-ups. They've got seven boys on the floor, wearing a mismatched array of black-and-white jerseys and shorts. Their coach is the older brother of two of the boys. Their star, a senior named Chris Moses, is limping with a bad case of tendinitis. He may not be able to play tonight. This is the first team Fort Yukon's met this season that is shorter than they are. Moses is only five-ten, but plays center. What the Blazers lack in size, however, they make up for with at least the appearance of toughness. One of their guards, a skinny freshman, has a black silk do-rag tied over his head. The refs make him remove it just before the introductions. The kid does so, slowly, with a smirk. His village sits two hundred miles west of here, on the banks of the Koyukuk River, even more remote than Fort Yukon, but his swagger is straight out of Compton, off the streets of the 'hood.

The bleachers are jammed, with Trader Dan settled into a soft cushioned chair set up near midcourt. When Doc and Georgie heard about that sofa in the bleachers at Nikolaevsk, they thought it would be fun to raffle off the same kind of thing here. That's what the chair is about, with Trader Dan buying enough tickets to make sure he'd be tonight's winner.

Moses is indeed on the bench when the game begins. Fort Yukon's starting five look like they belong there as well. They commit six turnovers in their first seven possessions. Their shots are hurried, off target. Allakaket's shots are no better, but one thing they have is speed. They're cat-quick, the first team Fort Yukon has faced this season that's as fast as they are. That's part of the reason for all those turnovers. Josh, in particular, keeps coughing up the ball. Three minutes into the game, the score is 4–0, Fort Yukon. Six minutes in, the score is 11–7 and Dave calls time-out. He's livid.

"Christ," he says, glaring at his starters, "we're only ahead of these people by four points. I can't *believe* the way you guys are playing."

He pulls Tim and Josh, inserts Derek and Wade, and they close the quarter with an 11–2 run. Matt has eleven first-quarter points, outscoring Allakaket by himself. Halftime, the score is 41–17. Third quarter, Justin hits back-to-back threes, and Dave hollers, "Hot hand!" for the first time this year. That's the highlight of this game, as far as he's concerned, seeing Justin come out of his shell and start shooting. The final is 81–41, but Dave is worried. Josh went scoreless tonight and looked lost at times against Allakaket's quick guards. Johnny simply looked awful, going scoreless as well.

The next morning the boys open the paper to find themselves ranked number three in the state. They see that Tok got some votes in the 2A poll, which makes them even prouder of their NIT achievement. That night, they arrive at the gym for the rematch against Allakaket intent on staying focused, the way Dave's been telling them to. Minutes before game time, however, as they sit in the locker room suited up and waiting for Dave to finish sweeping and picking up trash from the girls' game, Jack Shewfelt's drinking buddy, big Billy Gjesdal, lumbers in, takes a seat among them, pulls out a pint of whiskey, pours some in his cup, offers a sip to the kids, then begins regaling them about his latest sexual exploit. Dave can't believe it when he comes in and finds Gjesdal there, holding court. He politely asks him to leave. He's careful not to arouse the big man. Gjesdal is a nice enough guy when he's sober, but he can be dangerously violent when he gets liquored up. One night he got upset about something and fired several gunshots into the gym. Nobody was inside, but no one in town thinks it would have made any difference to him if there were.

Gjesdal gets up but doesn't quite leave. He hangs by the bathroom stall door and continues muttering even as the boys bow their heads for the prayer, even as they line up and run out onto the court for their pregame layups. Dave makes a mental note to call Doc about this in the morning, get the school to get the police to go over and have a chat with Billy about not doing this again. Neither of the village's two on-duty cops are in the gym this evening, or Dave would have asked them for help.

So much for focus. Thirty seconds into the game, Fort Yukon trails 5–0 and Dave calls time-out. He sits the boys down on the bench . . . and says nothing. For a full sixty seconds he stands there in silence, gazing at the kids as they squirm, avert their eyes, pray for the refs to whistle them back on the floor.

When they finally retake the court, they continue playing as if they're asleep. The Moses kid is out there tonight, and he looks good, taking the ball to the hole without fear. The cocky guard, the one with the do-rag, is simply outrunning Fort Yukon's entire team, hauling in one length-of-the-court pass in full stride, like a split end, taking it in for a layup. Matt is back to the wild showboat passes he was throwing a few weeks ago. "I think Matt and Josh both left their games in Nenana," says Dave.

One minute in, Allakaket leads 7–0.

Two minutes in, it's 9–0.

Three minutes in, and Fort Yukon's still scoreless, trailing 10–0. The gym is hushed. The home crowd is stunned. They can't believe this is the same team that just won the NIT.

Dave puts in Derek and Johnny and Wade. Johnny sinks a foul shot for Fort Yukon's first point—the only point he'll score tonight. They're all off their game, everyone on the team. A three-ball by Matt and a couple of jump shots by Derek, sandwiched around several steals and layups, put Fort Yukon ahead, but just barely. At halftime they lead by just six, 28–22.

Dave is matter-of-fact in the locker room. Low-key. Deliberate.

"They actually look a half-step quicker than you," he says. "You're giving them confidence, the way you're playing.

"They're ready to run with you," he continues. "But you're a much better team than they are. A lot better than you're showing."

He looks at each boy. He draws a deep breath.

"So let's start showing it," he says, sending them back out on the floor.

They open the second half by going scoreless again for three minutes. They lead just 28–24 when Matt finally breaks the drought with a pair of three-pointers to widen the margin to ten. They still lead by ten with two minutes left in the game, when Dave orders them into a stall. Even that looks shaky, as they throw the ball away twice before the clock finally, mercifully, runs out on a 57–49 win.

Dave doesn't have to tell the boys how ugly this game was. Their friends and families will take care of telling them that. He does say that this is the kind of speed they're going to face next week at Tanana. Meanwhile, he tells them, they've got Mat-Su coming in in the morning. Go home, he says. Get some sleep.

The next morning, Friday, it's snowing again. Earl's set some traps down near the river, where the remains of a half-eaten pup were found yesterday, with fresh wolf tracks running off into the woods. "Just the head was left," says Earl. "It picked up the rest and ate as it went." The wolf won't be back for a while, says Earl. It's got enough food in its belly for maybe five or six days. "That was a good-sized dog," he says.

Dave's up at the airport, unloading freight and trying to figure out what's going on with his boys. Big Billy certainly didn't help things last night. That locker room scene was disturbing, but it seems to always be like this when the boys play at home. They seem to simply play worse when they play here than they do when they're out on the road. Dave came to understand that a long time ago. What's got him worried about these last two nights is the issue of speed. Playing teams slower than they are has hurt this team, in a way. They weren't ready for Allakaket's quickness. That's precisely what they're going to see at the State Tournament—seven teams just as quick as they are, and far, far more talented than Allakaket. His boys have got to be focused to face that kind of speed. Speed over size is one thing. Speed against speed is quite another. That's what Native ball—bush ball—is all about. Speed.

The Mat-Su kids are not Natives. Dave's boys beat them with half a team down in Nikolaevsk, so he doesn't expect much of a challenge tonight. And he's right. Fort Yukon scores the game's first eleven points. The first quarter ends 30–7. It's more like a scrimmage, a chance for Dave to shuffle his kids in and out, try different combinations, give his reserves some court time. Zach takes full advantage, hitting two shots, to the delight of the crowd. Again, Justin is the bright spot, nailing three more threes. He's showing a confident stroke, something they're going to need down the road. The final is 69–35. Josh is high scorer with sixteen points, all in the first quarter. But sixteen points in a rout like this is next to meaningless. There'll be no Mat-Su to feast on in Anchorage—assuming they get there.

The next day word comes that Matt's grandmother—Grandpa Stanley's wife—has passed away at a Native nursing home down in Fairbanks. So the village must now prepare for its first burial of the winter. Dave mentions this before the boys take the court for the afternoon finale against Mat-Su. He mentions it again after their 71–42 win.

"We'll play the rest of the week by ear, in terms of practice," he says. "We know there's going to be a funeral. And we know we'll be flying out of here Thursday, to Tanana."

FOURTEEN

Tanana

MIDMORNING MONDAY — VALENTINE'S Day—Dave is out in the terminal lobby making a fresh pot of coffee when a light plane glides in for a landing. He has no idea who it is. Small planes like this drop in all the time, especially in summer, when they fill the air like mosquitoes. For bush pilots, the Fort Yukon airstrip is like a rest stop on a remote roadway—a place to get out, stretch your legs, maybe have a cup of that coffee, check out the local map tacked to the wall, then move on.

But the pilot who climbs out of this Cessna wants more than a cup of coffee. He's got questions. He doesn't say why, but he wants to know if Dave can tell him where he can find a man named Jay Cadzow. Dave's careful in answering. He doesn't know who this guy is, though he's got a pretty good hunch he's with the Alaska Department of Fish and Game. Dave's seen so many game wardens—"Duck Dicks," as some villagers call them—come through Fort Yukon that he could just about pick one out with his eyes shut. The fact that this man's asking for Jay Cadzow makes it even more likely he's a warden. Jay is one of the busiest hunting guides in the village, meeting small planes like this one and joining the pilot and one or two hunters as they fly into the wilderness, looking for bear or moose or wild sheep. Jay knows right where to take them: beyond Arctic Village into the foothills of the Brooks Range, or up the Chandalar River, or northeast, toward ANWR, past Vundik Lake. These people pay big money to come up here to the Arctic to hunt—as much as $20,000 or more for a guaranteed kill of, say, a grizzly. That price covers everything: transportation, food, lodging in the wild for a week, the guide, the kill fee ... everything. The guide's job is to make good on the guarantee, and Jay's one of the best around. To him, it's easy money. "Take guys out, kill a moose." That's how Jay describes it. He gets about $2,500 per hunter for one of these trips. More often than not, he gets to keep the meat, too. Some of the people he works for—the "expediters" who advertise these trips on the Internet—run them illegally, skipping the licensing procedures and fees and other restrictions they consider inconvenient. It's all the same to Jay.

But not to the government. Which explains why this guy has dropped in this morning. It turns out Dave is right. The man wants the name of one of Jay's "employers," one of those expediters. This one happens to live in Georgia. The game warden is here to give Jay a choice. Give up that name, or face some jail time himself.

Dave thought at first that this guy might be here because of Matt's grandmother's death. When a game warden flies up to Fort Yukon this time of year, it's usually to check on illegal winter moose hunting. The legal moose season is in early fall. The only exception to the ban on out-of-season kills is a funeral. When there's a death in the tribe, the Gwich'in are allowed to kill one moose, to feed the dozens of relatives and friends who fly in from all over the region for the burial and for the ceremonial potlatch that follows. It's a tradition that goes back beyond anyone's memory. There are some in the village, however, who take advantage of the situation in order to fill their own freezers. Dave's brother-in-law, Jim Carroll, has a wry way of putting it. "Every time someone dies in this country," he says, "ten moose die."

Dave tells the warden he doesn't know where Jay is. Which he doesn't. The warden leaves, heads on into the village. The phone rings in Dave's office. It's the Fairbanks airport. Matt's grandmother's body will be coming in this evening, on the late Frontier flight. Matt's uncle Brewster is already building a casket at the school shop. Jack and some others have begun digging the grave. The funeral will be Wednesday, which gives them time to get everything done, including lining the casket with silk, which Georgie will handle, and hand-lettering the large wooden cross that will mark Matt's grandmother's grave. Georgie's taking care of that, too.

The fact that Dave's boys are facing a critical basketball tournament this weekend in Tanana is almost an afterthought at the moment. Only eight of them show for the Monday night practice. A couple are out cutting firewood for the potlatch. Two others—Aaron and Wade—shot a moose yesterday, which they're butchering tonight. They found the animal out near Black River, about twenty-five miles east of the village. They tried chasing it on foot through the chest-high snow but couldn't keep up. Then their snowmachine engine froze, and they had to spend an hour and a half, at thirty-five-below, getting it started again. On the way back, near Twentymile, they picked up some fresh tracks, and this time they got their moose. Wade put it down with one shot. It took them about two hours to ride back to the village, grab some knives, and go back and cut up the moose so they could haul the meat home. Now, tonight, they're getting it ready for the women to cook.

Matt and Josh aren't here either. They're over at the school cafeteria, waiting tables at a Valentine's Day dinner the senior class is throwing to raise money for that spring trip to Hawaii. Tickets are twenty dollars a person for a full-course candlelight meal. Roast beef, mashed potatoes, gravy, corn, dessert—the whole nine yards. Dave's ordered two of the dinners delivered to his house after practice, candles included.

He's been thinking about last week's games, about this issue of speed. It's going to be telling to see how the boys do at Tanana, against more of what they saw against Allakaket. This little tournament will essentially be a dress rehearsal for the Regionals. Every serious 1A team in Fort Yukon's region will be at Tanana this weekend. Allakaket. Huslia. Hughes. And, of course, Tanana. Nulato won't be there, but from what Dave has heard, Nulato doesn't have much this season.

Dave hasn't seen Tanana yet, but he's been following them in the papers, the same way he's sure they've been following Fort Yukon. Their star, Tyler Hyslop, has been scoring ungodly numbers of points. He went for fifty and forty-two last weekend against Nulato. But Dave is actually more concerned about Hyslop's teammate, a lanky six-footer named Norman Carlo. Norman is kind of a crazy kid, likes to pretend he's from the barrio, talks and walks like a Hispanic street thug from South Central L.A. The only South-anyplace he's ever been is South Fairbanks, but that doesn't keep him from strutting like a pachuco, especially around girls.

Norman has a dangerously flamboyant game, more dangerous, as far as Dave is concerned, than Hyslop's. Hyslop is, as Dave puts it, a "frequent" shooter. Norman, on the other hand, is an uncannily accurate one—when he's hot. He transferred to Galena last year as a sophomore, to live in that village's small boarding school and play for the school's 2A basketball team. That's where Dave first saw him, when Fort Yukon faced Galena last season. Norman is back home this year in Tanana, teaming with Hyslop to give the Wolves the highest-scoring one-two punch in the region, if not the entire state. Norman went for thirty-five and twenty-two against Nulato this past weekend.

Dave goes over all this at Monday night's practice, and again Tuesday, with the entire team there. The boys hardly have room to shoot, what with the tables and chairs stacked in the gym, waiting to be set up for Wednesday afternoon's service and potlatch. More people are flying in for this funeral than for any in recent memory. Matt's grandmother, Madeline Jonas, was strongly connected to this land and her people. She was born up the Porcupine River, in 1927, in a tiny settlement called Old Rampart. Her family moved to Fort Yukon when she was a child. She and Matt's grandpa Stanley married and raised thirteen kids here in the village, including Matt's mother, Mary. They had thirty-nine grandchildren and forty great-grandchildren by the time Madeline moved into that nursing home down in Fairbanks. Family members are flying in today and tomorrow from all across the Interior, as well as from Anchorage, from Fairbanks, from Seattle, and from Canada's Yukon Territory, up around Old Crow, where some of Madeline's relatives still live. The Gwich'in Nation, as the tribe likes to say, knows no borders.

Wednesday morning the boys are gathered in the school office, studying the sports section's box scores from last night's games played down in Fairbanks. They can't believe the score of the game between Hutchison, a brand-new, first-year 4A school, and Monroe, a perennial local powerhouse. The final was 96–8, Monroe. The boys are incredulous, trying to imagine what it's like to take a beating like that.

Doc walks in, steaming mad. It seems somebody slipped some Windex into the geometry teacher's coffee. The suspect list includes Kyle, Johnny and Bruce. Doc summons the boys into his office and speaks to each one. He calls Wade in, too, to congratulate him on making the eligibility list once again this week. "Just barely," Doc says, but that's enough to send Wade almost floating out of the office.

School is dismissed at noon, so the kids can all go to the funeral. It's a clear day. The sunlight is piercingly bright. The temperature is ten-below, almost balmy. Dozens of men and women and children file into the gymnasium, finding seats in the bleachers or in the ten rows of folding chairs set up on the floor. An ornate hand-beaded altar cloth covers a table at midcourt. Madeline Jonas, like many of the older women in the village, was known for her beadwork, including this cloth, which she stitched for the village's Episcopal church—the same church in which the old missionary, Hudson Stuck, delivered his sermons nearly a century ago.

Her coffin, bedecked with flowers, surrounded by candles, sits before the altar. Its lid is open. A long line moves past as people pay their respects. Georgie's father, Mardow Solomon, stands silently at the head of the casket, wearing the white pleated robe of an Episcopal priest. A Native priest. Hudson Stuck would have loved that.

The line files past for close to an hour. Then the people are seated, and five men in the front row rise. They are each wearing a fringed, tanned, caribou-skin vest. The eldest of them grips a cane, his hand quivering as he steps to the casket, leans in, kisses his fingertips and presses them to the forehead of his wife.

Two younger men then step forward, close the lid, and screw it shut with hand drills.

There is weeping. And prayer. And the singing of hymns. The last one, "Amazing Grace," is sung as the casket is carried outside, placed in the bed of a pickup and driven to the cemetery, followed by several dozen vans, trucks, automobiles and snowmachines.

The sunlight is sharp, slicing through the snow-coated branches of the spruce and the birch and the willow trees that surround the grave. A single chair is set up for Stanley to sit in. The people assemble, gather around him, children scrambling up onto the snowbanks to get a better look. A crow flies past, its caw carried away on the afternoon breeze.

Six men carry the box to the hole. They gentle it down, with work ropes from their trucks. Then they each grab a shovel and begin dropping spadefuls of dirt onto the coffin. A fine cloud of dust, finer than snow, rises into the air, coating the jackets and jeans of the men. After several minutes, without speaking, the six hand their shovels to six others, who continue the work. By the time the hole has been filled, every man here has taken his turn.

The last six include Jack, who scrapes and squares off the edges, making the mound just so, as the villagers and guests begin filing past, dropping flowers onto Madeline's grave.

There is no basketball practice that evening. The next day, the kids gather at the airport, prepared to fly to Tanana. Wes, Bruce, Zach and Tim Woods will be staying behind. This is the team's first village-to-village trip this season. It's a bright, brilliant morning. Their plane rises and banks to the southwest, following the ice-locked Yukon, passing over the white frozen wilderness. An occasional group of two or three cabins appears below. These little clusters of homes actually have names on the map. White Eye. Purgatory. Rampart. The Flats gradually recede as the land pushes up into foothills and mountains. The river narrows here, squeezed between steep forested slopes. Finally, where the Yukon merges with the Tanana, two hundred miles from Fort Yukon, the airplane descends, banking over a good-sized village, its airstrip flanked by a ridge and the river.

Tanana.

They have a long love-hate relationship, Fort Yukon and Tanana. They are both Athabascan villages, both almost entirely Native, both dependent on hunting and trapping and fishing. Tanana is better known for its sled dogs than Fort Yukon. The U.S. Army once maintained a government dog yard here. The two villages' men and women have met and intermarried for generations. They consider themselves bound by blood. But there is an "upriver"—"downriver" distinction they just can't seem to shake. Eons ago, before white men arrived, there were spats between these two tribes, transgressions and retributions, nothing approaching actual war, but bad blood nonetheless. That was long, long ago, but something remains. It could be simple rivalry, a sheer matter of size. It could be that Tanana, with half the population of Fort Yukon, resents its big brother simply for being bigger. Whatever the reason, there's an intensity when these two villages meet that reflects a long past. Where they meet most often, and most intensely, is on the basketball court.

A bus is waiting at the airstrip to carry the kids to the school. The ones who have never been here before marvel at the massive dollops of snow curling off the roofs of the village's cabins. The snow looks like peaks of meringue, hanging suspended from the edges and ledges of Tanana's homes. People who study snow call this phenomenon "sintering." Fort Yukon, out on the Flats, is a relatively windless place. Its snowfall essentially settles and sits there, loose, granular, like sand, like sugar. The most it will do is blow into soft drifts. Tanana, on the other hand, is whipped by gusts of wind rushing down from those hills. The force of those prevailing winds pushes the snow into these smooth curling peaks and compresses the ice crystals, locking them into a hard solid mass, turning the snow from the texture of sugar to that of concrete. The effect is captivating, these billowing white waves suspended in midair, all bending west.

The bus rolls up Front Street, Tanana's main drag. It's sixteen-above—thirty degrees warmer than Fort Yukon was this morning. There's a small grocery store here, Tanana's own AC, right on the river. It's got a community bulletin board out front, just like Fort Yukon's. Among the fliers and For Sale cards tacked to the corkboard is a notice, posted just this morning:

"HELP NEEDED"
Karl Bushby, "The Walker," needs assistance
In walking to Ruby.
Deep snow is slowing him down!!
Karl is willing to pay for
2 snowmachines
$400 per person
Help is needed to break trail from his location

50 miles downriver from Tanana to Ruby
Be a part of the Goliath Expedition
WALKING AROUND THE WORLD
www.earthtrekuk.net

Dave and the boys have read about this guy in the paper. The *News-Miner* published a story on him around Christmas. He's an ex-British paratrooper attempting to circle the planet on foot. He set out seven years ago from the southern tip of South America and is headed for England, where he plans to arrive in three more years. He aims to cross the last stretch of his journey, the channel between Europe and the British Isles, wearing an inflatable "water-walking" suit. But right now he's dealing with snow. Apparently he's gotten socked in downriver in drifts too high to push through. He and his gear—two hundred pounds that he pulls on a sled—have been stuck for the past three weeks about fifty miles west of here. He's been camping out. He needs someone to come break trail for him so he can get on with his trip. That's what the flier's about. So far there are no takers.

People like this come up here all the time—adventurers, headline seekers, flat-out loonies who, for one reason or other, in one way or another, come to the Arctic to begin or end some kind of journey. The villagers in Fort Yukon still talk about the four Spaniards—three men and a woman—who showed up in town about ten years ago with all kinds of state-of-the-art hiking gear. Their plan was to walk, ski, bicycle and kayak five thousand miles from Fort Yukon to San Lucas, Mexico. "From the Arctic to the Tropics"—that's what they called their expedition. They had corporate sponsors. They planned to make a documentary about their journey; they had a high-tech video camera as well. The day before they set out, they came to the school to speak to the children, to tell the Fort Yukon kids all about their exciting trip. The kids looked at these people's sleek Gore-Tex clothing, emblazoned with patches touting their sponsors' products, and they asked where were their fur hats, their canvas boots, their beaver mittens.

The temperature was above zero that day, exceptionally warm for mid-January. By the next morning, when these four set off to begin their trek, walking east into the woods, the temperature had begun dropping. By that night it was fifty-below. Three days later, with the weather remaining ferociously cold, they hadn't yet reached their first checkpoint, the village of Circle. Search parties were sent out. They found nothing. Three days after that, the foursome straggled out of the woods at roughly the same spot where they'd entered the forest almost a week earlier. They were hardly able to walk. Someone called the police, who picked them up and rushed them to the clinic. Deb McCarty was there when they arrived. She'd seen plenty of frostbite before, but never anything like this. Two of the men's fingers and hands were frozen solid. Their feet had turned black. "Like giant burnt sausages" is how Deb describes it. The third man was injured, but not quite as severely. The woman, inexplicably, was not frostbitten at all.

As the men's limbs and extremities began to thaw out, the pain was excruciating. Deb put the three of them on morphine and called down to Fort Wainwright, asking for a military helicopter to come medevac these people to Fairbanks. The chopper arrived that evening. Deb later heard two of the men lost both of their feet.

The bus pulls up at the Tanana school, and everyone unloads their gear. They'll be staying three nights here, along with the teams from Allakaket and Huslia. Hughes had to pull out after a suicide in their village earlier this week. The victim, a young man, was a cousin, it turns out, of the cocky Allakaket guard, the kid with the do-rag. He won't be here this weekend, says Allakaket's coach. He's got his cousin's funeral to attend.

There's big news awaiting Dave's boys in the school's office. The morning paper just arrived, with this week's new state rankings. Fort Yukon is now number one. Only once has a Fort Yukon team ever been ranked this high. That was two years ago, the 23–1 team, Ryan's team. They rose to the top spot near the end of the season, only to lose to Noorvik at State.

The boys are elated. Josh grabs the clipping and tapes it to the door of the classroom where they'll be sleeping. Dave has no idea how this will affect the boys, whether it's a good thing or not. But he figures, hey, let them enjoy it. Why not?

They've got their first game this afternoon, against Huslia. Last year Fort Yukon had to beat Huslia twice to win the Regionals, after losing to the Hustlers in the opening round of the double-elimination tournament. Huslia was tough last season, but this year only three boys came out for the team. So Huslia has done what Allakaket had to do last season. They've filled out their squad with girls—in this case five of them. There's no question it's beyond strange for Dave's boys to play their first game as the top-ranked team in the state against a patchwork mixture of girls and guys.

The game is blessedly brief. One of Huslia's three boys is injured, leaving them with just two guys and three girls on the court. The refs don't mind that the scorer lets the clock run for this one when it's supposed to be stopped. The final is 91–30, with Dave's reserves playing more than the starters. His guys are more excited about getting their first look at Tyler Hyslop and Tanana tonight than they are about winning this game. They've got a street-ball kind of respect for Tyler. They're in awe of the fact that he went for 50 in one game last weekend. They've heard he's averaging thirty-one a game this season. They're even more in awe of the fact that he can dunk. There aren't many dunkers in Class 1A ball. Aaron's come close in practice, but he can't quite get it over the rim. He can't imagine doing it in a game. Tyler has done it in a game, an achievement that's near mythical to the Fort Yukon kids.

The teams—boys' and girls'—all break for dinner, served buffet-style in the school's little library by a group of the Tanana moms, including Tyler's and Norman's. The mothers all want to know how everyone's doing up at Fort Yukon. They ask how Madeline Jonas's funeral went. They knew Madeline. They wonder why Paul Shewfelt's not here, doing the games for the radio. They remember Paul, and Jack, too, from back when they both played for Fort Yukon. One of the mothers says, laughing, that Jack and Paul's sister Roberta called last night to tell them to keep those Tanana boys away from her daughter Ruby. As for the Tanana girls, they're apparently smitten with Fort Yukon's boys. They've been asking if they can trade their guys for Dave's, send their boys back to Fort Yukon and keep Dave's team here.

While the kids eat their dinner—tacos and rice—the referees are off in the corner, watching HBO on the library's TV. There are just two of them here, calling five games a day for the next three days, eating with the kids here in the library and sleeping, like them, in a classroom. One of the two is Jesse Myles, the army sergeant who did Fort Yukon's first two home games last month against Anderson. He's been following the team in the paper, he says. He was mighty impressed with that NIT win. Fort Yukon's 12–2 record looks very good, he says, especially considering that those two losses came so early, without all their players, and against larger schools. He's interested to see how they'll do tomorrow against Tanana.

That night the gym is packed with a raucous, roof-raising crowd as the home team takes on Allakaket. They love their basketball here. The Wolves are only 4–4 so far this season, but they're a blast to watch. High-scoring. Wide-open. The Tanana gym is a little larger than Fort Yukon's, but only a little. The strange thing about it, besides the melon-sized lump near that one foul line, is how dark it is. There's something wrong with the lights. They just barely come on. It's like playing in twilight, and it will be all weekend. The Tanana principal tried to fly a technician up from Fairbanks, but he can't get here till the start of next week.

The game reminds Dave of the way Fort Yukon played before he began coaching. Minimal defense. Maximum offense. Tanana's coach is a young guy, a villager, looks like he's in his late twenties, has on a leather coat and a Seattle Seahawks ball cap. He's sipping a Capri Sun and chatting with a group of his friends while his team warms up.

Discipline is not Tanana's game. From the opening tip, it's a run-and-gun shootout, Tyler against Allakaket's Chris Moses, mano a mano. Tyler's got a goatee this season, which he didn't have last year. It's bright orange, like his closely shaved hair. His skin is pale, ghostly white. That's his Scottish roots, says his mom. There were lots of Irish and Scottish trappers around here back in the day, she says. They left their mark, mingling with the Natives just like the Russians did out on the coast with the Eskimos, just like the British and Canadians and Americans did up in Fort Yukon. The term "half-breed" gets a chuckle from most Native Alaskans, as if anyone's pure anymore.

No question Tyler's got game, on offense at least. He's even quicker to the basket than he was last season, taking the ball to the rim with an array of spin moves and midair whirls. He hasn't got much of an outside shot, but his inside game is spectacular. At five-ten he's a flier, playing most of the game up over the rim. It helps that he's got Norman to take away some of the defensive pressure, make the other teams play him a little more honestly.

Dave makes a note that Tanana plays nothing but straight man-to-man on defense. Tyler's idea of man-to-man is if you score more than the man you're covering, you win. His man tonight is Chris Moses, who goes for thirty-eight points, most of them with Tyler nowhere around him. Tyler, for his part, scores thirty-nine. Tanana wins, 79–72. After the game, with the fans roaming the floor, Tyler pulls off his jersey, showing off his chiseled physique, and proceeds to put on a dunking exhibition, to the applause of his friends and neighbors. It's a strange little ritual, this performance. Josh wonders aloud, "Does he do that when they lose?"

The final game of the night pits Fort Yukon's girls against Tanana's, which sets up the odd situation of Dave's boys cheering for the Lady Wolves and the Tanana guys backing Fort Yukon. Matt and company are as taken with the Tanana girls as the girls are with them. As for the Tanana boys, Norman is entranced by Tahila Tremblay. Tahila is Dave's favorite among the Fort Yukon girls. She's a sweetheart, he says, and as far as basketball goes, she's one of the few girls on that team who plays with her head and not just her emotions. Norman is unabashed about his affection for her, sitting directly behind Tahila whenever the Fort Yukon girls come to the bench. Unfortunately, she doesn't share his feelings. She completely ignores him. She wishes he would go away. But Norman is relentless. He keeps grinning and calling her name, in his fake-Spanish accent.

The next day goes by slowly. The boys don't play until evening. They pass the time doing homework, wandering the halls, watching the other teams play, strolling down to the village's store to buy chips and soda. An hour before game time they suit up. They're eager, ready for their first real test as a number one team.

Dave comes in, looks them over. He does not want them to make the mistake of slipping into the kind of game they watched Tanana and Allakaket play last night.

"I know you're all thinking about Tyler," he says. "The danger is letting a player like that turn our team concept of defense into a one-on-one concept, me against you. We can't let that happen."

He knows this is easier said than done. Kids will be kids, especially when they're boys on the verge of young manhood. They've all got egos, and they're ready to test them, all the time, against the world, against each other, and of course against other basketball players. Tyler Hyslop is the king of the hill, as they see it. Everyone wants to bring the king down. But if they try to do it one-on-one, Dave tells them—the way Tyler would like them to—it won't work.

The gym is packed solid as Fort Yukon comes out on the floor. Snoop Dogg and Tupac blast from the sound system. The Tanana boys are warming up at their end of the court. All except Tyler. He's slouched on the bench, wearing a hooded sweatshirt over his red-and-white uniform, leafing through a copy of *Sports Illustrated,* yawning, looking like he's bored out of his mind. The kid is confident, says Dave. He'll give him that.

The game begins, and Tanana turns the ball over on three of its first four trips up the floor. Tyler loses it twice, daring Fort Yukon's guards to take away his crossover dribble, which they do, flashing the other way for quick scores. Matt hits two threes to build a fast six-point lead. Norman scores seven first-quarter points for Tanana on a variety of spin-reverse dribbles, his favorite move. Tyler has only two, and the period ends 20–16, Fort Yukon. So far the speed Dave expected from Tanana has not been a factor.

Norman's first shot of the second quarter is a twisting turnaround fadeaway from twenty-one feet, the kind of nutty shot Dave is only too happy to see this kid take.

He hits it.

Not only does he hit it, but he's fouled by Josh in the process. Norman sinks the free throw for a four-point play, tying the game just like that.

The crowd is up on its feet, going crazy.

Matt responds with a three of his own from the top right side of the key. Wade follows with a steal and a layup. Tyler loses the ball the next two trips up the floor, still trying to dribble through Fort Yukon's traps. His teammates, however, are playing well, keeping the game close. Halftime, Fort Yukon leads by just four, 36–32.

"You're shutting fifty-five down well," Dave says, back in the class-room. Tyler's number is 55.

"But there's too much staring at the ball on defense," he continues. "That's what's allowing those other guys to score. And there's no excuse for fouling someone on three-pointers. That should never happen."

He looks right at Josh, who looks right back at him and nods.

"Okay," he says. "It's our fault we're only up by four, not theirs. It's our fault defensively. Let's keep making fifty-five work hard. Make him feel like a caged animal. And let's not forget about the others. Make them work hard, too."

Done.

Fort Yukon comes out and simply obliterates Tanana. The Wolves open the half in a full-court press, which Fort Yukon shreds easily. Derek is the beneficiary, feasting on three-on-two breaks, sinking a string of short jump shots and layups. He scores fourteen points in the quarter. The entire Tanana team scores only nine. The period ends 66–41, Eagles.

Tyler doesn't even pretend to play defense in the fourth quarter, choosing instead to hang at half-court and yell for the ball after each Fort Yukon score. He pads his total for the game to twenty-five, still well below his average. Norman is invisible the entire second half, scoring just one point. Derek finishes with twenty-two—the fifth different high scorer for Fort Yukon this season. The final score is 83–54.

As for Josh's question about Tyler's postgame dunking displays, the answer is yes, he puts on the show even when Tanana loses. There's not quite as much zest to it as last night, but as the disappointed home crowd files out into the night, a few little kids stay behind to watch number 55 strip off his jersey and start throwing it down.

The next day, Saturday, Fort Yukon meets Allakaket in the afternoon, with the championship game later that evening. It's a little event, this tournament, nothing compared to the NIT, but it's important to Dave, not only as a preview of the postseason but also to put some fear in the hearts of the teams they'll be playing in the Regionals. He wants the 1A teams in this region to believe they have no chance against the Eagles. Last weekend, Allakaket left town feeling like they could give Fort Yukon a game. That's what Dave meant when he told his boys they had given the Blazers some confidence by playing so badly. Don't make that mistake today, he tells them, as they dress and get ready for the two P.M. tip-off.

Dave wants to throw something new at Allakaket today, catch them off balance. Instead of the 1-2-2 half-court trap, he sends his kids out to begin the game in a full-court 2-2-1 press. They practiced this all week, just to surprise Allakaket. The Blazers are indeed caught off balance. Their first three possessions, they cough the ball up, with Fort Yukon scoring each time for a quick 6–0 lead. But even without their star guard, Allakaket is quick. They've got a tight, swarming press of their own, which gives Fort Yukon trouble. Josh and Matt turn the ball over three straight times themselves, with Allakaket scoring each time, including a long three-pointer and a Moses head fake inside that sends Aaron into the rafters. Allakaket jumps ahead, 7–6, and Dave flashes time-out.

"Aaron," he snaps, "did he show you the ball? If he didn't show you the ball, why did you go for it? A head fake is a *lousy* fake, son. You know better."

He turns to the others.

"We're getting nothing on the boards. One and out every time. They're getting three shots at a time, and we're getting *nothing*.

"And I want you to run the press break, run it the way we practice it."

First play out of the huddle, against Allakaket's full-court press, Aaron inbounds to Justin, who snaps a pass to the left, hitting Josh on the run. Josh cuts to the middle, as Matt flashes up from the right, takes a pass from Josh in full stride, slices into the key, and releases a soft eight-foot floater that finds nothing but net.

Dave jumps up, clapping his hands.

"Now *that's* the way to run a press break," he says.

A 9–0 run puts Fort Yukon back ahead. The quarter ends 22–14, with Matt scoring half his team's points. The Fort Yukon press is taking its toll. Justin and Josh are pinching the middle, forcing Allakaket's guards toward the sideline, where Matt or Tim comes up to stop them, making the guards pick up their dribbles. Justin or Josh then moves in, windmilling his arms, forcing a weak, desperate pass or simply stripping the ball from the panicky guards.

Allakaket can manage only six second-quarter points. Halftime, Fort Yukon leads, 37–20.

Dave goes to his backups the second half, mixing in Johnny, Chris, Derek and Wade with the starters. He wants to see how they respond, how well they come off the bench and fit into the defensive scheme, as well as the patterns on offense. He needs them, if not now, later.

They look, quite simply, awful. Wade winds up scoreless. So does Johnny. "They look brain-dead," says Dave. If not for Matt and Tim Fields picking up the slack with some nice shooting, they could have let Allakaket back into the game.

The final is 63–47, setting up a rematch with Tanana that evening for the tournament title. But Dave's far from happy.

"We made way too many mistakes out there," he tells his boys back in the classroom. "We were in the wrong place; we didn't respond; we didn't anticipate.

"Our style of play depends on me being able to sub," he says, looking at his reserves. "It's your responsibility to be *ready*, to understand what's going on when you come in the game. We struggled the second half out there because you weren't ready. Your heads weren't in it at all."

He draws a deep breath.

"Play a game like this down at Anchorage, and we go home. Play a game like this in Regionals, and we might not make it to Anchorage. Other than that . . . well, you won by sixteen points. Congratulations."

He leaves. The classroom is dead silent. Matt tosses his warm-up on the floor.

"Thanks for the negative input," he says.

Dave's kids while away the afternoon, watch Tyler and his teammates lay waste to Huslia, then watch the Fort Yukon girls win, to set up their own championship game against Tanana. All the teams break for dinner, and by the time they return to the gym for the girls' title game, the bleachers are once again filled. Cheryl's girls came into this weekend with five losses, but they've played well here, led by Mandy and Ruby. Their problems will come when they run into Nulato, the powerhouse girls' team in this region. The Nulato girls are ranked third in the state at the moment. They've won the Regional title the past four years in a row. They came within one win of the state championship last season, losing to King Cove in the title game. They're a cut above Fort Yukon, and everyone knows it. Still, anything might happen. They'll find out next month.

Again, Dave's boys root for the Lady Wolves, lust trumping loyalty. By the time they leave to get dressed, Cheryl's girls are safely ahead. The home crowd is already turning its sights to the evening's finale, cheering its boys as they leave to suit up.

The Wolves come out for the warm-ups dressed in their road uniforms: black jerseys and shorts with white and red trim. The Eagles wear their home whites. The Red Hot Chili Peppers blare from the loudspeakers. The Tanana boys look looser than last night. They've got nothing to lose after that blowout. Again, it's Norman Dave's worried about more than Tyler. Norman is the quintessential streak shooter. If he gets hot, anything can happen.

Dave likes what he sees off the opening tip. Tanana brings the ball up, Tyler once again trying to break the trap by himself. Matt strips him, goes the other way for a layup.

Norman answers with a spin-leaner in the key, and he's fouled.

Tim hits a short bank shot.

Norman answers with another spin-shot in the key, this one a fade-away.

Aaron misses.

Norman goes coast-to-coast, spin-reversing his dribble twice to break through the traps, laying it in over Aaron.

7–4, Tanana.

Norman's on fire.

Dave doesn't like what he sees, calls time-out, tells his kids to switch from their half-court trap to the full-court press they used against Allakaket this afternoon.

It hardly affects Tanana at all. Unlike last night, when Fort Yukon's defense bedeviled both Norman and Tyler, the pair are running past Dave's boys tonight. And Norman is simply unconscious from the floor. With three minutes left in the quarter, he gets the ball in the far corner, facing away from the basket, doesn't even look before he goes up, twists in midair, leans away from the defender and squeezes off a long arching shot that settles into the net.

The crowd explodes, screaming, dancing, shaking the bleachers.

Two minutes left in the quarter, Tanana is up 15–10 when Matt picks up his second foul. The refs are calling it tight. Dave takes Matt out, tells him he's got to be aware of how they're blowing the whistle.

One minute later, Aaron picks up his second, and he, too, comes out. "Guys, you've got to adjust," Dave says.

The quarter ends 19–12, Tanana. The house is rocking. Dave can hardly hear himself as he talks to his kids, tries to settle them down. He can see it in their eyes. They're a little glazed. Their breathing's a bit rapid. They're on the edge of something like confusion—the first time this season Dave's seen them like this.

He puts Matt and Aaron back in. But their rhythm is off. They're getting the same open shots they got last night, but tonight those shots are not falling. Dave's warned the boys that they can't count on their shooting to bail them out of tight games. The night's going to come, he's told them, when the shots just aren't dropping. It's their defense, he's told them, that they've got to be able to count on at all times.

Tonight the shots are not dropping. Josh continues to believe in his long-distance knucklers, firing four of them in the first half without hitting one. Derek is off target as well, going scoreless so far. Matt has fourteen points, but Aaron has only two. If not for Tim Fields stepping up and knocking down three big shots, including a long three, they might be trailing worse at halftime than they are. Tanana leads by ten at the break, 35–25. Norman's got fifteen. Tyler's got ten.

"You're rushing your shots, boys," Dave says, as they sit on the classroom tables, staring down at the carpet, breathing hard. "Tim's keeping us in the game."

"They're not having any trouble with our press," he continues. "I'm tempted to go man-to-man, but I'm fearful because you haven't adjusted to how the refs are calling the game."

He stops, sighs, decides, yes, they'll go man-to-man.

"Josh, you'll take twenty."

20 is Norman.

"Matt gets fifteen. Aaron's got twenty-one. That leaves Tyler."

He looks over at Tim.

"Tim," he says, "you're too slow to take him, so you get thirty-three."

Tim nods.

Dave looks over at Justin.

"You're too small for him," he says.

Justin nods.

"So, Derek," Dave says, "you'll start the second half, and you'll take Tyler."

Derek's head stays down, his eyes on the floor.

"All you've got to do is turn him. Turn him, and turn him, and turn him. Do that, and you'll get help from Tim or Aaron."

Derek nods.

"Okay, boys." Dave motions them together. "Let's take back control of the tempo. It's up to you now. Let's see what you're made of."

The second half doesn't start well. Josh breaks away for a wide-open layup and clanks it off the rim.

"Point *blank*," Dave says, slapping his forehead.

Matt loses the ball, dribbling it off his foot.

"What the hell's going on?" says Dave. "What happened to the fundamentals?"

Josh picks up a foul, shoving his forearm into Tyler's back.

"Josh!" Dave yells. "Don't do dumb things!"

Other than that, though, the man-to-man's working. Tanana's off balance, a little unsettled. Derek hits his first shot of the night, a three-pointer, and Aaron gets hot, nailing a baseline jumper, followed by a putback and a breakaway layup to bring Fort Yukon within two, 39–37.

Norman answers with two scores of his own, both fadeaways in the key. Last night he couldn't buy a shot. Tonight he can't miss.

The quarter ends 45–40, Tanana.

"We're okay, guys," says Dave. "We've cut their lead in half. Keep pushing."

Tyler scores on a sweet up-and-under to start the fourth quarter. Derek responds with an air ball from the left side. Next trip up the floor, Josh draws an air ball of his own. The Tanana fans are merciless, chanting and mocking the two dreadful misses.

"Wade," Dave says, reaching over and grabbing Wade's forearm, "we need some more offense."

Wade checks in for Josh. But the bleeding continues.

Norman drives and dishes to Tyler, who drops the ball over the rim for a 49–40 lead. Tyler's cousin, number 15, hits a turnaround bank shot to push the lead to eleven. Dave signals time-out, and the Tanana crowd goes berserk.

He puts Johnny in, but there's no magic tonight. Johnny's first shot is a wide-open three. It's long. Tyler grabs the rebound and dashes the length of the floor, finishing with a soft left-handed layup over Aaron's outstretched hands.

The bleachers are rocking.

53–40 with five minutes left.

Dave can see his kids getting tight. Matt flings up a wild three-pointer from the top of the key. It barely draws iron. Derek grabs a rebound, goes up and completely bricks the putback. Josh travels. Derek loses the ball out of bounds.

Josh finally breaks the drought with a layup. He follows that with a steal and a line-drive jumper from the baseline. Tanana is called for three seconds. Matt comes upcourt, stops at the arc and fires a long three with Norman right in his face.

Bang. It's good.

The Tanana coach leaps to his feet and signals time-out.

A seven-point run for Fort Yukon. They trail by just six, 53–47, with 2:43 left.

Dave studies his boys' faces. They don't look distraught anymore.

They know what they need to do. Just keep coming. Keep pushing. Don't let up, not now.

They return to the court, pick up their men. Norman takes the inbound pass, works the ball up the floor against Josh. He reverse-spins to the foul line, makes a crossover dribble into the key, plants, leans back, with both Josh and Aaron in his chest, and lofts a high arching mortar that falls through the net as the whistle sounds.

The basket is good, and he's fouled.

The crowd is up once again, stomping the bleachers.

Norman misses the foul shot. Wade misses a three-pointer. Norman grabs the rebound, flies upcourt, spins out of two traps and drops in a layup to push the margin back to ten points with one minute left.

The crowd breaks into a chant: "We are mighty, mighty Wolves!!"

Norman caps the night of his life with one last three-pointer as the buzzer sounds and the crowd dances onto the floor.

63–49, Tanana wins.

"What a blessing," Dave says as he heads toward the classroom. "No more number one."

He hates being the favorite. Doesn't like what it does to his teams. He prefers coming up from below, knocking the bigger guy down. Like Tanana did this evening.

"Hey, this was bound to happen," he tells his kids as they pull off their jerseys. "And that's okay. No reason to hang your heads. There are nights where the shots just don't fall. Nothing you can do about that."

"Yeah," says Matt. "You win some, and you lose some."

"That's right," says Dave. "It will be a different story when they come to our house in two weeks. We're going to make them pay the first night, and we'll make them pay *again* the second night."

He looks his kids over.

"It's not like they're going to ride this into the Regionals, guys. Remember that. This was *not* the Regional."

With that, he leaves. The boys dress and join him back out in the gym, where the crowd is still packed in the stands and all four schools' teams have gathered on the court for the awards ceremony.

Cheryl's girls step up to receive their first-place trophy. Mandy is named MVP. Someone hands her a microphone to say a few words.

"*Mahsi Choo*," she says shyly, drawing a huge cheer from the crowd. They may not all speak Gwich'in, but they all know "Thank you very much" when they hear it.

Matt steps up to accept the second-place trophy for his team.

"Some of us are thinking about moving here," he says, drawing a laugh from the crowd as he looks over at the Tanana girls.

Last come the Tanana boys. This is the biggest win they've had in years. Tyler is named MVP, though Dave and his boys have no doubt Norman deserves it.

The Tanana coach takes the microphone to speak for his kids.

"This is the best team we've played all season," he says, turning toward the Fort Yukon boys. "I've been telling my guys all year, we haven't won nothin' yet. Well, now we've won something."

He holds the trophy aloft as the crowd gives one last ovation. Then everyone heads home. The kids walk back to their classrooms. They're tired. It's been a long day. Tomorrow they fly back to their villages, back to their homes and families.

Or, as Matt puts it to his teammates as they settle into their sleeping bags and the classroom lights are turned off, "Well, fellas, it's back to the Fort."

FIFTEEN

Tok

I T SEEMS EVERYONE in the village is dissecting the loss to Tanana. Paul and Willie are almost happy about it, as if it vindicates their criticism of Dave. John and Ryan have been relentless with Matt, chiding him, giving him grief about being only the second-best player in the house at the moment. They point out that Gina and the girls won down at Tanana. Matt lost.

Matt grins and bears it. The team is 14–3 right now. That's pretty damn good, as far as he's concerned. Yeah, they lost to Tanana. On Tanana's floor. In Tanana's tournament. In front of Tanana's fans, on a night when he couldn't hit shit, and neither could anyone else on his team. That Carlo kid played out of his mind. He had—what?—twenty-eight points in that last game. Those were some sick shots he made; Matt has to give him that.

Dave tells the team pretty much the same thing at practice Monday night. He puts the loss in perspective, points to their rematch with Tanana the week after this. Then he whistles them out on the floor and runs them hard, not in a punitive way, but simply to prepare for the push from here to the postseason. The boys understand. Their tongues are hanging down to their shoes after Dave starts them out with sixteen gassers, but they're upbeat, almost giddy, as if the loss to Tanana never happened. They're all teasing Johnny about that little Allakaket girl, the Lady Blazers' point guard, who barged into the boys' classroom over the weekend and cornered Johnny, asking him to give her a hug. Johnny turned five shades of red, he was so embarrassed. He kept backing away from her, and she kept pushing in, till she had him pressed up against the wall. Her nose came up to about Johnny's navel. For all his hip-hop stylizing, Johnny's by far the shyest kid on the team. The guys were all over him, yelling at him to go ahead and hug her. He wouldn't do it. No way. She finally gave up and left, but she mooned over Johnny the rest of the weekend, gazing at him wherever he went.

Dave motions the boys to the bleachers. He's been wracking his brain over this issue of why they run so hot and cold. It's one thing to say the shots simply weren't falling Saturday night. It's another to figure out *why*. Dave couldn't sleep last night, thinking about this. He believes he's come up with the answer.

"I mean no prejudice here," he tells the boys. "But when we play these white teams that are slower than us, we eat their lunch. It hurts us, though, because we tend to play only as fast as we need to. Then, when we go up against a team that's as fast as us, like Allakaket or Tanana, we're not ready to play full speed.

"Here's the point, guys. Matthew is one of the few on this team to whom it doesn't matter how fast the other team's playing. He plays at top speed, all out, all the time. The rest of you tend to turn it on and off, and that doesn't work. You've got to be *on* all the time.

"When I tell you over and over in practice to shoot at *game speed* or to make a pass at *game speed*, this is what I'm talking about. That stuff you do when you're shooting around—dribbling, faking, juking, taking these relaxed shots—it has no point. If we're used to taking our time in practice or against these slower teams, then, when we have to speed it up, we wind up *rushing*. That's why we shot so poorly against Tanana. Because we were rushing.

"Fellas, there's a big difference between a quick shot and a rushed shot. The difference is that a quick shooter is prepared to shoot *before* he gets the ball. He's in the place he wants to be; he's positioned his body the way it needs to be; he's *ready* to shoot the instant the ball arrives in his hands. The same with passing. Before you receive a pass, you need to be thinking about what you want to do with the ball when you get it. Where are the cutters going to be coming from? If you're looking at a zone and we want to reverse the ball, be ready to snap it right back the instant you get it. Don't give that defense a split second to catch up. *Move* it. *Snap* it. Make it *quick*.

"That's how we're going to practice, starting tonight. Catch, shoot. Catch, shoot. Catch, pass. Catch, pass. *Game* speed. *Quick*. Got it?"

They seem to get it. That night and the next, they do nothing but passing and catching and shooting drills, all at top speed. Justin, in particular, shines. He and Johnny can't seem to miss. The boys all seem more focused than at any other time this season. Certainly more than last week. It's coming on crunch time now, and they know it. They've got the Tok Round-Robin this week, their last chance to play against larger schools. Then Tanana visits to close out the regular season. Then comes the Regional. And then, god willing, they'll go down to State.

The Tok tourney, like the NIT, is a big event for Alaska's smaller schools. Like the NIT, eight teams are invited from all over the state. Unlike the NIT, the round-robin format has all matchups scheduled beforehand. Dave asked Tok's athletic director to give him the toughest three games he could, and that's what the Eagles have got. Dave found out today that his boys will open against the host team Thursday night. No surprise there. Tok is hungry for another shot at Fort Yukon. Friday, the boys will play Galena. Word is Galena's got a pretty good team this year, as always. They've been getting some votes in the 2A state poll, for whatever that's worth. Finally, Saturday, Dave's kids will face Wainwright, the team that beat them in last year's 1A state finals. They can't wait for that one. It would be sweet to get some revenge on those Eskimos.

The other five schools who will be in the tournament are Skagway, Ninilchik, Tanana, Northway (just the girls' team), and—there they are again—Anderson. But Dave's boys will play none of these teams, not this weekend.

Now that they've got the schedule—the girls open the tournament first thing Thursday morning—Dave's kids and Cheryl's prepare to fly out Wednesday, in order to get to Tok Wednesday night. Kyle and Bruce will stay behind. Josh will miss this trip as well. He's got that Junior Iditarod dog race this weekend—to honor the promise he made to his dad. He and his parents are driving down to Anchorage Wednesday to get ready for that.

Wednesday morning, the weather is unseasonably warm—fifteen-above—when the kids step off the plane at the Fairbanks airport and load up the vans. The boys all shed their jackets. It'll be T-shirts and jeans from now through most of the weekend.

It's a three-hour drive down to Tok. They've got time to kill, and it makes more sense to kill it here in Fairbanks than down there, where there's nothing to do. Dave runs a few errands, hits the bank to cash a school check for meal money, takes the boys to McDonald's for lunch, stops at Wal-Mart and, finally, he drops his team at the Bentley Mall, where—wonder of wonders—they run into the Tanana girls. Both Tanana teams just flew in from their village, and they, too, are killing a couple of hours before hitting the road. Matt makes no secret of his attraction to these girls—he's got the words LADY WOLVES FAN stenciled on his ball cap. Dave watches them peel off in groups of four and five, his boys mixed in with Tanana's girls, roaming the empty little mall on a slow Wednesday afternoon.

Two thirty, they load up and hit the road. This time, rather than heading southwest, as they did on their trips to Nikolaevsk and Nenana, they point southeast toward Tok, on the fabled Alaska Highway. It's no longer the notorious road it once was—loose gravel and mud, frost heaves and mountainous pitches, ninety-degree cutbacks and potholes the size of bomb craters. But it's still quite a drive

It was built in a feverish rush, in the spring and summer of 1942, hacked fifteen hundred miles through the Canadian and Alaskan wilderness as a response to the Japanese attack on Pearl Harbor. With Alaska considered a vulnerable target for another attack (the Aleutian Islands would indeed be invaded that June and occupied for nearly a year), Franklin Roosevelt authorized the construction of a military supply route to the Arctic. On April 11, construction began. A *Time* magazine writer visited the work crews that summer and filed a report on their progress: "This was a job for Paul Bunyan; to wrest an all-weather road from the jealous Northland between early spring and autumn; to span the fierce, death-cold rushing rivers, the black custard quagmires; to cut switchbacks across the Great Divide, to make the way between the Arctic and the U.S. for a highway which some day may be as common as the Boston Post Road."

For years the Alcan—Alaskan-Canadian—Highway remained a twisting, unpaved, single-lane trail fit only for bulldozers and trucks. The carcasses of family sedans and station wagons destroyed by the journey were scattered in the roadside brush, testimony to how damned-near impossible it was to drive to Alaska.

It's still a long trip, but the roadway is paved now, with occasional rest stops and cafés and motels along the way. It's busy in spring and summer but almost deserted this time of year, this far north.

The late February sky grows gray and overcast as Dave and the boys roll out of Fairbanks, along the frozen Tanana River, past the glaciers and ice fields of the eastern Alaska Range. Clouds swirl around the jagged alpine peaks of Mount Silvertip and Mount Kimball. Gusts of wind rock the van. Dave's got the headlights on. The radio plays Queen, T. Rex, ABBA. Whirling ribbons of snow dance across the blacktop. The boys, slumped on their bags, on each other, lie asleep.

By the time they pull into Tok, night has fallen. The sky has cleared. The buttery light of a full moon bathes the snow-covered slopes of the mountains flanking the village.

It's more a crossroads than an actual town. Tok was built as a work camp that summer of '42; some say its name came from shortening the word "Tokyo." It's grown over the decades into a neon-lit cluster of roadside shops, service stations, motels and restaurants—the first significant stop in Alaska for drivers who have crossed the Canadian border, some ninety miles southeast. Travelers headed to Anchorage can leave the Alcan here, take the Tok cutoff and merge onto the Glenn Highway, which snakes over, through and around the Wrangell and Chugach mountains, until it finally reaches the state's largest city, 330 miles away.

That's the route the Ninilchik boys' and girls' teams drove to get here tonight—a twelve-hour trip, all told, counting their drive up the Kenai and an overnight stay in Anchorage. The Skagway teams drove here as well, ten hours up the Alaska Highway from the southeast, most of it through Canadian territory, from their home down near Juneau. As for Tanana, Wainwright and Galena, they all flew into Fairbanks this morning and, like Fort Yukon, drove down from there. The Anderson players and coaches had a relatively short five-hour trip. Only the girls' team from Northway, just sixty miles down the highway from here, and host Tok aren't completely exhausted this evening.

Almost all the visiting teams have convened at a large roadside restaurant called Fast Eddie's. Dinner at Fast Eddie's is another treat Dave looks forward to each season. They'll be eating in Tok's school cafeteria for the next three days, so the boys make the most of this meal, studying the menu to squeeze every cent out of the ten dollars each they're allowed.

The kids and coaches from Wainwright are seated one table over. Dave recognizes a couple of their players but doesn't see the point guard who tore Fort Yukon apart in last year's title game. He doesn't see the head coach from last season either. It would be hard to miss that guy: He was seven feet tall, no kidding, says Dave. A white guy. He had to bend down to get through the locker room door.

Dave reaches over, shakes the hands of several Wainwright boys, asks about the point guard.

"He quit," says one of the kids. "Two weeks ago."

"Quit?" says Dave. "Why?"

"Xbox," says the kid. "He'd stay up all night playing Xbox, and he'd sleep all day. Finally, he just decided to quit."

Dave is incredulous. The starting point guard for a state champion basketball team gives up the sport, his education, his future, for video games.

"What about your coach?" Dave asks. "Where is he?"

"He went back to school to get his master's degree," says the kid.

"He *quit* on us," says one of his teammates.

Dave was right to wonder about that early number-one ranking for Wainwright. They're struggling this year. They've already lost twice to Nuiqsut, in their own region. Their chances for returning to State don't look good.

"That's so sad," Dave says later, out in the parking lot. "It's like everything they had going has crumbled."

Dave and his boys will be spending the next four nights in a church. There isn't room at the school for all the visiting teams, so some have been assigned to accommodations around town. Fort Yukon—both the boys and the girls—has drawn the basement of the Faith Chapel, a little whitewashed wood-frame sanctuary just off the highway.

Dave loves watching his boys unload and settle in wherever they're spending the night. There's a military-type precision to the routine, like an infantry supply corps setting up camp. As in the military, there is a clearly defined pecking order, with shit filtering down from the top. Matt and Josh, being seniors, take care of nothing but their own gear. They get first pick of where to lay down their sleeping bags in the room. They decide what music the team will listen to, which movie they'll watch on the DVD player. A freshman like Zach, on the other hand, must shoulder as much of the team's gear as he can carry: the sack of basketballs, the two first-aid boxes, the pallets of food. Zach is also the continual target of ridicule. Wes, too, must work like a mule, but he escapes most of the barbs, largely because, unlike Zach, he rarely opens his mouth. Johnny, although he's one of the team's key players—its best offensive weapon off the bench—is also a gofer when it comes to the team's equipment. That's because he's only a sophomore. The same with Tim Woods and Kyle and Bruce, when they're here. Everyone else is a junior, which exempts them from all but the most necessary labor.

Beyond their well-oiled efficiency, what delights Dave about these boys—not just this particular team but every Fort Yukon team he's ever coached—is the fact that they rarely complain. Dave can only imagine taking fourteen typical American teenagers, stuffing them into a van, driving eight or nine hours in one day, the way these kids did on that Nikolaevsk trip, stopping to rest or to eat or to piss only when and where he says so, sleeping on hard concrete floors—like the basement floor of this church. He can only imagine how much bitching and whining there would be from most kids in this culture today. God knows his guys can complain with the best of them. He's watched them grow up. They're no angels. But something clicks when they go on the road. It's as if they're so happy just to be here that there's nothing they could possibly complain about. Some of them have it so hard, in so many ways, in their homes, in the village, that getting away like this is a vacation, a respite, a relief.

The fact is that these boys know what "hard" really is. Anyone who's slept in the Arctic forest on frozen ground in subzero temperatures for days at a time, under makeshift lean-tos or beneath canvas tarps, shaking the hoarfrost off their sleeping bag when they awake, eating nothing sometimes but beans if they're lucky, breaking trail through ice-crusted snow, the way these boys do when they go out to hunt moose in the fall or run traplines in winter—anyone who's had to smear themselves with muskrat grease or moose tallow or lard to keep the mosquitoes away in the summer, the way these boys' grandparents had to—anyone who's raised and run dogs the way Josh has, cutting and gathering goose grass in the fall for their bedding, catching and slicing and hanging chum salmon for their food, cooking that food night and day in those dog pots, tending the teams like a nurse when they're out on the trail, slipping hand-sewn booties over their paws and makeshift jockstraps over their penises—"peter heaters," they're called—to keep the animals' extremities from freezing—anyone who's done any of this would never dream of bitching about having to sleep on the floor or having to share one bathroom with thirteen other boys.

It's sharing that bathroom with the *girls* that's a pain in the ass. That's what's bugging Tim Fields as the team settles in for the night. The girls take so damn long in there, he says. Tim's the team clown, no question. He loves goofing with accents—fake lisps and speech impediments. Right now he's got the guys doubled over with a bit about "shlapping penishes." The others have their own routines. Justin begins every sentence with the word "Christ," as in "Christ, who drank all the juice?" Or "Christ, who farted?" Or "Christ, the girls all talk at once. Listen!" Aaron is always appropriating Wade's headphones. Right now he's listening to an Eminem CD. Johnny just lies on his side on his sleeping bag, a broad easy smile on his face, soaking it all in.

Eleven o'clock, it's lights out. The chatter continues, in the dark, in both the boys' and the girls' rooms. Gradually, it fades into silence.

Next morning, the boys are up early, to have breakfast at the school, then to watch the girls kick off the tournament with a nine A.M. game. Cheryl, unlike Dave, did not request a tough draw for this weekend. The new weekly rankings are out this morning, and three of the top five 2A girls' teams in the state are here: Ninilchik (ranked first), Skagway (third) and Galena (fourth). But the Fort Yukon girls will play none of them. They've got Anderson—yet again—this morning. They've got Northway tomorrow and Tok Saturday night. They will win one game this weekend—this morning against Anderson.

As for the boys, they aren't surprised to find that they've dropped back to number three in the 1A poll. They're happy to still be that high, after losing to Tanana. They see Emmonak is in the top spot, and they notice that Nuiqsut, with those two wins over Wainwright, has climbed up to second. They also see that Galena has broken the top five among 2A schools.

The day passes slowly. Late morning, the boys get their first look at the Ninilchik girls—"the Machine," as Dave calls them. Four years ago *USA Today* featured a sports section cover story on the Lady Wolverines' dynasty. A dozen or so Ninilchik fans, mostly parents, have caravanned up with the team this weekend. They all wear bright yellow T-shirts proclaiming their girls' string of state championships. On the backs, the shirts read:

FIVE STRAIGHT
Alaska State Record
Any School—Any Sport

After watching the Machine rout Wainwright's girls, Dave and the boys drive back to the church to do homework. It's been almost thirty hours since they boarded the plane yesterday morning in Fort Yukon. "Christ," says Justin, "this trip seems like forever, and we haven't even played yet."

Five o'clock, they head back to the gym to watch Galena's boys play Wainwright. Galena looks loaded, with a pair of quicksilver guards—both Native—and a six-foot-three black kid at center, a lanky freshman who can jump out of the gym. They don't see many black kids on village teams, and this kid is good, very good. It's hard to believe he's only a freshman.

What's harder to believe is how far Wainwright has fallen. Galena turns the game into a rout early on; the freshman will finish with twenty-

six points—and the Wainwright players begin bickering among themselves on the bench. During one time-out, one of the players yells at the
coach, a young guy from their village who's volunteered to take over
the team after last year's coach left. To make matters worse, their best
remaining player takes an elbow to the head in the second half and has
to be driven to the Tok clinic to be stitched up. He's out for the rest of
the tournament. Dave feels terrible—for him, for that coach, for the
whole team.

At dinner, the boys hear word, through the Tanana girls, that someone
told someone that they heard from somebody else that Josh Cadzow
was driving all the way up from Anchorage today to surprise everyone
and play against Tok tonight, like he did down at the NIT. The rumor
is still drifting around as Dave and his boys settle into the bleachers to
watch the first half of the Tanana–Tok girls' game, before getting dressed
for their own. The gym is filled, with close to a third of Tok's 1,400
residents squeezed into the bleachers and along the walls to watch the
hometown girls and boys play. Sure enough, late in the second quarter,
Josh appears, pushing his way through the throng to get to his teammates.

"It's just for tonight, fellas," he says, as they make room for him to
sit down. "I've gotta drive back tomorrow."

A flash of disappointment crosses Chris's face. If Josh hadn't shown
up, Chris would have started tonight. Other than that, though, the boys
are ecstatic.

Halftime, they leave for the locker room to suit up. There's no need
to spring any surprises tonight, Dave tells them. They'll go with the
same half-court trap they used in Nenana, the same trap they've used
virtually all season. "Let's see what *they've* decided to change," he says.

The Tok players look especially intense during warm-ups. It couldn't
have been easy coming home after losing to Fort Yukon in that NIT
final. Their center looks particularly pumped, exhorting his teammates
as they run through their layups. They're wearing their home white
uniforms. Fort Yukon is in blue.

The big man opens the game by swishing a soft jumper from the foul
line. For a kid who carries so much weight—three hundred pounds, plus

that Mohawk—he's got a nice touch. Two free throws by one of his teammates gives Tok a quick 4–0 lead before Matt nicks the backboard with a lucky three-pointer from the corner—a replay of Josh's improbable three against Tok in Nenana.

Tok's defense is clearly keying on Matt, hardly giving him room to sweat. They're watching Josh, too, which leaves Justin roaming the perimeter by himself. But Justin still seems reluctant to do anything but pass.

"Shoot the ball!" Dave yells. Justin looks over, almost startled. The next time he touches it, he turns and squeezes off a picture-perfect three-pointer.

"Bingo!" says Dave.

Tok is handling the traps well tonight. Number 21, their point guard, is splitting the seams and feeding his teammates. The rims in this gym are notoriously loose. Almost anything that hits them, from any angle, no matter how hard, just dies on the rim and falls in. Shooters love loose rims like these. The Tok kids clearly know them well. They hit four three-pointers in the first quarter, three of which bounce around the basket before rolling in. The bright spot for Fort Yukon is another Justin three—"Bingo" again—from the top of the key, to close out the quarter. The score at the end of the first is 20–16 Tok. Justin's got half of those sixteen.

Tok comes out in the second and quickly stretches the lead to ten. The big man is wreaking havoc inside, and 21 is playing a tremendous floor game, shooting and passing with crisp confidence. Both have ten points by halftime. If not for back-to-back threes by Johnny coming off the bench midway through the period, the score would be worse than it is at the half: 42–32, Tok.

Dave's surprisingly upbeat. You'd almost think his team was ahead. With no locker room to go to—Tok's boys are in one, and the Tok girls are still getting dressed in the other—he leads his kids to a stairway vestibule in a darkened hallway just outside the gym.

He likes what he's seeing, he tells them.

"They're not turning the ball over . . . yet," he says. "That's going to come, I'm certain. Just keep pushing."

Be aware of Tok's weak side, he advises, both on passes and shots. "They're getting too many off-side rebounds," he tells his kids. "Too many second shots."

He asks Matt how that ankle is feeling. Matt twisted it again late in the first quarter and has been limping since then.

He nods that it's okay.

"All right then," Dave says, looking back at the others. "We clean up these little things, and those ten points disappear."

With that, they return to the court. Up on the gym's second level, Paul is broadcasting the game. He couldn't make it to Tanana last week— "Couldn't afford it," he says. But he spent the past several days on the radio, asking Fort Yukon's villagers to chip in to send him to Tok. He arrived here this morning—got up at four A.M. to drive down from Fairbanks—did the girls' game, and now he's up there this evening, not happy at all with the way things are going and not shy about telling his audience why. The boys just look so disorganized, he says to his listeners. And that defense of theirs, they should call that stuff off. Tok is beating it every time up the court.

Tok keeps beating it in the third quarter. The pace is frenetic, both teams playing nose-to-the-chest defense all over the floor. Number 21 hits two more three-pointers, giving him four for the game. But Matt's come alive, dropping two bombs of his own. Josh, after scoring just two points in the first half, makes several steals and hits two knifing layups over the big man that bring the crowd to its feet. The fans love watching this little guy play, even if he's not wearing a Tok uniform.

The third quarter ends with the Wolverines pushing their lead to twelve, 58–46. Still, Dave seems strangely sanguine. The frantic pace is just what he wants. If Tok can keep it up these last eight minutes, more power to them; they deserve to win. But he's not sure they can. He has no doubt about his own guys. That's what all those gassers have been about.

Fort Yukon opens the quarter with three quick buckets: an up-and-under drive by Derek over the big man, a steal and a layup by Wade, and a five-footer by Derek off a smooth feed from Josh.

Six minutes to go, it's 58–52 Tok.

The Wolverines push their lead back to eight with four minutes left, before Matt nails a three-pointer from the right wing and Josh strips 21 for a layup, bringing Dave out of his seat.

"The game is *on*," he says, slapping the floor.

64–61 Tok, with 3:30 to go.

The big man scores, shaking Aaron inside and dropping the ball over the rim with both hands—gently, like he's handling an egg.

Matt misses a three.

Josh steals and pulls up for a three of his own. He misses, as well.

"*Not* a good shot," says Dave.

Tok coughs up the ball again. "They're tired," says Dave. Tok's boys' faces are strained—especially their guards'—with utter exhaustion.

Derek grabs a defensive rebound, takes the ball the length of the floor, all the way to the hole, where he's mauled by the big man. He hits both free throws, cutting the lead back to three, 66–63, with 2:45 left.

The crowd's in a frenzy. They were celebrating earlier. Now they're pleading for their kids to hold on.

Tok responds, scoring a layup off Fort Yukon's press, then hitting a baseline jumper after a turnover by Matt.

With 1:55 to go, the Wolverines lead by seven.

Justin pushes the ball up the floor, passes to Matt far out on the right wing. Matt turns and, in one motion, flings a wild twenty-three-footer that barely grazes the rim before glancing out of bounds. He's got nineteen points right now, high man on the floor. But that shot smells like desperation.

"Matt," hollers Dave, "don't ruin a good night!"

Before he can finish his sentence, Wade strips a Tok guard and shoots the other way for a score.

70–65 Tok, with 1:30 left.

Another Fort Yukon steal, this one by Josh, who hits the breakaway layup.

The ref blows the whistle.

Intentional foul on the big man. He was trailing the play, nowhere near Josh, but in his frustration, he shoved Matt from behind.

The crowd groans as the refs clear Fort Yukon's end of the court for two free throws. Tok's coach, a bearded redhead in a flannel shirt and a NASCAR ball cap, calls his boys over to try calming them down. The big man is dripping with sweat. His Mohawk is slightly askew.

Matt steps up for the shots, sinks one to make it a two-point game, 70–68, with 1:14 left. And it's Fort Yukon's ball on the baseline.

Dave signals the boys' pet inbounds play, a stack under the hoop, with Matt simply lobbing the ball high to Aaron, who, if the play works the way it's designed, leaps up, rising a beat sooner than the defenders, grabs the pass at its apex and lays the ball in. Simple. It never ceases to amaze Dave how often this play works. It's worked half a dozen times already this season.

It works this time as well. Matt lobs the pass perfectly. Aaron rises above Tok's flat-footed big man, catches the ball at almost rim-level, flips it point blank into the hole . . . and misses.

The crowd gasps. They can't believe it. Neither can Dave.

Tok grabs the rebound and calls time-out. They still lead by two with 1:10 left.

Dave is relaxed. Conversational. He knows his kids take their emotional cues from him, especially at times like this. What he's showing them right now is calm. Don't foul, he tells them. There's plenty of time left. Tok may try to hold it, he says, but don't change what you're doing. Keep running the trap. They can't freeze it for long against that. He checks with the scorer to see how many time-outs he's got left. He's only used one. He's still got four remaining.

Sure enough, Tok comes out in a stall. Fort Yukon doesn't panic. The clock ticks down under a minute, below fifty seconds, as Matt, Wade and Josh chase the Tok guards, while Derek and Aaron protect the front court.

Forty-five seconds, Wade dives, flat-out, parallel to the floor, and slaps the ball loose. It careens toward the sideline. The ref is right there, set to blow his whistle as soon as the ball sails out of bounds.

But somehow, Wade, scrambling on all fours like a sped-up cartoon, like the Road Runner in full flight—"Like a seed spit out of a water-melon," Dave will say later—catches up to the ball just as it reaches the sideline, and scoops it back into play as he hurtles head first into the scorer's table.

Josh snares it, snaps it upcourt to Matt, who lets go a three from the corner.

It's wide.

Aaron rebounds, fires the ball right back to Matt, who shoots it again.

Another miss.

Tok rebounds.

Thirty seconds to go.

Tok brings it across half-court. Justin and Josh flank the ball handler. He picks up his dribble—just what they want—desperately looks for an open man . . . and drags his foot in the process.

Whistle. Traveling. Fort Yukon's ball at midcourt.

Dave calls time-out.

Twenty-four seconds left, Tok is still up by two.

Dave pulls out his wipeboard, draws up a play. He has to shout to make himself heard over the crowd. He wants Matt to inbound the ball, then break to the corner for a return pass if he's open. Remember, who's the most dangerous man on the floor? The guy who just passed the ball, right? Meanwhile, he wants Aaron and Derek to exchange down low. If the pass back to Matt isn't there, he says, look for Aaron or Derek inside. Justin and Josh nod their heads.

The pass isn't there. Tok is all over Matt as he inbounds the ball to Josh. Matt cuts to the corner, drawing two Tok players with him.

Under the basket, Derek flashes across the key, sets himself in the path of the big man and braces himself as Aaron slices the other way, running the big man into Derek's pick.

Aaron breaks open.

Josh hits him.

Aaron goes up, lays the ball off the backboard. The shot comes off hard, pumped by Aaron's adrenaline. It hits the rim, bounces, hits the rim one more time . . . and falls through.

The gymnasium erupts.

A Tok guard signals time-out.

Thirteen seconds left.

The score's tied at 70.

Dave gathers his guys by the bench, squats on the floor as they circle him.

"Okay," he shouts over the thumping and chants of the Tok fans. "The big guy or twenty-one, that's who they're going to, understand? Twenty-one or the big guy. Do *not* let either of them get open."

The boys nod their heads, breathing hard, sweat dripping from their brows onto the bright hardwood floor.

They break from the huddle just as the ref strides over from the scorer's table.

"Coach," he says. "We've got a technical foul on the white team."

Dave doesn't understand.

"They had no time-outs left," says the ref.

Dave turns, calls his guys back, tells them what's happened.

"Chris Webber," mutters Matt, a half smile on his face. Matt knows his basketball history. He remembers Michigan in the NCAA finals twelve years ago, when their freshman star, Chris Webber, called time-out with eleven seconds left, his team down by two to North Carolina. But Michigan had no time-outs left. That flub cost the Wolverines the national title. Webber said so himself.

Now these Wolverines face the same thing. Dave sends Matt out to shoot the two free throws.

The crowd is wailing, stomping, shaking the walls.

Matt hits the first, misses the second.

71–70, Fort Yukon.

Their ball at midcourt.

Dave huddles the team one more time, sketches the play. He wants Aaron to slide one way off a stack, Matt to peel off the other, for a possible breakaway, and Josh to cut to the ball.

"If it ain't there for Matt," Dave says to Josh, "just dribble like *hell*, you understand?"

It's not there. Neither is Josh. He's smothered on the inbounds. But Wade breaks open. He gets the ball and is immediately fouled.

Eight seconds left.

"Wade," Dave hollers as both teams line up for the free throws. "'Bout time you *made* a couple, huh?"

Wade looks over, grins. The bench cracks up. There goes Old Dave again, with his jokes.

Wade makes the first.

72–70.

He misses the second.

The big man rebounds for Tok. There's still time for something to happen.

But Josh scoots in from behind, flicks the ball away, retrieves it and is fouled with three seconds left.

It's still not over.

"Matthew! Wade!" Dave shouts as the teams line up for Josh's one-and-one. He points at number 21.

"Like white on rice, boys," he yells. "Stick on him like white on rice!"

Josh misses.

The bench groans.

But the ball caroms straight back to Josh. He grabs it and is fouled again.

One second left.

Josh hits the first shot, misses the second. Tok has no time-outs left.

The game's over.

73–70, Fort Yukon wins.

Dave leaps off the bench and punches the air. That's not like him. But this was no typical game. Fort Yukon, for all their effort, had no business winning it. The Tok players and fans still don't believe it. So many things had to happen for Fort Yukon to win. And they did, including that technical foul at the end.

Dave sees the kid who called the time-out, sitting alone on Tok's bench, his head in his hands. He walks over, puts his arm around the boy's shoulder, consoles him, tells him it wasn't his fault.

"Frankly," he says a few minutes later, as his team showers and celebrates in the locker room, "that was their coach's fault. I hate to say it, but it was. He should have made sure his kids knew they had no time-outs left. That's why I always save at least one for the end, for situations just like that."

Dave's wrung out. They all are. It's been a long day—a long two days, for that matter—waiting to play this game. But it was worth it. No matter what happens the rest of the weekend, this trip is a success, as far as Dave is concerned. Beating Tok on their home floor? Beating them twice, in two pressure-packed games like these have been? Nothing could better prepare his boys for what they're going to face at State. This is what it's all about. This is why Dave schedules matchups like these. Just playing well against higher-tier teams is all he asks of his kids. Winning, the way they did tonight, the way they did down at Nenana, well, that just makes it sweeter.

They all sleep like babies that evening. Next morning, at breakfast, they hear even more bad news about Wainwright. The night before, out in the parking lot, after Fort Yukon's win, two of the Wainwright kids got into an argument over who would get the front seat in their van. One of the two, the one who had gone to the clinic that morning, cold-cocked the other one. Somebody called the police. It was a mess. And those boys still have two games left to play this weekend.

Dave can't get over last night's win. It was textbook, the way it played out. Their trapping defense paid off at the end. That's some-thing Paul and Willie and the others don't seem to understand. They can't see that even if the other team has success breaking that defense, it's still taking a toll, because it forces the other team to work so damn hard every trip up the court. Sooner or later the turnovers will come. Last night was a perfect illustration. Tok owned that ball game for the first three quarters. But the price they paid was enormous. They finally wearied. Number 21 missed a couple of shots toward the end that he normally nails. His legs were just a little bit shaky. Fort Yukon, on the other hand, seemed to get stronger. That's where conditioning comes in. The scorebook from last night shows it. Dave's guys scored sixteen points in the first quarter, sixteen in the second, fourteen in the third . . . and twenty-seven in the fourth. They outscored Tok by fifteen in those final eight minutes. What more can Dave say? That says it all.

The day passes in a blur of jerseys and warm-ups. More than 170 boys and girls basketball players from nine villages roam Tok's hallways, wearing their school colors. Skagway's blue and gold. Tok's red, white and blue. Northway's black and red. Anderson's purple and gold. Galena's yellow and blue.

At one point Paul joins the Fort Yukon kids in the bleachers, as they watch Ninilchik's boys rout Anderson. He's got a sheet of paper in his hands—a "stat sheet" from last night's game, based on Paul's play-by-play. Paul's pointing at the numbers, diagnosing them. You guys didn't win that game last night, he's telling the boys. Tok lost it. Dave's watching from a seat down by the court. He just shakes his head. What can he do? Thank god his kids know enough to let that kind of nonsense go in one ear and out the other.

Two thirty, the boys suit up for their three P.M. game against Galena. After yesterday's results, with Tok and Wainwright both losing, this is today's marquee matchup, along with Ninilchik-Skagway on the girls' side. There's always an edgy intensity when Fort Yukon plays Galena. It comes from the coaches. They've faced each other for years. Unlike Dave, Galena's coach, a thirty-something redhead named Orin Wear, came to Alaska as a kid, with his family. He was born in South Bend, Indiana, which always comes up because he looks so much like the Hoosier State's most famous basketball son, Larry Bird. Whenever people first meet Wear, they note the resemblance. He was a big high school star at Delta Junction, just up the highway from here. Played a little junior college ball down in Washington State, then came back to Alaska to teach and to coach. Like Dave, Wear has spent his career out in the villages, establishing himself at Galena, 350 miles downriver from Fort Yukon, near Nulato. He's a good coach, works well with his kids, knows what he's doing. What bugs Dave about him is Wear's demeanor during games, the way he never sits down, paces the sidelines, barks at his players, works the referees, harangues them, complains, tries to push every button he can. Dave's also heard the rumors that Wear takes advantage of the boarding school they've got there in Galena by recruiting top players from other bush schools, inviting them to come board at Galena and play for his team. Wear says he does nothing of the sort. But just this morning, Wear and the girls' coach from Galena were in the coaches' hospitality room talking about getting Norman Carlo to come back from Tanana and about trying to get Tyler Hyslop to come with him.

Still, the guy knows how to coach. Last year, his team whipped Fort Yukon twice, including a forty-point slaughter. The way Galena looks in their warm-ups today, they're expecting to win easily this afternoon. Those two guards of theirs—11 and 22—look beyond confident, beyond cocky, as they watch Fort Yukon's kids shoot their layups. The expression on their faces is one of utter disdain. Dave warns his boys about exactly that as they gather before the tipoff.

"They want to play a macho type of game," he says. "Don't get pulled into that. Don't get pulled into a physical push-and-shove game with these guys. Just do what *you* do."

There's no Josh today. He took off early this morning to drive back to Anchorage—wearing the Player of the Game medal from last night. So Chris gets his start. Wade and Johnny have more talent than Chris, but Dave likes to have them come off the bench, provide that jump-start when it's needed.

It's needed early today. Five minutes into the game, Matt is whistled for a foul. He doesn't like the call, mutters his favorite word under his breath. The ref hears it, whistles him again, this time for a technical. Dave motions to Wade to check in for Matt. Matt heads toward the bench, extremely upset, bends down and slaps the floor on the way.

Another whistle.

Another technical.

Matt's out of the game.

It's all happened so fast, Dave can hardly believe it. The ref comes over, explains. Dave still doesn't quite understand. The first whistle, okay. He's told Matt a hundred times that that mouth of his is going to get him in trouble. But the second one, it seems to Dave that the ref got carried away there. The kid had already gone to the bench. His substitute had already checked in.

Whatever. Matt's out now, not just for this game but for tomorrow's as well, against Wainwright. That's the rule for ejections.

What makes this sting even more is Matt was zeroed in today. He already had a steal and a layup and a three-pointer before he was tossed. Fort Yukon was ahead 7–2 when he got thrown out.

Next thing they know, they're down 9–7. After coming off the bench red-hot last night, Johnny's back in the ozone this afternoon. He air-balls his first shot, misses the next one almost as badly. The quarter ends 13–9, Galena.

The one bright spot is Aaron against Galena's center—the black kid, the freshman. Aaron blocked three shots in the game's first two minutes, letting Galena know nothing inside is going to come easy today. He won't score as many points as his counterpart—the black kid will finish with eleven points in this game, to Aaron's four—but that's not Aaron's role on this team. Rebounding and defense, that's what Dave needs from Aaron. With Matt gone, he'll need even more of it this afternoon.

The game's pace is fierce. Galena plays defense as trenchantly as Fort Yukon. Every point for each team is earned. The lead swings back and forth, never more than three points. Wear has been on his feet since the opening minute, storming up and down the sideline, all the way to half-court at times. Dave can't believe how much the officials let him get away with.

"Set him *down*, ref!" Dave yells at one point. "*He's* calling the game!"

With 1:40 left in the half, Galena leads 23–21 when Johnny brings down the house by catching a Galena guard from behind on a break-away layup and swatting the shot into the bleachers. It never ceases to amuse Dave how fans and players respond to blocked shots and dunks, no matter how meaningless they might be in terms of the score. There's something primal, something visceral, something straight off the street about these kinds of plays that has nothing to do with winning or losing or Xs and Os. The people who put "And 1" on TV have tapped into that something. They know what those blocks and dunks and in-your-face passes are all about. They're about showtime.

Nine seconds to go in the half, Galena leads 26–23, when Wade strips the ball from Galena's point guard and zips a pass upcourt to Justin, who's blocked on the sideline as the clock ticks to five.

Justin whirls and passes to Derek at the top of the key, with the clock down to one.

There's a man right on Derek. No time to put the ball on the floor. No time to fake. No time to do anything but shoot.

He rises straight up, the defender rising right with him.

The shot just makes it over the defender's outstretched fingertips, a high arching spinner. The horn sounds as the ball is still rising, just as the horn sounded for Matt's shot at Nenana, against Su-Valley.

Just like that shot, this one splits the net, another buzzer-beating three-pointer for Fort Yukon.

The score's tied, 26–26.

Today, they've got a locker room to go to at halftime. Dave looks around. Josh isn't here. Matt's in his street clothes. Tim Fields is icing his knee, which he banged badly in the first quarter. They're playing the fifth-ranked 2A team in the state. And they're tied. Not bad, not bad at all. The boys feel the same way. They look more relaxed than they do at most practices. Keep it up, guys, Dave tells them.

They come out, and Aaron continues to make Galena's big kid, the freshman, work hard at both ends of the floor. The kid had three fouls at halftime. Three minutes into the third quarter, he picks up his fourth. Wear takes him out. Without his height in the middle, there's nothing to stop Wade from penetrating, beating Galena's guards and rocketing to the hoop, drawing fouls or scoring, or both.

"All *day*, baby!" Dave hollers as Wade hits a double-pump layup through three Galena players, and then hits another, drawing a foul, putting Fort Yukon ahead, 33–32. "Keep doing that till they show they can stop it."

They can't, not with their big man on the bench. Fort Yukon's trap is bothering Galena. Their guards are coughing it up. Aaron is dominating the middle. He grabs an offensive rebound with two minutes to go in the third and puts it back in for a three-point Fort Yukon lead. Wear is furious, screaming for the refs to call fouls.

With twenty-eight seconds left in the quarter, Wade pulls up and launches a three—a rarity for him. He's got the quirkiest outside shot on the team, even quirkier than Josh's. He cocks the ball beside his right ear, as if he's shaking a Christmas gift to guess what's inside. Then he snaps it from there, the ball spinning sideways like a corkscrew. It's a roll of the dice when Wade shoots from long-range like this—anyone's guess whether the ball will come anywhere close to the hole.

This one goes in, pushing Fort Yukon's lead to six, 38–32.

Galena comes down and misses. Aaron grabs the rebound with seven seconds to go. He passes to Johnny, who crosses half-court and spots Justin at the top of the key.

Justin's already set, got his legs under him, ready to receive the pass. Just like they practiced. Catch, *shoot*. Catch, *shoot*.

He catches the ball as the clock ticks past one second.

He shoots as the quarter expires.

It's good.

Dave has no idea what to say as his kids swarm Justin and come to the bench. Are the stars aligned? He's had teams go through their entire schedule without making one buzzer-beating three-point shot like that. This team's had four already this season—two this afternoon.

Four minutes ago Fort Yukon was down 30–32. Now they're up 41–32. An eleven-point run to close out the quarter.

It's the Derek-and-Wade show in the fourth. Galena's center is back in the game, but it makes little difference. Wade is making mincemeat of Galena's guards, and Derek is on fire at the offensive end, feasting on open jump shots as the Hawks' defenders are a step too late to stop him. He scores Fort Yukon's final nine points of the game, shutting the lid on a 56–44 win. It's all Wear can do to shake Dave's hand when it's over. He was not ready for this. Neither were his boys. They were sure they'd be playing Skagway tomorrow for the tournament title.

Instead, Fort Yukon blitzes depleted Wainwright the next morning, 81–36, to emerge as the Tok Round-Robin's only unbeaten boys' team. Wade is selected Player of the Game, as he was against Galena. He doesn't say much, but he packs those two medals with care in his bag— a bag he didn't use once last season because of his grades.

The Eagles are 17–3 now. They could just about fly home to Fort Yukon from here, without an airplane.

"Nice weekend, guys," Dave tells them as they pack up and pull out of the snow-packed church parking lot. "Nice weekend."

Now it's back home for Tanana. And then on to Fairbanks, where the real season begins, with the Regionals.

SIXTEEN

Payback

ALL WINTER, THE issue of drilling for oil in Alaska—in ANWR and right here in the Flats—has been heating up. This week, the first week of March, it's coming to a boil. Five U.S. senators, all Republicans, are flying in tomorrow from Washington, D.C., to visit the North Slope and gather more "facts" to inform their debate. Hundreds of protesters are massing in Anchorage to mock this junket, to expose it as nothing but a façade, masking the foregone conclusion that this administration is going to start drilling in ANWR, and soon. The protesters point out that the Senate debate may not even take place; a parliamentary move by the Republicans may bypass any discussion on the floor and simply move the ANWR bill straight to a vote.

Here in the bush, among Alaska's Natives, the debate is raging, setting tribe against tribe, villager against villager, even family members against one another. For them, the issue is simple, clear-cut. All that talk down in Washington and in the national media about America's energy needs, about national security, about homeland defense is beside the point, as far as they're concerned. For them, this is personal. It's about the land that their people have always lived on, and whether that land is for sale. Everything else is just noise.

There's no question they're talking about a lot of money here. Estimates are that if drilling in ANWR gets the green light, about $1.2 billion in lease payments and royalties will begin flowing into Alaskans' pockets within the next two years. Exactly how much of that money would flow into whose pockets is another question. How much would go to Natives is another question beyond that. How much would go to *which* Natives is yet another question altogether. To most villagers—even to many who support this drilling—it feels like it's 1970 all over again, with wads of cash being waved in their faces, but with little assurance that they won't somehow get screwed, not just by the whites but by their own leaders, the corrupt ones, the ones Dacho Alexander's dad, Clarence, called the "Athabascan mafia" back when he was chief.

To those Natives opposed to the drilling, it doesn't matter how much money the tribes might receive, or who might receive it. The land is what matters, they say, and they can't give it up. To Woodie Salmon, the Yukon Flats state representative—the brother of Paul Shewfelt's old Fort Yukon basketball teammate, Willie—this is the same old story, one that goes all the way back to the white man's arrival here in the Arctic. The Gwich'in lived on this land for twelve thousand years before the white man showed up, says Salmon, and they will be here for twelve thousand more, "unless you people kill us."

"We used to be the real Alaskans, the real true Alaskans," he says. "Now we've been invaded by this—I don't know—it seems like the devil or something."

Salmon will speak those exact words this week on the floor of the statehouse in Juneau, and he'll wind up apologizing the next day after newspapers around the state trumpet his "devil" comment.

But no one's about to apologize here in Fort Yukon. Chief Adlai Alexander and the Tribal Council are preparing for a village meeting tomorrow afternoon with representatives from the Doyon Corporation and the federal government. Tribal leaders are determined to do all they can to block this land swap. They've mobilized everyone in the village who can possibly be at this meeting to show up.

Meanwhile, Dave and the boys gather at the gym for their Monday practice. The sun is still up when they begin arriving just before five. It will still be up when practice is over an hour and a half later. The village is gaining more sunlight each day. Only last week, it was dark out when practice ended. The week before that, it was dark out when practice began. Everything is accelerating now: the daylight, the coming of spring, the basketball season itself. It's hard to believe they've played twenty games since the middle of January. That opening home stand against

Anderson seems like ages ago. It's hard to believe the regular season will wind up this week, with Tanana coming to town.

As the boys drift in, Dave is still savoring the weekend, what he calls "the best three games back-to-back that any of my teams have ever played." The comeback against Tok, after trailing by twelve at the start of the fourth quarter—that took guts. Guts and faith. Beating Galena without Josh or Matt, and with Tim Fields limping like a lame race-horse—that was a team win. That displayed depth. It's amazing to Dave how much depth this team has, how the players keep emerging. When the season began, he knew he could count on Matt and Aaron and Tim. Everyone else was a question mark. Josh and Derek were completely unknown quantities. There was no way to know that Johnny, who hardly played at all last year, would blossom as the team's best pure offensive player, even better than Matt. Wade's emergence has been in the class-room, where he's kept himself eligible, something he was unable to do last year. Then there's Justin, who stepped up this weekend with those clutch shots against Tok and Galena, and went for a game-high, career-best twenty-one points against Wainwright on Saturday. That makes seven different high scorers Dave's had this season. Amazing. The Tanana boys watched those three games in Tok and had to wonder how in the world they ever beat this team. That was a question everyone was asking Dave at the tournament: How did Tanana beat you guys?

Dave doesn't intend to let it happen again this weekend. One thing that's bothering him is Matt's continued hot-and-cold play. He's leading the team in scoring, as expected, averaging more than sixteen points a game. He had those dream performances at the NIT. He was high scorer in last Thursday's Tok game, with twenty. But he continues to look downright awful at times, making senseless passes and taking ill-advised shots. And his temper seems to have gotten worse as the season's progressed. That's not what Dave expects from a senior, a team captain. He expects maturity, leadership, steadiness. Most of the time, Matt provides all three. But sometimes he slips.

There's some kind of pressure eating at Matt, Dave can see that. Some of it's got to be coming from home. Everything he does is compared to Ryan or John. Matt's got the upper hand this week, after beating Galena.

Neither Ryan nor John ever beat a Galena team. But the constant comparisons have to weigh on him. It's as if he's playing against seven opponents each time he steps on the floor: the five players on the other team plus the specters of Ryan and John.

Not to mention the presence of Paul. Dave knows it's got to be messing with Matt's head, how Paul is constantly waving his "stat sheets" in Matt's face, pointing out how badly Matt and his teammates are playing. Thank god it looks like they may not see Paul on any more road trips this season. After broadcasting those first two days last weekend, Paul missed both the girls' and the boys' games on Saturday. Word is he went out Friday night to some party in Tanacross, just up the highway from Tok, stayed well past midnight, drinking and singing karaoke, then simply blew off both broadcasts the next day. As a matter of fact, according to Jay Cadzow, Paul flew back to Fort Yukon a day early, stepping off the plane at the airstrip on Saturday night just as the girls were taking the court down in Tok for their last game of the weekend.

Word's gotten around about Paul going AWOL. It doesn't look like he'll be getting another red cent from anyone in the village. Which is okay with Dave. If the team makes it to State, they'll use that same freelance broadcaster they had down at Nikolaevsk. That's their focus now—getting to State. That's what Dave wants to talk to the boys about this evening.

"Every game from this point on," he says, "you have to treat as if it's the last game of the season. There can't be any letdowns, no off nights, not one. You have an off night at Regionals, we go into the loser's bracket, and the loser's bracket is hell. You have an off night at State, and the season is over."

The only player missing from practice is Josh. He's still down in Fairbanks, getting his dogs settled after finishing ninth in the Junior Iditarod—ninth out of twenty-one mushers. The winner was a sixteen-year-old girl from Nome, which might be surprising to someone unfamiliar with the world of competitive dogsled racing but is nothing new to anyone who follows the sport. Like jockeys in horse racing, women have an advantage in mushing because of their lighter weight and lower center of gravity compared to men. They've shown they can match any man in terms of the skills and the savvy of driving. The sport's most legendary musher is an Alaskan named Susan Butcher, who established herself as the Lance Armstrong of the sport in the late 1980s by winning the Iditarod three years in a row, a record that still stands. The year before she began that streak, another woman—Libby Riddles—was the winner. A popular bumper sticker around the state reads: ALASKA, WHERE MEN ARE MEN AND WOMEN WIN THE IDITAROD.

Dave wraps up the practice with a warning about not letting the schoolwork slip this week. It's the stretch run now, he tells the boys. If they can all stay eligible for just this one more week—and he looks straight at Wade when he says this—they'll be good to go for their final road trip of the year, the postseason.

Tuesday is clear, bright, zero degrees by midafternoon as the Native Village parking lot fills with snowmachines and pickups, all come for the meeting about the land swap. Three dozen townspeople are already inside, fixing cups of coffee and taking a seat in the Tribal Council's meeting room. Six U.S. Fish and Wildlife employees in their khaki and dark-chocolate uniforms are roaming the room, straightening stacks of stapled handouts and glossy brochures, focusing the lens on a slide projector, making sure everyone knows there are two trays of free cookies back by the door.

Three on the dot, the lights are shut off and a PowerPoint presentation begins. Pristine images of Yukon Flats wildlife and woodlands flash on the screen as one of the uniformed staffers provides the narration. He refers to "impacted acreage" and drilling "footprints," outlining the deal the federal government would like to make with Doyon. The villagers already know the details. This "swap" has been in the works for a long time. It's been written about in the papers. There have been public meetings just like this in other Interior villages. Only a handful of Doyon's fourteen thousand shareholders live up here in the bush, compared to the thousands who live in Fairbanks or Anchorage. The vast majority of those nonvillage Natives support this agreement. The deadline for the final decision is next month, but most of the Natives out here in the bush believe it's already a done deal. That's why more of them aren't here today. To them, this is nothing but a dog-and-pony show staged by the government and Doyon for the sake of appearance, to pretend they actually care what the people of Fort Yukon have to say.

A Doyon corporate spokesman is here, flew up this morning from Fairbanks along with the Fish and Wildlife team. He's smooth, dressed down in a flannel shirt and white Arctic "bunny boots," trying his best to fit in. He's laid-back, conversational. He leans on a table as he speaks. He pooh-poohs the ramifications of this plan, says it does nothing more than "rearrange" ownership of the land. "Kind of moving some pieces around on the board" is how he puts it. He assures the audience that "local access to traditional activities will be preserved." He reminds everyone of the bottom line, of the gas that possibly lies beneath these icy forests and streams. "We want to maximize dividend payments to you," he says.

The villagers listen politely, but they're starting to fidget. They can hardly believe it when one of the Fish and Wildlife staffers explains his agency's part in this agreement. "It doesn't mean we support development," he says. "Our purpose is to *confine* it."

Eyes roll at that one. None of the villagers have come here today believing that anything they have to say could possibly change the minds of these people. Nonetheless, they've come—some with prepared statements—to put their words on the record, to declare their feelings, if for no other reason than to show that the people of Fort Yukon, the Gwich'in, are not fools. They may be powerless in the face of these forces, they may be unable to stop this, as they've been unable to stop so much that has gone before, but they are not fools.

Adlai Alexander, the chief, is the first to stand and speak. He's been to the North Slope, he says. He's seen what he calls "the yellow sky" above wellheads. He knows what emissions from drilling can do.

"Where is it gonna' go?" he says, facing his friends and neighbors. "It's gonna' go into the land, the water, the trees, the animals. It's pretty scary."

He points to a map on the screen showing proposed drilling sites.

"I walk that valley in snowshoes," he continues, pointing to a section around Birch Creek. "I've got a trapline going right through that area, and I'm afraid that land's gonna' go to hell, literally.

"I'm thinking thirty years down the road. What are *those* folks gonna' do? It's our future generations that are gonna' be depending on what we decide here."

That's the message of almost everyone in this room, everyone from Fort Yukon.

"Shame on you," one of them says to the man from Doyon, pointing out that not one of the corporation's seven board members who will actually vote on this deal next month even bothered to show up today, that they sent a mouthpiece like him instead.

"We've gotten lied to, run over for years by you people," says someone else. "Where have you been all these years? Why haven't you helped us? Why haven't you promoted *our* interests? This is why you were *created* thirty years ago, to act in our name, to help villages like this one that are still living in third-world conditions today."

The Doyon spokesman has taken a seat. His elbows are on his knees. His head's down. He's running his hands through his hair.

Paul Shewfelt stands and spins off a riff about the *Beverly Hillbillies* and Jed Clampett and bubbling crude coming up through the ground. It's a little disjointed, but everyone gets the point.

Craig Fleener rises and speaks. As the director of the Council of Athabascan Tribal Governments, he represents not just Fort Yukon, but the interests of Native villagers throughout Interior Alaska. He's lean, dark-haired, strong-jawed, about forty. He grew up in this village. He lives here, with his wife, Charlotte, and their kids. He makes the point right up front that he is not necessarily opposed to all drilling.

"I think it would be hypocritical of me, who uses a snowmachine, drives a car, operates a chain saw, sits under lights in my house, enjoys the warmness of this room, wears clothes that were all produced through oil and gas—I think personally it would be hypocritical for me to say I'm one hundred percent against oil and gas development.

"What I can't *stand*," he says, "is the idea of Native people losing any more of our land."

That's the issue here, he maintains. Not money, or oil, but land. Not what the land might be worth in terms of any other commodity, but what the land *is*, in and of itself, and what it has always meant to the people who live on it.

"*You* own what we used to have," he says, gazing at the man from Doyon. "The state of Alaska owns what we used to have. There's a lot of folks that own what we used to have. And now we have nothing, nothing except these last vestiges of Native-owned land in the form of corporations."

He pauses, turns back to his fellow villagers.

"Now, I don't like the idea of everybody picking on Doyon too much, because that's what they're there for, to make money for their shareholders, which includes us. If we don't like what Doyon's doing, then we ought to oppose the structure of Doyon, and we ought to oppose the Alaska Native Claims Settlement Act in its entirety and try to fight that. These guys are just doing what they're supposed to do. They're supposed to make money. That's their job. So I'm not going to get on their case.

"I'm more mad at the federal government." He turns to the Fish and Wildlife employees. "Because I think the federal government has a responsibility to make sure that Native people don't get screwed.

"This is the closest thing to sovereign Indian territory that exists anymore," he says. "Any of this land that is lost is a total travesty, if you ask me. And I think it's incumbent upon the federal government to make sure that they fulfill their responsibility to the Tribe to protect our ownership of this land. The federal government should be doing all it can to see that our land stays in our hands. They are supposed to represent us, to protect our land for us. Instead, they're 'protecting' our land in the interests of the U.S. government, not in *our* interests."

Finally, a small elderly man in the front row stands, with the help of a cane. He's wearing a tattered red-and-black-checked wool jacket torn at the elbow, and dark blue workpants tucked into a pair of thick black rubber boots. His gray hair is bristly, cropped close to his head. He has on a pair of eyeglasses.

"My name is Jonathan Solomon," he says. "I come from Fort Yukon, Alaska."

He was chief of this tribe thirty-five years ago, when the ANCSA agreement was originally drafted. He was a signatory to that agreement. He sat at the table with the state's Native leaders back then, facing the federal and state government negotiators who wanted so badly to make a deal for the pipeline to go through. He was among the architects of the Native corporations—including Doyon—that were created to represent the business interests of tribes throughout Alaska. In the decades since, he has watched those corporations disappoint and betray the interests of the people they are supposed to represent. It's happening again today, he says.

"I was there," he says of the ANCSA discussions. "Never was oil and gas development in the Yukon Flats mentioned at all. *Never.*"

He leans on his cane with one hand, raises the other to point a wrinkled finger at the corporate spokesman and faces the room.

"These guys are working for Doyon," he says. "They don't give a shit about you as long as they get paid. As long as they get their thousand-dollar-a-day meeting fee in their pocket, they don't give a *shit* about you. And they never will."

The room breaks out in applause. The man from Doyon will gather himself, finish his spiel. The Fish and Wildlife employees will finish their slideshow. But the meeting, for all intents and purposes, is over.

By the next day, the whole village has heard about Chief Jonathan dressing down that man from Doyon. Not that anything will come of it. There was nothing in today's newspaper about the meeting. No reporters were there. To the world beyond Fort Yukon, it's as if it never happened.

Dave's big concern at the moment is Wade—Wade and his grades. Matt, Josh and Derek all have 3.0 averages. The rest of the team is rock solid. But Wade's carrying three Ds at the moment, and they're not high Ds. If he slips in any one of his classes, he's out when the team leaves next week for the Regional tourney in Fairbanks. Which means he's out as well for State.

Dave tells the kids at Wednesday's practice that their objective right now is to sweep Tanana this weekend, which will earn Fort Yukon the number one seeding at the Regionals, giving them a bye in that tournament's opening round.

Thursday, the boys learn that they're back at the top spot in the state 1A rankings, after their sweep down in Tok. They see that Galena has dropped out of the 2A top five. They also see that the top-ranked 2A team is Cook Inlet Academy, unbeaten at 18–0. Josh says if Fort Yukon wins State, they ought to challenge those Cook Inlet boys, show them the Eagles have got more than they showed down at Nikolaevsk.

The business at hand, however, is Tanana. Dave ran the team especially hard Wednesday night—so hard that Wade has to sit out Thursday's practice with shin splints. He's ready on Friday, though. They all are. One good thing about that loss at Tanana is the boys seem relentlessly intense as they dress for their final home stand of the season. It's Justin's birthday today, a fact the standing-room-only crowd acknowledged by serenading him when he walked into the gym. It's also the final home stand of Matt's career, and Josh's as well. Dave points this out as he gathers the boys in the locker room before they take the court.

"For a couple of you," he says, "this is the last time you'll play in this gym in an Eagles uniform. I want you to make it a weekend you're proud of. I want you to give those people out there and yourself something to remember you by. Play it like it's Su-Valley, boys. Play it like it's Tok. Play it like it's Galena."

The gym explodes as the team bursts out the door. More than a hundred kids and adults are on the floor, forming a corridor through which the boys sprint. "Thunderstruck," as always, blasts from the speakers. Tanana, wearing their black road uniforms, looks lost in a sea of Fort Yukon blue and white.

Up in the wet section, everyone's standing, Jack leading the cheers. Bobby Solomon—Paul's old teammate, Georgie's brother—sips on a whiskey-and-Coke and expansively points toward the crowd.

"See this?" he shouts. "It was like this every night back when we played here. Every *night*."

He turns and points toward the boys.

"This is *history* here tonight," he says. "The last home stand of the first Fort Yukon team to win the state championship. That's what I think; these guys are going to go all the way."

Doc is especially fired up this evening. He asks the crowd to join him in honoring the team's two seniors, Matt and Josh, introducing them last, each to a standing ovation.

…n it's game time.

…on wins the tip, and Tim Fields wastes no time putting Fort Yukon …he board, faking Tyler Hyslop into the air and swishing an eight-…oter from inside the key. A Tanana miss, and Justin comes down and nails a three from the left corner.

Just like that, it's 5–0, Fort Yukon.

Dave likes what he sees. They're primed. Tim, in particular, is playing as if this is *his* last home stand. He slides outside, dumps a pass in to Aaron, takes a quick return pass and buries a three. Two possessions later, he does it again, banging a long three from the right side to make it 15–4. Tanana calls time-out and Tim is pummeled by backslaps as he comes to the bench. He's got eight points in less than four minutes. Not bad.

Meanwhile, Tanana looks like they're lost. It doesn't help that Norman's limping, wearing a heavy brace on his left ankle. He's already air-balled two shots. It doesn't look like he'll be much of a factor tonight. As for Tyler, he's got two white jerseys on him wherever he goes. He's forcing his shots and his passes, trying to carry his team by himself, playing right into Fort Yukon's hands.

Two minutes left in the first quarter, there's a scramble under the Tanana basket. Justin comes up with the ball, and both teams burst the other way. All except Tim. He's down, writhing in pain and clutching his right knee. A hush falls over the gym. The only sound is Paul's voice, telling the radio audience what's going on.

It takes two of the boys to help the big guy up and shoulder him back to the bench. He winces just putting the slightest weight on that leg. He's out for tonight. No doubt he's out for tomorrow as well. Anything beyond that is anyone's guess. No one's more disappointed than Tim, except possibly his dad. Willie's shot chart will show that his son was on his way to a career game tonight. Now it looks like he might be out for the season.

Derek checks in. A quick five-point run by Tanana quiets the crowd, but the boys regain their balance, closing the quarter with a layup by Matt and a putback by Aaron for a 19–11 lead.

Wade checks in to start the second quarter and ignites three rapid scores with his passing and steals: a three-pointer by Justin, a layup by Matt and an unlikely three-pointer by Wade himself, another one of those spinning corkscrews off his right ear. The score's 27–11 with four minutes left in the half when Norman goes down, holding his ankle. Like Tim, he needs help from his teammates to get to the bench.

"I think that's the ball game," says Dave. "I think that's it."

He's right. It's a romp the rest of the way. Aaron gets a rise out of the crowd by blocking a Tyler layup at the rim. Justin is zeroed in once again, sinking four threes for the night. The defense is stifling, holding Tanana to six second-period points. The reserves—Zach and Tim Woods, Wes and Kyle and Bruce—play most of the fourth quarter. The final is 65–44. As both teams head to the locker room, Tyler stays on the court, strips off his jersey and puts on his show once again, dunking for an audience of Fort Yukon children.

The big news the next day is not the boys' win, but what happened after the game. It seems that three Tanana girls slipped out of the gym during the second half. Two were freshmen. One just got back from rehab at a clinic for teens called Raven's Way, down near Sitka. The girls were "looking to party," according to some of Dave's boys, who were over at Chris's cabin when two of them showed up there. The girls had already found something to drink, somewhere in town. A search party of adults, led by Georgie, found them close to midnight and drove them back to the vo-tech center.

Doc is furious. He called a meeting of both schools' coaches this morning, was ready to suspend Matt, who gave the girls a ride sometime during the evening. Matt insists the girls waved him down by the side of the road, that he did nothing but give them a short lift. Anyone else would have done the same, he says. It was cold out there last night.

Matt winds up off the hook. As for the girls, they were flown back to Tanana this afternoon. Dave has no doubt he's going to hear about this from his sister-in-law and from Buzzy at the next School Advisory Committee meeting. He can't wait to get tonight's game out of the way, get these boys out of town next week, get away from all this.

Sure enough, his kids come out for the Saturday night rematch sluggish, lethargic. They open a quick lead, then sleepwalk the rest of the way, letting Tanana stay just close enough for the crowd to be worried. They win by nine, 60–51, but the feeling is anticlimactic, both among the fans and the team. Last night's game was the one that really wrapped up the season. Tonight's was a coda.

Now it's time for the second season to begin, the one they've been aiming toward all year.

Regionals.

Then State.

PART THREE
Postseason

SEVENTEEN
Regionals

DAVE WAS WRONG about his sister-in-law and Buzzy. The School Advisory Committee met Tuesday night, but the episode with the Tanana girls was not even mentioned. The discussion focused completely on what to do about the school board's decision to cut Fort Yukon's funding. With the entire activities budget threatened—not just the money for basketball—everyone's on the same side, at least for the moment. They talked about possibly hiring a lawyer, a big-name attorney, someone who could draw some attention, put this case under the media spotlight, thrust it into the court of public opinion. The meeting ended with a decision to call a town forum, get the whole village mobilized, let the board see that the people of Fort Yukon are not going to take this lying down. They've scheduled the forum for the week after the State Tournament. Doc has agreed to run it.

Dave's got everything set for the trip down to Regionals. It's always a bigger production than any regular-season road trip, and more expensive—especially this year, with fourteen boys going. Doc brought the word to Tuesday's practice: Everyone's eligible, even Wade. Dave's booked a motel suite in Fairbanks, an end-of-the-year treat for the kids. The girls get one, too. Both teams have been told to pack and prepare to be gone for two weeks. If either—or both—win Regionals, they'll drive directly to Anchorage.

Fort Yukon has never brought this many players before. Alaska's state high school athletic association rules limit each team's postseason roster to twelve names. That means two of Dave's boys won't be allowed to suit up. They're permitted to travel with the team, sit on the bench, but that's as close as they'll come to playing. Dave's decided to let the boys decide for themselves who those two players will be. Wednesday night's practice—the last practice before they fly out for the last time this year— ends with a vote on which two will not dress. The boys each write two names on a slip of paper and hand it to Dave. Somebody mentions "Survivor." Dave takes a few minutes to tally the votes. It's a clear-cut decision: Kyle and Zach won't be bringing their uniforms. Tim Fields's bum knee may keep him from playing at all, but if there's even a chance he can recover, the boys want him out there. He won't have healed by this weekend, but if they make it to State, he may well be ready by then. They all want to keep that option open.

Thursday morning, as the team arrives at the airport, gusts of wind are whipping the runway, driving the snow into chest-high drifts. The wind is unseasonably warm for this early in March, pushing the temperature to ten above zero. These are vestiges of the fabled Chinooks, swirling up from the Pacific Northwest. The word "Chinook" means "snow eater" in the language of the Chinook Natives who inhabit the lower Columbia River valley in Oregon, where warm temperature inversions often collide with frigid Arctic air masses over the Rockies, creating dry, ovenlike winds that sweep down to the lowlands, raising temperatures as much as seventy degrees in a matter of hours. After the icy stillness that pervades the Interior for most of the winter, these winds are yet another sign that spring is approaching.

It's forty-three-above when the plane lands in Fairbanks. Snowmelt is dripping off the terminal roof. The tarmac is slushy. Organizers of the city's annual Winter Carnival, which kicked off this week, are in a panic—the display of ice sculptures in a park near downtown is in danger of melting. The Iditarod, which began last week down in Wasilla, is a mess. Rain and wet snow have slowed the race to a crawl. Mushers are telling reporters it's more like swimming than sledding. Their poor dogs are roasting in their thick coats of winter fur.

The first thing the boys do is grab a newspaper, tear it open to see this week's rankings. Fort Yukon is still number one. But the rest of the top five are schools that haven't been listed all season: Newhalen, Shishmaref, Savoonga, Russian Mission. The only one Dave's even heard of is Shishmaref. They won the state title three years ago. Two of the teams—Newhalen and Russian Mission—have already won their Regional tournaments, which were played last weekend. By this Saturday night, all eight State slots will be filled.

After a stop at Fred Meyer for groceries, Dave drives the team to their motel. It's a sweet setup, with a kitchen, a living room large enough to sleep half a dozen, and a bedroom big enough to take care of the rest. The boys are delighted to find that the Tanana girls are staying in the same building. Their room is one floor below Fort Yukon's. Dave's going to have to keep his eye on that.

A quick lunch, then it's over to the University of Alaska–Fairbanks' fieldhouse—by far the largest gymnasium Fort Yukon has set foot in this season. The boys who haven't been here before marvel at the spacious complex: the Olympic-sized swimming pool, the handball and racquet-ball courts, the weight rooms, the indoor shooting range where the six-time defending NCAA champion UAF Nanooks rifle team practices. The gym itself looks enormous. It seats 2,700—thirteen times the capacity of Fort Yukon's. The floor—a regulation-length ninety-four feet—looks like it goes on forever. Fort Yukon's home court is almost ten feet shorter. It will be a good test the next three days, getting used to running on a floor this long. The floor at UA–Anchorage, where the State Tournament will be played, is the same length.

The afternoon's "play-in" game between Nulato and Huslia has already begun. The winner gets Fort Yukon tonight. Huslia, with its mixture of girls and boys, has its third boy back, the one who didn't suit up when the Hustlers played Fort Yukon last month at Tanana. Nulato looks terrible. Disorganized. Sloppy. Huslia, with its girls contributing a couple of three-pointers, drops the disheveled Wolves into the loser's bracket. The Hustlers are ecstatic, leaping around the floor and hugging one another. This win makes their season, no matter what happens the rest of the weekend.

Next comes Allakaket-Tanana. Norman is in a hot-temper mode, screaming at the refs, cursing, flinging his headband, drawing an early technical and spending much of the first half on the bench. Tyler is unable to carry his team by himself. Allakaket's freshman guard—the one with the do-rag—is woofing for the crowd, showboating after every score, tearing his jersey off during time-outs and whirling it in the air. Dave can't believe how out of control this kid is. The entire game is out of control, both teams racing up and down the court in a series of mad dashes. It's playground ball at its rawest, with Allakaket having the upper hand. The long floor is perfectly suited to that Allakaket guard's speed. He's simply outrunning Tanana, releasing whenever the Wolves take a shot, breaking long for wide-open layups. Dave points this out to his boys, in case they're not paying attention.

By the time the Fort Yukon girls beat the Tanana girls in overtime in their first-round game, the gym's lower level has filled for the evening's finale: Dave's boys against Huslia. The crowd is almost entirely Native, from the outlying villages and from Fairbanks. Jackets and T-shirts bearing the Doyon Corporation logo are everywhere. Most of the men in the stands will be playing next week on this court in their own tournament, the North American games, which pits the best of the Interior's Native adult teams against one another. Zach's and Derek's dad, Jerry Carroll, is a perennial star in that tournament. But he won't be there this year, not if Fort Yukon wins this weekend. He's here tonight, cheering his sons on, and he'll be in Anchorage next week if Fort Yukon makes it that far.

There's a good-sized contingent of Eagle fans who have flown down to cheer for the kids. The hard core are all here: Trader Dan, Georgie and her husband and children, the Solomons, the Fleeners, the Cadzows, the McCarty sisters, the Rozells. Diane is here and will travel with Dave and the boys on to Anchorage, if they win this weekend. Doc is handling the PA system, getting a kick out of introducing the teams for each game. The crowd loves his thick Okie accent, the way he hams it up for the "Tanana *Wooooooooooolves*" and the "*Hoooooooooslia* Hustlers." Paul's up in the top section, hooked to his headset. Again, Jack's not here. Neither are Ryan or John.

Any drama this game might have had is gone by the first quarter, which ends 17–0, Fort Yukon. Dave can't blame his boys for losing their focus the rest of the way. They're more excited about getting back to the motel and hooking up with the Tanana girls. Halftime, it's 32–6. The subs play the rest of the way. The final is 48–18.

That night, Dave drives the team to Fairbanks's lone cineplex, where the boys join the Tanana girls to take in the horror film *Boogeyman*. Then it's back to the motel, where Dave camps by the door to ensure against any middle-of-the-night excursions.

Friday, they watch the Nulato girls, now ranked fourth in the state, easily beat the Fort Yukon girls, dropping them into the loser's bracket. Then, all the players from all eight teams in the tournament come down on the court, girls at one basket and boys at the other. They form two long lines, single-file, for an event the tournament organizers stage each year: the Regional Free Throw Contest. The rules are simple. Each player, in order, shoots a free throw. Those who make it go back to the end of the line and move forward. Those who miss go back to the bleachers. It continues like this until only one shooter's left standing.

Forty players form the boys' line. Within minutes, the number's been whittled to four, including two from Fort Yukon: Justin and Johnny. Two misses later, only Justin and Johnny remain. They've each made ten shots apiece. Justin's eleventh caroms off the back of the rim. Johnny, without blinking, steps up and swishes his. "Ice," says Dave. The boys are all over Johnny. He's embarrassed, half-smiling, blushing the same way he did when that Allakaket girl cornered him in that classroom.

By the time the team suits up for the evening's winner's bracket final against Allakaket—after watching the Tanana boys eliminate Nulato—the bleachers are filled with Fort Yukon fans waving blue-and-white feathered boas. "We Will Rock You" booms from the sound system. Dave knows Allakaket is ready to run, and so are his kids. His biggest concern, with the length of this floor, is whether the refs will be able to keep up. "They better be in shape," he says, looking over at the three officials as his team shoots their layups.

"Okay, guys," he says as the boys gather beside the bench before taking the court. "Good decisions now."

He glances over at Allakaket's number 12, the kid with the speed and the attitude. And number 15, their captain, Chris Moses—he went for thirty in the Blazers' first-round win over Tanana.

"I don't want either one of those two kids getting off, understand?" he says.

He turns to Josh.

"I want you to get under fifteen's shirt," he says. "Don't foul him. Just get under his shirt. He has to take that funny step of his before each move. If you're under his shirt, he can't *take* that step."

Dave's right about that step. It's an odd little splay-legged, knock-kneed fake that Moses makes each time before putting the ball on the floor. He does it the first time he touches it tonight, twenty seconds into the game, and blows past Josh and Aaron for the night's opening score.

After Josh puts Fort Yukon on the board with a three from the wing, Moses answers with a three of his own. Number 12 then sneaks down-court twice on Fort Yukon shots, hauling in two long passes for layups, one of which he makes, the other on which he is fouled. Three minutes in, the score is 8–3, Allakaket. Dave is up, and he's all over Justin.

"Twelve is *releasing*," he yells. "You've got to go *with* him!"

Derek, starting in place of Tim Fields, sinks a three, but Moses answers again with one of his own. Dave can't complain about his kids' defense. They're all over Allakaket. And Allakaket is all over them—literally. The referees are calling the game loose, and the Blazers are taking advantage, shoving and grabbing without getting whistled. It looks to Dave more like an alley fight than a basketball game. He calls time-out. As his kids come to the bench, he motions to one of the refs.

"They're getting *pounded* out there," he says.

Before the official can answer, number 12 steps between them, turning to Dave.

"Sit *down*," sneers the kid, putting his face right in Dave's before moving on to his bench.

Dave doesn't blink. Doesn't utter a word. Neither does the ref, which both surprises and disappoints Dave. A player chiding the other team's coach, a high school student showing such thuggish disrespect for an adult—there should be absolutely no tolerance for such behavior, not in a setting like this, not with these kids representing their schools, their communities, their tribes. That's how Dave feels, but he doesn't share those feelings. Not right now. There's no point. If the ref is going to let something like that go, so be it. They've got a game to win here.

"Okay, guys," he says, huddling his players. "I know you're getting hammered out there. You can't let it get to you. Just play your game."

Moses scores off the time-out to make it 13–6, Allakaket. The Blazer fans are going ballistic. Dave has been here before. It happened three years ago, when his kids came into the Regional seeded first and lost the opening game to Cornerstone Christian. They had to battle back through the loser's bracket, playing five games in three days, including two more against Cornerstone, in order to survive and move on to State. They did it, but it was hell. It was exhausting. He doesn't want that to happen again.

Wade steals and scores to make it 13–8.

Matt hits a short running bank shot to make it 13–10.

Wade scores again off a steal.

Josh rebounds and scores on the follow to put Fort Yukon ahead, 14–13.

Twelve seconds left in the quarter, Wade takes a pass in front of the Allakaket bench, cocks the ball by his ear, and lets fly a long spinner from beyond the arc.

Swish.

An eleven-point run to close out the quarter. Fort Yukon leads, 17–13. The blue-and-white boas are twirling now.

"That's better, boys, much better," says Dave. "Wade, you helped us a lot. Thank you."

He looks up at the scoreboard, then back at his boys.

"Now, you guys need to look around more on defense, keep track of where everybody is. We're losing people, and we can't do that. Especially Moses. You can't lose him, because he'll disappear. He knows how to move without the ball. He's very good at getting to where he can hurt us if we let him move like that."

He taps Johnny's shoulder, tells him to check into the game.

"Okay guys," he says. "Way to suck it up. Let's put the hammer down now."

Allakaket inbounds to Moses, who turns, drives and is fouled by Derek. Six fouls on Fort Yukon, to one on Allakaket. One more foul, and the Blazers will be shooting bonus free throws for the rest of the half.

Moses makes one out of two.

Justin pushes the ball upcourt, zips it to Johnny on the right wing.

"Big shot?" says Dave, rising out of his seat.

Johnny cradles the pass and shoots in one motion, splitting the net.

"*Big* shot!" says Dave, flopping back in his chair.

Derek follows with a short bank and a long three.

24–16, Fort Yukon.

Number 12 breaks away for a cherry, but his teammates are dragging.

"They're tired," says Dave.

All but number 12. He releases yet again on a Fort Yukon miss, hauling in a long baseball pass from Moses to close it to 24–20. He dances back upcourt, tugging at his jersey the way the NBA players do, showing his number to the Fort Yukon crowd.

"*Justin!*" Dave yells.

Justin nods, purses his lips, slaps the floor. He won't let that happen again.

Derek scores on a soft jumper, after four brisk passes around the perimeter.

"I *like* it," Dave says. Catch, pass. Catch, pass. Catch, pass.

Matt nails a long three from the left corner.

29–20 with two minutes to go in the half.

Matt makes a steal, veers off to the side, sets up the offense. Four rapid passes and Aaron winds up with the shot, banking in an eleven-footer from the right side.

31–20.

But 12 is not finished. He hits a short bank of his own with one minute left, then follows with a long three to close out the half.

Fort Yukon leads 31–25 as Dave and his kids head to the locker room. It's the most spacious such room they've been in all season. Dave's voice echoes off the long rows of metal lockers as his guys sit on the floor and the bench. The refs are here, too, toweling off in a corner, catching their breath.

"Listen," says Dave. "You weathered their best shot. They're going to suck it up here at the half and come out with their *last* best shot.

They only have so much left. We're going to counter that by subbing. They've got no answer for that.

"Understand?"

They understand.

Both teams trade baskets to open the half, before number 12 scores on an eight-foot jumper to cut the gap to three, 32–29.

"Here comes their run," says Dave. He calls time-out and inserts Wade and Johnny. There's a flurry of steals by both teams but no scores. Finally, Justin breaks the ice with a three from the top of the key. Allakaket answers with a two-pointer. Derek responds with a follow of a short Aaron miss. Number 12's backcourt mate then hits a three-pointer to close it to three once again, 37–34, with 3:40 left.

Then Matt steps up.

After a foul on the Blazers, he inbounds the ball in front of the Fort Yukon bench, slides to the corner and takes a return pass from Josh for a wide-open three.

Swish.

"The most dangerous man on the floor," chants Dave.

Wade sneaks behind number 12, strips the ball at half-court.

"He smelled it," says Dave.

Wade passes to Matt near the top of the key. Matt fakes left, pulls back and launches a skyball from beyond twenty feet.

Swish.

The boas are whirling. Fort Yukon's lead is suddenly nine, 43–34.

Derek pushes the gap to eleven with a soft ten-footer with one minute left in the quarter.

Dave was right. That was the Blazers' best shot, their last one. He continues to rotate his subs off the bench, running Allakaket's beleaguered five into exhaustion. Midway through the fourth quarter, the lead has ballooned to twenty-two points. Allakaket calls its last time-out with three minutes left.

"Okay, guys," Dave says. "Let's take it home."

They do. The final is 68–51. Both teams, as always, line up and shake hands before leaving the court. Number 12 makes a point of trying not to shake Dave's. Dave makes a point of finding his hand and letting him know he played a nice game.

So did Derek, who led all scorers with eighteen points. And Wade, who scored seventeen off the bench. And Matt, who hit fourteen, including three threes. Number 12 had sixteen for Allakaket, but Moses was held to a mere eight.

Dave likes that number best. His boys did just what he asked them to do, locking down the other team's key player on defense. If they do that tomorrow, they're headed to Anchorage.

It's Friday night, but there's no time or money for movies this evening, so the boys invite the Tanana girls up to their motel room to watch TV and hang out. Dave positions himself in the middle of the living room floor, where he can see into the bedroom and guard the front door as well.

He lets the boys sleep in the next morning. They leave around lunchtime, passing a pond on the way to the gym. A flock of ducks floats on the shimmering water—the first open water the kids have seen since their drive down the Kenai. Wade raises his arms as if holding a rifle, squeezes off three phantom shots as the van passes by.

By the time they get to the gym, the Allakaket-Tanana loser's bracket final is under way. The winner gets Fort Yukon, whom they'll have to beat twice for the title. Tanana has eliminated both Nulato and Huslia to get here, with Tyler going for thirty-six points in each game. But he's out of rhythm today. So is Norman. Allakaket is simply running the Wolves out of the building. By halftime, the game is all but over. Half of Dave's boys have moved out to the crowded lobby, mixing with kids from other villages. What they miss is a third-quarter comeback by Tanana that defies belief. It doesn't look like the same game. It's as if someone pulled the plug on Allakaket. Maybe it's fatigue, although Tanana should be even wearier. This is the Wolves' fourth game in three days. With Allakaket continuing its fade into the fourth quarter, Tanana pulls away for an improbable eleven-point win, after trailing by seventeen. They'll face Fort Yukon in the finale this afternoon—their fifth game of the tournament. If Tanana wins, the two teams will play yet again. That would be six games in three days for the Wolves. That's what Dave meant when he called the loser's bracket pure hell.

The Fort Yukon girls face the same circumstances as they take the court to once again face Nulato. Cheryl's girls knocked off Tanana for the second time this weekend to get here, and they'll have to beat Nulato twice if they want to move on to Anchorage. Ashley Hildebrand, the Nulato girl Matt had that fling with two seasons ago, doesn't intend to let it happen. She plays as tough as she looks, with her piercings—the eyebrow, the tongue—and her cocky demeanor. She's dominated the girls' side of this tournament as Nulato has churned through its bracket. She was the girls' winner of yesterday's free-throw shootout, receiving the same medal and ribbon as Johnny. And she's on top of her game today, as the Lady Wolves control Fort Yukon from the opening tap. Late in the fourth quarter, with Nulato up by double digits, Mandy shows her frustration by giving Hildebrand a hard shove, sending her into the wall. The refs miss Mandy's push, but they've got a clear view of Hildebrand's retaliation as she springs to her feet and knocks Mandy to the floor. The crowd goes crazy. There's something about a girlfight that excites them. Hildebrand is whistled for the flagrant foul and tossed from the game, which means nothing today—Nulato wins easily—but could change the entire course of the rest of their season, since she'll have to sit out the next game as well. The next game is the opening round of the State Tournament.

Now comes the boys' final. If there's a watershed game each winter, this is the one. If there's one game Dave aims at, one game that makes or breaks the entire year, this is it. For every team from the bush, the State Tournament is Valhalla. And this game, the Regional final, is the gateway to State. All that has come before—the twenty-two regular-season games Fort Yukon has played, the two wins this weekend—is simply a prelude. This is the one that counts most.

The boys understand as they suit up. The referees are once again here in the same locker room, putting on their black slacks and striped shirts. Harder to believe is that the Tanana team is in here as well, dressing two rows away from Fort Yukon. Both teams are keenly aware of each other, lacing their shoes in silence, the only sounds the opening and shutting of the steel locker doors.

Dave waits for the Tanana boys to leave before huddling his team for their prayer. As he reaches the part about the wings of eagles, a toilet is flushed and out of the bathroom walks a lone Tanana player. No one looks up as the boy walks past. Dave waits till he's gone to finish the prayer.

The gym is hot and loud as the boys burst through the doors for their warm-ups. Everyone's here, including Mike Doppler, a beefy, mustachioed North Dakota native who taught in Fort Yukon and coached the basketball team back in the late 1970s and early '80s. He was Jack's coach, and Jerry Carroll's. He's sixty-five now. He and his wife, Mary, a Fort Yukon Native, live here in Fairbanks, where they both work at a rehab center for Native kids with substance abuse problems. Doppler follows Fort Yukon's teams each season in the newspaper, and he always tries to catch at least one Regional Tournament game. He says he likes what he sees in this year's team: speed and depth.

Tanana draws first blood, with Tyler taking the ball straight to the hole off the opening tip. Fort Yukon misses its first four shots, but Tanana's off target as well. They staged a tremendous comeback against Allakaket four hours earlier. It's asking a lot to expect them to now face Fort Yukon's feverish defense. That's why Dave's sent his boys out in a full-court press rather than their usual half-court trap.

The press starts reaping dividends early. Norman's spin-reverse dribble—the move that did so much damage when Tanana beat Fort Yukon three weeks ago—is ineffective today. Matt, Josh and Derek strip the ball from him time and again. He's only a blink of an eye slower than normal, his legs just a tad heavy after their workout against Allakaket, but that blink makes all the difference. Again, without Norman at his best, Tyler can't carry the load by himself. The score at the end of the first quarter is 20–5, Fort Yukon.

Halftime, it's 35–18. Dave's only worry now is how close the referees are calling the game. Three of his boys have two fouls, and one—Aaron—has three. But Norman erases all suspense by drawing two technicals midway through the third quarter, ending his season, and, effectively, Tanana's, with an ejection.

The final is 61–44.

The fans flood the floor at the final buzzer. The boys dump a cooler of water on Dave. He's surrounded by well-wishers, not just from Fort Yukon but from the other villages as well. From this point on, his team is their team, they tell him. The Eagles will carry the hopes of the Interior against the rest of the state next weekend.

And they'll come in as the number one seed, the top-rated 1A team in Alaska, the only one making its seventh straight trip to the dance.

Seven straight.

Dave likes the sound of that. He'll take time to savor it tonight. Let the boys celebrate. Then, tomorrow, they'll pack, gas up the van, and hit the highway for the last time this season, for the drive Dave's been aiming at since the first day of practice last November.

The drive down to Anchorage.

EIGHTEEN

State

I T'S A SEVEN-HOUR drive from Fairbanks to Anchorage. The van's dashboard is adorned with trophies: the team's Regional Championship plaque, Johnny's free-throw medallion, All-Tournament ribbons for Matt, Josh, Aaron and Wade. Derek missed the All-Tourney team by one vote.

The trip starts out, as always, on the snowbound Parks Highway. Then up once again through the wind-whipped passes of the Alaska Range, past a jackknifed eighteen-wheeler slammed into a snowbank, down through the Mat-Su Valley, where the snow turns to rain, sheets of it washing over the van's windshield. It's the first rain the boys have seen since last August. A bank clock in Wasilla flashes forty-six-above. As they approach the outskirts of Anchorage, they see blossoms of willow catkins peeking up through the snow. The ice on the roadsides is rotting and filthy. The air is heavy with dust from a winter of sand spread on the streets, now revealed by the sun and churned up by the traffic. The first day of spring is one week away.

Dave's still miffed about what happened late last night. They celebrated with a movie after the game, then stopped at a late-night Safeway, bought ice cream, fruit and toppings to make banana splits back in the room. A little past two, they all went to sleep. About four thirty Dave was awakened by sounds from the bedroom—rustling and murmuring. He knocked on the door, heard the scurry of feet, walked in and cut on the lights. Aaron and Josh were aligned on one bed, their eyes shut like angels. A lumpy blanket lay on the floor beside them. Dave walked over, lifted the spread and there were three Tanana girls. He opened the closet door, and out stepped two more. They'd climbed up the balcony and come in through the window. Dave sent the girls back downstairs, chewed out the boys and went back to bed. He's a little upset, but not much. "Hey," he says, "it wasn't booze; it wasn't drugs. It was just hormones."

They pull into their home for the next week, a Comfort Inn by the railroad tracks, not far from downtown. The sun has come out, casting its afternoon glow on the slopes of the mountains that rise to the east. It's a beautiful sight, but the city itself is an alien place to Dave and the boys. The traffic, the sprawl, the chain stores and malls, the chrome-and-glass buildings and banks, a quarter million people commuting from condos and rowhouses crammed into cul-de-sacs—this is the world most people who come to Alaska are trying to flee. It's the world Dave left behind twenty-nine years ago. The way he feels—the way most Alaskans who live beyond Anchorage feel—he'd just as soon see this city split off from the state and drift into the sea.

The first thing Matt does once they've checked in is slip into the motel's "business center," log onto a computer, punch up the State Tournament Web site and find out who's made the field and what the pairings are for Thursday's opening-round games.

The only team he's heard of is Noorvik, the school that knocked off Fort Yukon two seasons ago. They're back again, playing some village called Golovin, from up around Nome.

The first game of the day matches Kwigillingok, an Eskimo community down on the Bering coast, with Atqasuk, another village of Eskimos from up north near Barrow.

The nightcap pits Newhalen, a small lakeside hamlet not far from Cook Inlet, against Kalskag, yet another Eskimo settlement, located on the banks of the Kuskokwim River, almost four hundred miles due west of here.

Fort Yukon has drawn Russian Mission, a village of Yupiks near Kalskag. Matt never heard of the place until last week's rankings came out. One of Dave's daughters says someone told her they've got a bunch of bad-ass gangsters on their team. A couple of them can dunk. That's what she heard.

For Dave, this is part of the kick of the State Tournament—the mystery, knowing nothing but hearsay about the other teams who are here. It's always a strange kind of thrill, finding out who you've drawn, figuring out what they've got, asking around and getting little but rumors and guesses. Few of the teams have actually seen one another play. Most have never even heard of each other. There's really no way to prepare for the opening game, other than do what you've done best all season. The second and third rounds are easier. You've gotten a look at the others by then. But the first round, it's a shot in the dark. "A crapshoot," Dave calls it.

He orders in pizza and chicken wings that evening, gathers the boys and reads them the tournament rules, which prohibit smoking and drinking, of course, but also chewing tobacco anywhere inside or around the arena. Tourney officials will be everywhere this week, he tells them, roaming the stands in their bright red shirts, some going incognito, making sure no one is breaking the rules. He tells a story, from two years ago, about a girl—a guard from Wainwright—who was caught watching a game with a plug of chew in her cheek and was sent home. Dave doesn't want that to happen this week. He looks straight at Wade and Tim Fields and Aaron as he speaks. They're the team's big chewers.

They've got three days to kill before play begins. Most of the other teams won't be arriving until Tuesday night. Fort Yukon's the only one to have played its Regional Tournament "on the highway." The others played theirs in outlying villages. Unlike Fort Yukon, they had no way to drive here when they were done. So they went back to their homes and will fly in later this week.

Monday, Dave takes the boys to the Dimond Center—a real mall, three stories high, with escalators, and a bowling alley in the basement. They spend a few hours there. Derek, who's never bowled before, beats everyone with a 182. Then they drive over to the university, to take a look at the gym.

It's like stepping into a cathedral for the boys. They gaze down at the glimmering hardwood floor, set below ground level, like a pit, row upon row of shellacked wooden bleachers rising up to where the boys stand, and—most entrancing of all—the jerseys, mounted on the wall near the ceiling, twenty-seven of them, one from each of the universities that have won the Great Alaska Shootout. The Shootout is a hallmark for basketball fans across the whole nation, a kickoff to each NCAA season, staged each November, televised by ESPN, featuring some of the most fabled Division I college teams in the country. Five NCAA champions have launched their title seasons on this floor. More than two dozen former national championship schools have played in this event. Duke, Kentucky, North Carolina, Kansas, UCLA, Syracuse, Louisville, Arizona, Michigan State, Marquette—they all have a jersey up on that wall. Past MVPs include Dwayne Wade, Ray Allen, Antawn Jamison, Drew Gooden, Glenn Robinson, Sean Elliott, Chris Mills, Brad Daugherty—all of whom went on to NBA fame. Vince Carter played on this floor. So did such legends as Len Bias, Derrick Coleman, Danny Manning, Glen Rice, Wayman Tisdale, Clark Kellogg, James Worthy, Sam Perkins. These are names the boys know—from TV, from their fathers, from growing up with the game in their blood.

They stand in silence, watching a janitor wet-mop the floor. Then they leave, back to the motel to pick up their practice gear, then out to the van for the forty-five-minute drive up to Houston, to a junior high gym next to the same high school gym they played in two months ago. One of Dave's friends, a former Fort Yukon teacher, is on staff there and has arranged for the team to work out this evening.

They look sharp. Even Dave looks on top of his game, pacing the sideline, blowing his whistle, clapping his hands, shouting instructions. He makes Aaron and Josh run extra wind sprints, paying the price for their Saturday night tryst. "Was it worth it?" he asks, as they lean, almost heaving, against the gym wall.

"Oh, yeah," gasps Josh.

"*Well* worth it," says Aaron, grinning.

Tim Fields circles the court, jogging on his tender right knee. "It hurts," he tells Dave, "but I like it. It's moving better." He may be able to play Thursday, if only a little.

Tuesday they hit yet another mall. Johnny runs into a cousin, a kid from Fort Yukon who now lives in Anchorage. He's admiring Johnny's clothing, asking him where he got his jewelry. The kid has a reputation back in the village. He actually tried to start a gang there. Never mind that there was no other gang to compete with. He got three boys to join him. They went so far as to tag the school one night—spray-painted the front of the building. It wasn't hard for the police to find them. The four of them wound up doing their penance in the subzero cold, shivering as they slapped fresh paint on the wall.

That night, Dave takes the team to an indoor water park, sets them loose for three hours while he and Diane sit at an upstairs deck table and read.

The next morning, Wednesday, all sixteen teams—boys' and girls'—report for scheduled half-hour practice sessions and photo shoots for the tournament program. The bleachers are filled with kids and coaches watching each team take the floor for the brief "workouts," trying to ferret out what they can about one another. There's not much to learn in thirty minutes. Some squads run through a few drills. Most do no more than simply shoot around. The Russian Mission kids spend the half hour playing a ragged game of "21" while their coach sits on the sideline chatting with his wife and some friends. Dave runs his boys through some layups and a couple of gassers.

The Atqasuk coach—a stocky, crewcut former wrestler from Montana named Mike Weatherbee—and his kids are particularly interested in Fort Yukon, since Atqasuk beat Wainwright, among others, to get here, and Wainwright beat Fort Yukon in last year's state final. This is Atqasuk's first trip to State. They've got only fourteen kids in their high school. Their village, sixty miles south of Barrow, was used by the military to mine coal during World War II. The name Atqasuk means *"the place to dig the rock that burns"* in the Inuit Eskimo language. One of their players has never been this far south, says Weatherbee. "He's never been off the Slope," he says. "He's never seen a tree." Atqasuk had to beat Kaktovik, who upset Nuiqsut to get here. Nuiqsut and Wainwright typically rule their region, says Weatherbee. He's quite impressed that Fort Yukon won the NIT, with Nikolaevsk finishing seventh. Atqasuk played Nikolaevsk this year themselves. They lost by twenty-five. "We didn't have an answer for that big Russian kid," he says. "He scored forty on us."

The Russian Mission contingent is sitting just down the way. They're friendly, engaging, nothing like the rumors Dave's daughter relayed, nothing like gangsters. Their coach, a burly, gregarious forty-nine-year-old Native named Art Vaska, has only seven kids on his squad. Three are his sons. The assistant coach is his wife. This is Russian Mission's first time at State as well. They knocked off Emmonak—the team that was ranked number one earlier this season—in their Regional final to get here. "Yeah," says Vaska with an unabashed grin, "they were crying." His boys played far fewer games than Fort Yukon this year—just fourteen, all in their region, around the southwestern stretch of the Yukon River, just before it spills into the Bering Sea. Their budget is small. Their village has only three hundred people. Their school has three dozen kids. Their gym is barely the size of a half-court. "We don't play any home games," says Vaska with a chuckle. "We don't even have a full set of white jerseys." He chuckles again. "It's always an away game for us." They travel to some of those games by snowmachine, he says, caravanning through the midwinter darkness. It took them about two and a half hours to drive eighty miles through the woods to play Aniak this year. They drove the same distance to play Holy Cross. His boys might not look like much when they walk into a gym—Vaska chuckles again—and that's okay with him. Ask Emmonak.

After the last team is done with its workout, the coaches all leave for a meeting, and the kids are called down to the floor. Two from each team have been chosen for the tournament's Three-Point Shootout. Modeled after the NBA's All-Star Game three-point contest, sixteen boys and sixteen girls will have one minute each to shoot five racks of four balls arranged around the arc. Each rack has a white-striped "bonus ball" worth extra points. The top two boys and two girls from today will shoot again at halftime of Saturday night's championship game, which will be televised statewide.

Justin and Matt take the floor for Fort Yukon. Justin draws first go, and he's hot. He hits four of the five bonus balls, for a total of thirty-eight points. "That would have won it last year," notes Matt. As shooter after shooter fails to top Justin's total, it looks like it might win it this year as well. At the least, it looks like it will get him into Saturday night's final. Matt is ice-cold, totaling an abysmal seventeen points. He's followed by a kid from Newhalen. The kid's short—about five-seven—squat, beefy, with a scraggly mustache and half beard, bushy hair and eyeglasses. He looks like John Belushi in *Animal House*. But he shoots like Steve Nash. Ball after ball sails through the hoop as the clock ticks away. The buzzer sounds, and the PA announcer gives the total. Forty-two. High fives all around from the other contestants. Justin's still in, but now he's in second. Belushi's teammate steps up next, another small guard, and he's even hotter. He puts up a forty-four, and that's it. Both Newhalen boys will be on TV Saturday night. Justin finishes third.

Dave returns from the coaches' meeting. The only news of note is the players from Kwigillingok have been held up by bad weather. They still haven't gotten out of their village. Their game tomorrow morning has been moved to tomorrow night, to give them more time to arrive. But this doesn't mean much to Fort Yukon. Kwigillingok is in the opposite bracket. If Fort Yukon wins tomorrow, they'll play the winner of Newhalen-Kalskag on Friday. If they win that one, they're in the finals Saturday night.

That evening, Dave drives the boys over to Aaron's grandparents' house—Jim and Annette McCarty, the parents of the McCarty sisters—Deb, Diana and Laurie. It's become a tradition each year, Dave and his boys having their last supper here before playing the tournament. They wend their way through a neighborhood of tightly packed condos and apartments. Josh gazes out at the driveways and trash cans and tiny front lawns. "Jesus," he says, "how would you like to live here?"

Tim Woods stares out his side of the van. "What kind of food do you think they're going to have?" he asks.

"Do you think they'll have moose stew?" says Josh.

"That would kick *ass*," says Matt. "Moose! Some *good* food before we play."

Josh mentions that his aunt Rosalie invited the team over yesterday to have duck soup. But Dave told her they couldn't make it.

"Duck soup!" says Matt. "Fuck! What's *wrong* with Dave?"

Dave isn't listening. He's trying to find the McCartys' address. He's been here before, but it's never easy. The houses and streets all look the same.

They finally arrive. A crowd's gathered inside, around a spread of homemade Mexican food: enchiladas, burritos, tacos and a big cake with candles. It's Aaron's birthday, his seventeenth. Trader Dan is here. So are Deb and Diana McCarty, but their sister Laurie is not. Her son Brandon is playing this weekend for Mount Edgecumbe in its 3A Regional Tournament down in Sitka. Brandon started at center his freshman and sophomore years for Fort Yukon. He's the same size as Aaron, only heftier. Dave can't imagine how strong the Eagles might be if Brandon had come back to play for them this year.

Everyone fills their plates and gathers in the living room to watch a videotape of last Saturday's game against Tanana. Then someone brings out the cake, and they all sing "Happy Birthday" to Aaron. Then it's time to leave. Dave wants the boys to turn in early, get a good night's rest. Or at least try.

They sleep in the next morning. Their game's not till three thirty. By noon, everyone's up. They've already checked out the newspaper. The new rankings are out, the final poll of the year. Fort Yukon remains number one. Newhalen is next, followed by Noorvik, Kwigillingok and Russian Mission.

Dave gathers the boys in the room, turns the TV set down—they've got the NCAA tournament on—and goes over the game plan.

"These guys play straight man-to-man defense, from what I've heard. So I want Matt to handle the ball. Aaron and Derek, I want you to post low and screen for each other, take turns popping up to the foul line. Justin, Matt, Josh—look for the kickout from the high post for a three. Wade, a man-to-man is right up your alley. I don't think there's a player in this tournament—I don't think there's a player in this *state*—who can keep up with your first step."

He goes over the defense, and the substitutions he'll make.

"Don't get your underwear in a bundle if I take you out. If I think someone can give me more on the floor at that moment, don't come to the bench and try to give me some excuse or explanation. I don't need to hear you make your case. We'll get Judge Judy in here later, and you can make your case to her. I don't care about excuses. I care about performance, mentally and physically. If I don't see it, I'll give someone else a chance to show me it."

He pauses, looks around, tips his Red Sox cap back.

"I expect you to feel a little bit nervous. That's natural. But remember, they're going to be at least as nervous as you, if not more."

The kids are stone silent, staring hard straight at Dave.

"The competition here is no different than the competition was at the NIT. It's no different than it was at Tok. You've proved what you can do."

He rolls up the sleeves of his Fort Yukon windbreaker.

"For at least two of you, this is it. I have never felt this good going into this tournament. I've felt good, but never *this* good."

He stands, rolls his sleeves back down.

"Okay, it's a three-game season now, boys. All you have to do is perform."

By the time they get to the gym, one boys' game has already been played. Noorvik destroyed Golovin, 71–34. Dave knew coming in that Noorvik could well be the team to beat. They've been here before. They've won four state titles—more than any other 1A school—all in the past ten years. Their coach, like Dave, has been at their school a long time. The Noorvik team's got that continuity, that tradition. Like the fans in Fort Yukon, the people of Noorvik expect their team to get here each season. And they expect them to win. Unlike Fort Yukon, they have. If the Eagles are finally going to bring home their first banner, Dave figures they'll have to beat Noorvik to get it.

The big news on the girls' side is top-ranked McGrath was beaten this morning by New Stuyahok. "The mighty have fallen," Dave says to his boys. "Take note."

By the time the Buckland girls have blown out White Mountain, the arena is jammed, more than twelve hundred Natives of all ages from all over the state, waving banners and flags, blowing noisemakers, beating the bleachers. Elders with canes are helped down the aisles by grandchildren. Parents wear buttons embossed with photographs of their sons and daughters, their ballplayers. Whole villages seem to be here, some chanting in Yupik, others in Inuit, some in Gwich'in. The Buckland fans wear T-shirts inscribed with the words RESPECT ALL, FEAR NONE.

Two forty-five, Dave leads his boys to the locker room. They've never been in one this nice. Their school's name is posted on the door. It's the UAA's varsity coaches' room—carpeted, low-ceilinged, intimate, buffed wooden cubicles with individual nametags above each one. It looks like those major league dressing rooms the kids see on *SportsCenter*. The first thing Johnny and Bruce do is pull out their Axe.

There's nothing more Dave can say. He lets the boys dress in silence, gathers them for the team prayer, then leaves them to huddle alone. Three minutes, he tells them. Come out in three minutes.

James Brown's "Sex Machine" thuds through the sound system as the packed house awaits both teams. Russian Mission's not here yet. They called from a cell phone, told the tournament officials they're held up in traffic not far from the campus, that they'll be here as soon as they can.

The Fort Yukon contingent has filled the section behind the team's bench. Doc is there, and Diane. Trader Dan sits beside Clifton and Janet and the Cadzow kids. Georgie and her husband and children are squeezed next to the McCartys. Jerry Carroll and his wife, Jackie, are here. And Dave's daughter Jolene. And Wes and Bruce's mom and dad, and their grandmother Vera. And Wade's parents—Alfred and Linda. And Johnny's aunt Daisy. And Louie John, who now lives in Anchorage—she's brought her granddaughter, a breathless seven-year-old waving a homemade blue-and-white Fort Yukon pennant. "I've never *been* to a basketball game before," she says, her eyes wide with excitement.

None of the Shewfelts are here. Neither is Willie Fields. There's a big party in Fairbanks this weekend, a blowout, with live music and all. Word is that's where they are—Paul, Jack and Willie. As for Ryan and John, there's no telling where they are. But they're not here. The radio man Dave contracted is beaming today's game back to Fort Yukon. He's broadcasting all the games this weekend, boys' teams and girls', back to each of the participating villages, a hundred bucks a game. That's eight hundred dollars per day. "Not bad," says Dave. "I should get into that."

His boys, wearing white, take the floor. Russian Mission still hasn't arrived. Ten minutes before game time they're still not here. Six minutes to go, the Raiders, all seven of them, straggle through the door, a couple still pulling on their blue jerseys. The crowd gives them a sarcastic ovation.

Dave looks them over as they shoot a few quick layups. One of the coach's three sons, Art Vaska Jr., is Aaron's size. He looks smooth. So does number 30, a five-seven guard with a nice outside stroke. They'll have to keep their eye on those two. This team beat Emmonak. That's all Dave has to know. They've got game. They're here.

Russian Mission wins the tip, takes the ball right into a Fort Yukon trap, and Matt makes the steal, feeding Derek for a wide-open three.

He misses.

The Raiders bring it downcourt and miss a shot from the key. Derek is fouled on the rebound.

Josh works the ball up, to one side, then the other, till Matt gets loose for a three of his own.

He misses, and fouls on the rebound.

Both teams look nervous. Tight.

Russian Mission scores first, on a foul shot.

Aaron is called for three seconds. Dave stands up, motions his kids to settle down, relax.

Matt rebounds a Raider miss, hits Aaron on the outlet, who throws it away trying to feed Derek.

Two minutes in, and the score is 1–0.

The crowd is restless, perplexed: *This* is the number one team in the state? They look awful. The other team doesn't look much better. The Noorvik coach is scribbling in a notebook, huddling with his two assistants, pointing down at Dave's boys.

Aaron finally breaks the ice with a follow shot as he's fouled. He makes the free throw to put Fort Yukon ahead, 3–1.

A block by Aaron, and another turnover by Matt. He's pressing, trying to do too much, too fast. Dave can see it. He's rushing.

Aaron fouls number 30, who hits both free throws.

Justin misses a three. One of Vaska's other two sons grabs the rebound and goes coast-to-coast to put Russian Mission ahead. These kids can run, Dave can see that. He's not surprised. Every team here can run.

Josh misses a short baseline push shot. Vaska Jr. scores at the other end to put Russian Mission up, 7–3.

Josh bangs a three-pointer wide off the glass, a terrible miss.

Aaron fouls again at the other end.

Dave pops up, walks down to Tim Fields, grabs his shoulder. "You ready?" he asks. Tim nods, pulls off his warm-up, reports in for Aaron. He's limping, but only a little.

The big Vaska kid scores inside once again, to make it 9–3 with 3:30 left. The refs call a radio time-out.

Dave gathers his boys by the bench. They're jittery, tense. The best he can do is stay relaxed himself, show he's not worried. He sends Wade in for Justin.

Wade wastes no time. After a miss by Fort Yukon, he strips a startled Raider guard and feeds Matt for a layup.

Number 30 comes back with a three. The kid can shoot, no doubt about it.

12–5, Russian Mission.

Wade is fouled on a hard, headlong drive, makes one of two free throws.

Derek rebounds a miss at the other end, spies Josh breaking away, fires a length-of-the-court bullet pass for a layup.

A steal by Tim, but he throws the ball out of bounds.

A travel by Russian Mission.

Josh finds Tim inside, on the right. He hits a short turnaround off the glass to make it 12–10.

Another defensive stop, and Wade finds Derek flashing through the lane for a layup.

12–12. A seven-point run for Fort Yukon. The crowd's buzzing now. The Eagle fans are out of their seats. The quarter ends with the score still tied at 12.

Dave huddles his kids by the bench. He's got to shout to be heard.

"Two things. We're getting killed on the boards. We've got to have at least three people going for rebounds. The other problem is turnovers. We've *got* to take better care of the basketball. Do you understand?"

Aaron stays on the bench. Tim's doing fine. Derek's hanging tough, going to the glass like Dave's asked him to. Wade's sticking his nose in there, too, mixing it up with the big boys, a fireplug, quick off the floor, with a sense for the ball.

One minute into the quarter, Tim slides out to the deep left side, takes a reverse pass and flips in a clean three.

A free throw and a short baseline floater by the big Vaska kid ties it.

Dave gets up, walks over to Johnny, tells him to check in.

Two trips upcourt, and Johnny gets his first touch. He nails it, an eight-footer from the right side.

"Instant offense," says Dave.

Justin chases down a Raider miss. Tim misses a three, but Derek rebounds and puts it back in for a four-point Fort Yukon lead. Dave's never seen Derek so strong on the boards. He's playing his guts out.

Russian Mission misses again, and Derek snares yet another rebound. He outlets to Justin, sprints up the sideline for a return pass and squeezes off a three-pointer.

It rims out.

Three minutes left in the half. Number 30 swishes a foul-line jumper to cut the lead to two.

Justin misfires a three.

Vaska Jr. rebounds, goes baseline to baseline and is fouled hard by Tim on the drive.

He misses both free throws.

Dave's noticed the last three times upcourt, Johnny's been open. He's out of his seat, imploring his guys to get the ball to Johnny.

Matt doesn't hear him. He splits two defenders, forces a floater from the right baseline that draws nothing but air. The Raiders push it upcourt, but Wade steps in from nowhere, slaps the ball away, grabs it and hits Matt in stride for a layup.

21–17, with 1:40 to go.

Number 30 gets the ball on the right wing, beyond the arc. Matt and Josh are both in his face. They're not letting him breathe.

It doesn't matter, not this time. The kid rises with both players draped over him and hits nothing but net for a three. It's the shot of the game to this point.

21–20, with 1:15 left.

Justin to Josh to Tim Fields in the middle. Tim flips a bank shot from just inside the foul line.

Good.

23–20, one minute to go.

The Raiders come down, miss, and Derek rebounds.

Thirty-six seconds left.

"One shot!" someone yells from the crowd.

"One shot, my ass," Dave says softly, watching Johnny sneak along the baseline, moving without the ball toward his favorite spot, the left corner.

Justin to Josh on the right.

Back to Justin at the top of the key.

Over to Matt and into the corner, to Johnny.

He pulls in the pass, squares and shoots in one motion.

Bang.

Three points.

The Fort Yukon bleachers explode.

26–20, Eagles.

Twenty-five seconds left.

The Raiders take it down to eight seconds and miss. Matt rebounds and passes to Johnny for a long three at the buzzer.

It rims out.

Dave grabs a stat sheet on the way to the dressing room. That's another thing he likes about the State Tournament, another thing that makes this event special—they've got computerized statistics, just like the college teams do. Just like the pros. Rebounds, turnovers, steals, assists, blocked shots, points off the bench—it's all there. The numbers don't tell Dave anything he doesn't already know. Derek's got eight rebounds. Fantastic. Number 30 leads all scorers with ten points. No surprise there. Tim—who would have guessed?—leads the Eagles with seven.

The number that worries Dave most is Fort Yukon's turnovers. Thirteen. Russian Mission's got fifteen, but most of theirs were forced by Fort Yukon's traps. Dave's boys, on the other hand, have simply been throwing the ball away. They're trying too hard to force the action. That's what Dave tells them as soon as they get in the dressing room.

"We need to cut back on the turnovers. And we need to be aware of thirty.

"They're crashing the boards like sons of a gun," he says. "Derek has sneaker tracks up his back. We've got to give him some help."

He pauses, takes a slug from his bottle of water.

"You're doing a good job of taking away the three, forcing them to bring it inside. They're fumbling it down there. At first I thought it was nerves. But I can see now that it's not. That's just not the game they like to play. They like it outside. They like the three."

He takes another swallow.

"Hey, all said, if I told you back in January that you'd be ahead by six at halftime of the first State Tournament game, you would've said, 'Right on.'

"So, right on, guys. Let's go out and get it done."

He puts his starting five back in. The second half begins like the first, both teams stuttering, misfiring, pressing. Two minutes in, neither has scored. Matt finally slaps the ball away on a trap and feeds Josh for a layup, pushing the margin to eight, 28–20.

Russian Mission throws it away, forcing it in to the big man.

"They're starting to get a little frustrated," says Dave.

Matt misses a three. He's 0-for-5 from the arc.

Dave's rocking in his seat like an autistic child. He's never looked this anxious, not this season.

Josh flashes in front of a Raider pass, makes the steal and feeds Matt for another layup.

30–20, Fort Yukon.

Russian Mission finally scores, after rebounding four straight misses inside.

"The *boards*, guys," yells Dave. "We've got to get on the *boards*."

He gets up, taps Tim and Wade on the shoulders, sends them both in.

Matt misses a drive, but Wade is there for the rebound and is fouled on the follow.

"Here's where we can put them away," says Dave.

Wade misses both free throws.

Vaska Jr. scores on a layup to cut it to six.

Aaron finds Tim on the right side for a short jumper.

It's good. Tim has missed only one shot all game.

32–24, Fort Yukon, with three minutes left in the quarter.

Dave sends in Chris. He responds, feeding Tim on the far left wing for a three.

It's good.

Incredible. The kid hasn't played in two weeks. Three days ago, he could hardly walk. Now he's having the game of his life.

Russian Mission scores on a free throw, but Wade answers with one of his headlong drives straight down the lane, through the teeth of the defense, popping out at the rim, flipping the ball into the hole.

37–25, Fort Yukon, with 1:05 to go.

Dave leaps from his chair, punching the air. He's hardly back in his seat before Matt gets the ball after a Raider turnover and launches a moon shot from well beyond the right arc. It doesn't matter that he's missed all five threes he's taken today. He could have missed fifty, and he wouldn't think twice about taking another. That's a shooter's mentality. That's what Dave counts on from Matt.

The shot splits the net.

40–25.

The Fort Yukon fans are going nuts.

The buzzer sounds. A 14–5 quarter for the Eagles.

"Time to put them away," Dave tells his boys. "They're tired."

The Raiders come out in a man-to-man press all over the floor. They're gambling now, going for steals.

Matt air-balls a three. Aaron picks up his fourth foul going over the back of the big kid. Dave leaves him in. "We're all right," he says.

The Raiders score on a layup after a flurry of loose balls.

Dave calls time-out with six minutes to go.

"They're forcing more pressure out front," he says. "Which means there are opportunities down low and in the post. Make them *pay* for those gambles."

No sooner is the ball inbounded than Wade drives the baseline, swallowed again in midair between three Raider defenders, popping out once again on the other side, still in midair, for an up-and-under layup.

"Like there's nobody *there*," says Dave.

42–27.

Russian Mission scores.

Matt fires a pass to Aaron, but a Raider cuts in front for the steal and is fouled on a layup.

"Step to the *ball*," shouts Dave. "They're gambling. You've got to step to the *ball*."

He pulls Matt and Chris, sends in Justin and Josh.

"We're still not taking care of the ball," he tells Matt.

"I know it," says Matt, flopping into his seat, grabbing a bottle of water, sweat dripping from his chin onto the floor.

The Raider guard makes one of two free throws.

42–30 with five minutes left.

Wade loses the ball. The Raiders score in transition.

42–32.

Dave's rocking again, rubbing holes in the knees of his jeans.

Josh drives to the middle, fakes the big man into the air, and flips in a layup.

Wade flashes from nowhere to strip the point guard.

Another layup.

Four points in six seconds. The lead's back to fourteen with four minutes to go.

Russian Mission misses inside. Aaron rebounds and is fouled. He misses both free throws. Number 30 comes down and nails a long three, his first points of the half.

"Come *on*, Josh!" yells Dave. "What did I say about leaving him alone?"

46–35, with three minutes left.

Justin shoots and misses.

The big man rims one in and out.

Aaron goes up for a jumper, is hacked hard, but no whistle.

Dave springs from his seat, stares hard at the refs, but says nothing.

The Raiders' point guard stumbles, and the whistle blows—traveling.

"Was that a *makeup* call or what?" Dave asks, looking at the scorer's table. Like a Greek chorus, the scorekeepers nod their heads, laughing. They love this guy's show.

Russian Mission calls time-out. Two minutes to go.

Fort Yukon huddles, puts their hands together.

"One, two, three, *finish!*" they shout.

Wade's trapped and is fouled. He makes the first free throw, misses the second.

47–35, 1:50 left.

Josh steals and is fouled. He makes one of two.

The big man comes down, pulls up for a three, misses, but Derek is whistled for the foul.

Three free throws.

"*Errrrr,*" Dave growls, "I *hate* that.

"*Not* the three-point shooter, Derek!" he shouts. "*Never* foul the three-point shooter."

The scorekeepers are eating it up. They can't keep their eyes off Dave.

The big man hits two out of three.

48–37, with 1:35 to go.

"They're not quitting," says Dave.

Justin hits Josh, who finds Aaron down low for a clean lay-in.

"Smooth," says Dave.

50–37, with 1:15 left.

A Raider guard heaves a wild twenty-five-foot air ball.

"Holy mackerel," says Dave. He's sitting back now, relaxed.

Wade is fouled, makes both shots, then Josh is whistled for a foul of his own with thirty-three seconds to go, stopping the clock.

"Josh, *why?*" Dave asks, spreading his arms wide.

Josh comes to the sideline for a quick drink of water.

"Get back *out* there," snaps Dave. "No water for *you.*"

The kids crack up. So do the scorers.

Nine seconds later, another whistle. Another foul on Josh.

"Josh, you're *killing* me," says Dave. "Will you just play basketball?"

The clock finally runs out.

Fort Yukon wins, 53–38.

They're in the semis.

Dave bounces off the bench, shakes Vaska's hand and the hands of the Russian Mission kids. A reporter from the Anchorage newspaper corrals him, asks a few questions, then moves on to Wade, who doesn't say much, then to Matt, who gives him a couple of quotes he can use.

The Fort Yukon fans spill onto the floor, surrounding their boys with hugs and handshakes. Louie John's granddaughter's pennant is in tatters.

They finally clear the court for the next game. Dave gets his team in the locker room, grins all around.

"Tremendous, guys," he says. "Eighteen second-half points, that's all they got. Nine people played for us, nine people contributed.

"Okay." He claps his hands. "Same thing tomorrow."

Tim is clutching a stat sheet, savoring it. He's Fort Yukon's high scorer with twelve—the eighth high man the team's had this season. Wade is next with eleven—ten in the second half. That's the number that stands out most—points off the bench. Twenty-eight for Fort Yukon, to two for Russian Mission, thanks to Tim and Wade, with Johnny pitching in five.

By the time they've showered and dressed, Newhalen and Kalskag have already started. Fewer than two hundred people live in Newhalen, all Natives, and every one of them seems to be here, backing their Malamutes. A Newhalen student in a furry gray dog getup romps on the sidelines, leading the cheers. Kalskag—the Grizzlies—has a mascot of its own, a kid in a big brown bear outfit.

Fort Yukon will face this game's winner tomorrow night. It looks like it will be Kalskag. They're lithe, athletic, with a center—a black kid, six-one—who's velvety smooth, both inside and out. Newhalen is smaller, not a six-footer among them. But they're ballers, especially Belushi, the kid with the scraggly beard and eyeglasses. He knows right where to be, doesn't waste a step, has a sense of the floor and the flow of the game that comes from thousands of hours—an entire boyhood—spent inside a gym.

Newhalen builds a nine-point lead and sits on it into the fourth quarter. Kalskag finally makes its move, cutting the lead to two with five minutes left. Newhalen is back on its heels. Kalskag ties the score with four minutes to go. The stadium's rocking. Whistling, pounding, chanting. The Kalskag fans, clad in blue and gold, are all on their feet. So is the blue-and-white Newhalen section.

It comes down to a shootout between the black kid for Kalskag and Belushi. The kid for Kalskag takes the ball inside, hitting two twisters. Belushi answers with two scores of his own, the second an area-code three-pointer that takes the roof off the building. He backpedals upcourt, waving both arms high in the air, working the crowd. This is the State Tournament at its best.

Newhalen scores with nine seconds left to break a tie. The kid for Kalskag takes the inbounds pass, dribbles the length of the floor, drives toward the basket, left side of the key . . . and loses the ball off his leg out of bounds.

Newhalen wins.

Hugs and howls on the Malamutes' bench. The Kalskag players are sprawled on the floor, devastated. To come so close, then to lose.

Dave and the boys leave to go find some dinner. There's a place called O'Brady's that someone told Dave is not bad. They drive clear across town, almost into the mountains, pull into the parking lot, circle it twice before finding a spot, then step out to a sight and a sound they can't quite figure out.

A band of kilted bagpipers is marching out of the restaurant, blowing its instruments full force.

"Oh jeez," says Dave, slapping his forehead. "I forgot today is Saint Patrick's Day."

It's a two-hour wait at O'Brady's. They get back in the van, find a pancake house downtown, then drive back to the motel to turn in early again.

Friday, they awake to a half-page photo of Wade on the front page of the *Anchorage Daily News*'s sports section. He's grabbing a rebound, beside the headline FORT YUKON SUPER SUB SPARKS WIN. The boys clean out the lobby's supply of the paper, devouring the news from yesterday's first round. They see that Kwigillingok finally arrived for the evening's last game, versus Aqtasuk. They lost by three. So it will be Noorvik against Aqtasuk in one semifinal, Newhalen–Fort Yukon in the other. They also see that the Nulato girls, without Ashley Hildebrand, still managed to win their first-round game against Scammon Bay.

Lunchtime, the boys finally get their fresh meat, courtesy of Chris's grandmother, who lays out a spread of fried moose, rice, potato salad and fruit at her home not far from the UAA campus.

Midafternoon, they return to the motel, gather their gear and watch Vermont knock off Syracuse in the NCAA's opening round. A major upset. Dave loves it. He picked Vermont. They're his kind of team. Their coach is his kind of guy—down-to-earth, personable, nothing pretentious about him. No way Vermont should have beaten Syracuse, but they did. Dave hopes his boys take note of this, should it come down to them against Noorvik. He hopes they take note of it tonight. Play as a team, he tells them, and they can win this whole thing.

He asks Wade to turn down the TV, pulls out some notes and goes over the game plan.

"This is a very, very active team," he says. "They do a lot of moving without the ball, a lot of baseline cuts to set themselves up for those outside shots. You're gonna have to be aware of where they're at at all times. You're gonna have to look around more than you usually do. Watch the baseline. Be aware of their cutters. Do *not* stare ball."

He tips his cap back, studies the boys' faces.

"There's going to be a loud crowd in that gym tonight," he tells them, "even louder than last night. This is the kind of team that feeds on that kind of energy. You saw it yesterday. But they can falter. You saw that, too. They almost ran out of gas yesterday against Kalskag. When they did, who did they go to?"

The boys answer in unison.

"Number thirteen."

Belushi.

"That's right," says Dave. "So we're going to key on him. Him and number twelve. Those are their go-to guys."

Number 12 is the kid who outshot everyone two days ago in the three-point contest.

With that, they shut off the TV, turn off the lights, head out to the van.

The sun has just set, it's a little past seven when they get to the campus. The night air is brisk, in the twenties, the coldest it's been since they arrived here last Sunday. As they cross the parking lot, they can hear the roar of the crowd inside the building. Dave was right. It's louder than last night.

They step inside, and the sound is near deafening. The first quarter's just ending, Noorvik leading Atqasuk by just two. Dave and the boys squeeze into a row of Nulato fans. The Nulato coach and his girls are sitting nearby. They're not happy. They lost this afternoon to New Stuyahok in the girls' semifinal, despite Ashley Hildebrand's eighteen points, including five threes.

Both Noorvik and Atqasuk look tight. Both coaches are intense, up and pacing the sidelines, barking commands to their players. The first-quarter score is abysmally low: 7–5. But Noorvik wakes up in the second, scoring twenty-two to Atqasuk's eleven. By the time Dave and the boys leave midway through the fourth quarter to head to the locker room and start getting dressed, Noorvik's ahead by sixteen.

Again, there's not much more Dave can say. Watch 13. Watch 12. Don't stare ball. Be aware of the cutters.

"Play hard, gentlemen," he says, gathering the boys for the prayer. "Show the people out there why we're here."

Newhalen, dressed in road blue, is already warming up when Fort Yukon comes out. The Malamute mascot romps on the sideline, mocking Dave's boys as they shoot their layups. The Fort Yukon fans do their best to match the roar from the Newhalen side, but it's hard. No village here is as loud as Newhalen.

The Malamutes take the opening tip and score right away off two quick passes, igniting their crowd even louder.

They're in a tight man-to-man defense all over the floor, as Dave expected. Josh takes his man on a drive to the right, forcing a left-handed push shot that's short off the rim.

Number 13—Belushi—responds at the other end with his first shot of the game, a quick-release jumper just inside the arc.

It's good.

4–0, Newhalen.

It's clear right away, this team is every bit as quick as Fort Yukon, and better drilled than any team the Eagles have faced this season. Their patterns on offense, their movement on defense, double-teaming the ball wherever it goes—there's not one wasted motion. Every pass Fort Yukon makes is contested. It's like playing a mirror image of themselves at their best. They'll need to be at their best to stay in this game.

Derek scores off an inbounds pass after a tie-up. Josh follows with a steal, misses the layup, but Matt puts in the rebound to tie it at four.

Dave likes it. They're making Newhalen work for every pass, every shot.

13 finds a seam on the left side, glides to the bucket and flips a soft shot off the glass, just past Aaron's outstretched arm, for a score. This kid knows the game. There might be nine better athletes out there on the floor, but there's no better player.

Aaron is fouled putting back a missed jumper by Josh. He makes the first free throw, misses the second.

6–5, Newhalen.

Dave sends in Wade. The Newhalen coach sends in two players himself. Fort Yukon's bench has been their advantage all season. But Newhalen has a bench, too. They've got twelve kids over there, and all twelve can play.

A flurry of misses and steals by both teams, before Matt rattles in a three-pointer from the right side to put Fort Yukon ahead, 8–6.

Number 12 comes right back with a high-arching three from the left corner to put Newhalen back up by a point.

A steal and a foul, and it's Newhalen's ball.

Time-out for the radio. The crowd's rocking. The Malamute's out at midcourt, doing a little jig.

"Watch for the cutters," says Dave. "Keep an eye on their cutters."

Newhalen scores off the time-out—a leaner in the lane by one of their subs.

11–8, Fort Yukon trails.

Another steal at midcourt. Dave doesn't like what he's seeing. His kids are starting to look rattled on offense. They haven't faced a defense this relentless all season. Tanana, Allakaket—they were nothing compared to these Newhalen kids. Neither was Tok, or Su-Valley, or Galena. These Newhalen boys don't let up, not for a second. All season, the Fort Yukon kids have swarmed and swallowed their opponents. Now they're getting swarmed and swallowed themselves.

Newhalen misses. Wade rebounds.

Justin finds Derek on the left wing, wide-open. Derek seems surprised to have such a clear look. He air-balls the three.

Newhalen misses again. Fort Yukon's offense may be sketchy, but their defense looks good. This is what Dave's preached all season: The shots may not fall, but the defense should always be there. Tonight, it is. If Newhalen is going to score, they're going to have to earn it just like Fort Yukon.

After a long miss by Matt, 13 comes down, finds a teammate slicing backdoor behind Aaron and hits him in stride for a layup.

"The *cutters*!" yells Dave. "Watch the *cutters*!"

Matt feeds Derek for a layup of his own, but Newhalen comes right back with a short jumper by another one of their kids off the bench.

15–10, with 1:30 to go.

Justin works it upcourt, through his legs, behind his back, the Newhalen defender right in his shirt. He spin-dribbles past his man, into the face of number 12, who's jumped off Matt for the double-team. 12 strips the ball from Justin's hands, takes off the other way all by himself. Justin catches him from behind at the foul line, but it's not enough. The kid's gone for a layup. Everyone can see that.

What Justin does next makes no sense. It's pure emotion, frustration. He reaches out and grabs number 12 from behind. The ref blows the whistle.

Intentional foul.

Dave can't believe it. He slumps to his knees in front of the bench, his head in his hands. Justin can't believe it himself. He knows what he's done. He walks back toward midcourt, hiding his face with his jersey.

Two free throws for Newhalen, and their ball out of bounds.

12 makes one out of two. On the inbounds, 13 feeds a teammate for a layup to push the score to 18–10, Newhalen.

Matt nails a three from the corner to close out the quarter, but Dave is not happy. His kids trail by just five, 18–13, but they look worse than that. Their rhythm is off. Newhalen looks fluid, cohesive, even when they don't score. Fort Yukon looks skittish, offbeat. They can't find their tempo. Newhalen won't let them.

Dave puts in Tim Fields. And Johnny. Shake it up a little. Find the right combination.

Newhalen picks up where they left off, number 12 swishing a long three on their first possession.

Justin brings the ball up, takes his man all the way, beats him into the key for a short floater, but it's off.

Number 13 comes back with a quick-trigger three from the left wing. It's good.

One minute into the quarter, and Newhalen has widened the gap to 24–13.

They make yet another steal, but Johnny steals it right back, hurtles into the key, slices free for an over-the-head reverse layup right at the rim . . . and misses.

Dave shakes his head. Give Johnny that shot ten times, he makes nine.

Newhalen comes down, is fouled inside, makes one of two free throws to push the lead to twelve.

Johnny's trapped on the wing, loses the ball out of bounds.

Newhalen misses.

Derek gets another look at an open three and misses again.

This is the worst Dave's seen his boys shoot all season. Part of it's got to be nerves. Part of it's certainly Newhalen's defense. Whatever it is, they just can't find the hole.

Johnny makes a steal off the wing, has it stolen right back by number 12, who scores and is fouled.

27–13, Newhalen.

Dave calls time-out, gathers his kids. They don't look too worried. They've been here before. They've got plenty of time to get it together.

They know that. Dave knows it, too. But it better be soon.

"We've got to take care of the ball, boys," he says. "Run that screen we talked about. And we've *got* to keep an eye on those *cutters*."

The horn sounds. Play resumes. Number 12 makes his free throw. Justin brings the ball upcourt, gets it over to Matt on the wing, who hardly touches it before Belushi flashes in from behind, flicks it away and takes it the length of the court for a layup.

30–13, with 3:30 to go.

Justin is fouled, makes one of two free throws.

Number 12 answers, yet again, with a floater from the left side.

Dave can't believe how these two kids are shooting—numbers 12 and 13. There's no way they can possibly keep this up.

Derek scores inside to make 32–16 with 1:30 left.

Number 12 comes down and pops a twelve-footer from just outside the key.

It's good.

Dave can't recall seeing a team shoot this well. They must be hitting close to 70 percent.

Wade busts past his man, hurtles into the lane for one of his knifing layups.

It's long—too high and too hard.

Newhalen comes down and misses.

Forty seconds to go.

Matt works himself loose for a three on the wing.

He misses it badly.

Newhalen turns the ball over, but Derek gives it right back for a breakaway Malamute layup and a 36–16 Newhalen lead with fifteen seconds to go.

Matt closes the half with another long three, but it's hardly enough to rouse the deflated Fort Yukon fans. The Eagles trail by seventeen as they head to the locker room.

Dave comes in, takes a seat alongside his boys. For a full sixty seconds they sit there, he and his kids. No one says a word. The only sound is their breathing and the occasional swallow of water.

Finally, Dave stands, draws a deep breath.

"Hey," he says gently, tapping Matt on the knee, "thanks for the three. Brought us back a little bit."

He's got the halftime stat sheet in one hand.

"They're picking you clean on defense," he says. "And they're not missing their shots. That's the scary thing, how well they're shooting. They pull the trigger real quick. They take the first open look, and they're hammering it."

He studies the sheet, looks at Newhalen's numbers. Their leading four scorers—numbers 12 and 13, and two kids off the bench—are a combined 14-for-22 from the field. Just under 70 percent, including the threes. Number 12's got eleven points. Belushi's got nine. The "points off the bench" figures are frightening: fifteen for Newhalen, zero for Fort Yukon. Nothing. Nothing from Wade. Nothing from Tim. Nothing from Johnny. Josh is scoreless as well, 0-for-5 from the field. If not for Matt's eleven—including three threes—the game would be over already.

It's damned near over right now.

"We've got a big lead to eat up, boys," says Dave. "We're going to have to go man-to-man, full court, to do it. That's going to give us a matchup problem with Aaron on twelve, but we've got no choice. That's the only solution. We've tried everything else."

He looks at their faces. He knows they can do this, if they only believe that they can.

"Hey," he reminds them, "we've done it before. This isn't that big a lead."

A head pokes in the door, tells them it's time.

"Any questions?" says Dave.

The boys shake their heads.

"All right, then. Let's go eat up this lead, shall we, gentlemen?"

It's Newhalen's ball to begin the half. They miss and Aaron scores on a strong move to the hole—his first field goal of the night.

Newhalen misses again, and again Aaron scores, on a soft jump shot from the foul line.

36–23, Newhalen.

Number 12 hits a twelve-footer from the wing. Dave glances up at the ceiling. Will this kid ever miss?

Aaron gets the ball yet again at the line, turns and releases a soft spinning floater that nestles into the net.

Three scores for Aaron in less than two minutes.

38–25.

The Fort Yukon fans are on their feet. They've been waiting all game for their boys to make one of their runs.

Newhalen is fouled. They hit both free throws.

Derek misses a drive after splitting a trap.

Number 12 gets the ball on the baseline, goes up for a jumper. Aaron goes up with him, swats it away.

The ref blows the whistle.

Dave can't believe it. Neither can Aaron.

Two free throws for 12.

He hits both.

42–25.

Josh takes his man to the hole, fumbles the ball on the drive, recovers . . . and misses the layup.

Newhalen's coach motions to his players. They work the ball around the perimeter. They're in no hurry to shoot. They're happy to eat up some of that clock. Almost a minute goes by before one of their forwards breaks loose in the key for a strong inside score.

This is one well-schooled team, Dave has to give them that. Every button they push rings the bell.

Aaron gets the ball on the right side, squares up and lets go his fourth shot in four minutes.

It's good.

Four for four.

Dave is up on his feet.

Number 13—Belushi—sits him back down with a clean twenty-footer, a three.

47–27.

Matt throws away a long crosscourt pass.

Dave signals time-out, motions his boys to the bench. They're doing everything they can, but they're still losing ground.

"Settle down," he says. "Don't get frustrated."

He puts Wade back in.

Newhalen scores inside.

Matt misses a runner.

Number 4, a reserve, hits a three for Newhalen.

52–27 with three minutes left in the quarter.

Newhalen steals, and 4 scores again, faking Aaron into the air before laying it up.

Another miss by Matt.

Number 12 comes down, shakes loose at the top of the key. He launches a three. The ball hits the rim hard, caroms high off the glass . . . and falls through.

Dave shakes his head. What can they do? They've run into a buzzsaw.

Matt beats the horn with another long three—his third end-of-the-quarter three-pointer tonight—but the Eagles are down twenty-seven, 57–30.

The Newhalen fans are raising the roof, beating the bleachers, dancing in the aisles. They're ready for Noorvik, right now.

Dave makes his last move, puts in Johnny for Aaron, prays for some kind of miracle.

Johnny's on fire. He nails four long three-pointers, one right after the other. But it's too late. With 1:30 left in the game, Fort Yukon trails 69–44. Dave calls a final time-out, gathers his boys in a circle, kneels down among them.

"We go out with our heads *up*, gentlemen," he says.

So do their fans.

It's over, the ride that began last November.

Four months. More than four thousand miles. Twenty-seven games. Only four losses. But the one that counts most is this one.

The kids are down, no question, as the final horn sounds and they drift into the locker room. They shower, dress, with hardly a word. No wisecracks from Justin or Tim. No speech from Dave, not right now. He leaves them alone, waits outside till they're ready.

They're hungry. It's late. Dave drives till he finds a restaurant still open, a nice sit-down place. He tells the boys there's no ten-dollar limit tonight. They can have anything they want, he tells them, anything at all, including dessert.

The boys order quietly, politely, as the waiter circles their table. Ribs, pizza, spaghetti. Hot fudge sundaes all around.

The waiter comes back after placing their order. He doesn't know who these boys are, where they've just been. But he likes kids. He's good with them. His one-liners are dry, deadpan. And he's got a few tricks to show them. He makes a coin disappear, makes water vanish from a glass. The boys are skeptical at first, but this guy's pretty good. Within a few minutes, they're wide-eyed, trying to figure out how he knew what number they all had in their heads. They're into it. Justin blows everyone away by tossing an olive into the air and spearing it on a toothpick held between his front teeth, just like the waiter's showed him. Within seconds, they're all trying it, laughing, hooting at each other's misses.

Dave watches them. His boys.

Soon enough they'll be back in Fort Yukon.

But right now they're here, a bunch of kids having a blast, into the moment, the meal, and the magic.

EPILOGUE
Spring 2005

THE WIND IS gusting, bending the trees, blowing the snow from the branches and sending it whirling through the bright sunlit air. The sky is achingly blue. It's ten above zero, the first day of spring.

Dave's in his office, watching ESPN. The Red Sox have started spring training in Florida. They scrimmage the Dodgers today. Their regular season begins in two weeks against—who else?—the Yankees.

They got back last night, Dave and Diane and the boys, after driving all day from Anchorage, then boarding the last Frontier flight to Fort Yukon. When Dave and Diane reached their house, her son, Andrew, was there with some heartbreaking news. Mickey the cat passed away. Andrew found him back in the bathroom, under the tub, in his favorite spot. His kidneys had failed. Dave called both his daughters to tell them the news. They took it hard. Mickey's been with them for most of their lives.

Dave couldn't be prouder of how his boys bounced back from the loss to Newhalen. They played the next day for third place against Atqasuk. It would have been easy to tank, to just go through the motions after missing their shot at the title. But they played their hearts out, took an early lead and held on for a 56–48 win. That night, they watched Noorvik beat Newhalen by eight in the championship game. Matt was named to the All-Tournament team.

The highlight of the night for the boys was a mash note some girl slipped in Josh's coat pocket while they were watching the final. "Damn baby," it read. "Ur so fine. If your free (which I doubt) you should hit me up." She wrote down her e-mail address. Josh thought it was funny.

He showed it to Matt and Aaron and Derek, then gave it to Wes.

The Elders are planning a luncheon this week to honor the boys for their season. Twenty-four wins and four losses. Third in the state. Championship trophies from the NIT and Tok tournaments. The boys did them proud. That's how most of the villagers feel.

But not Paul. He was on the radio just this morning, talking with one of the deejays about the Spring Carnival and other news around town. The subject of the basketball team came up, and Paul acted like somebody died. "My eyes are still swollen," he said. The deejay sympathized. "Well," she said with an audible sigh, "there's always next year."

The boys plan to enter their team in the Spring Carnival's basketball tournament this weekend. Several men's teams from surrounding villages will be playing, along with a couple of squads from Fort Yukon. Ryan and John and Simon are going to play, and Earl Cadzow's pulling together a team of old-timers. Word is Jerry Carroll may bring a group up from Fairbanks. The winning team gets a set of new jackets.

There's a lot going on in the village this week. The town meeting is Thursday, to discuss the school board's decision to cut Fort Yukon's activity funds. As for the land swap, Adlai Alexander has pulled together four other chiefs—from Venetie, Chalkyitsik, Circle, and Canyon Village—to issue a joint statement opposing the deal. They've gotten some headlines, stirred up a public response. The Fish and Wildlife office in Fairbanks was flooded last week with more than two thousand e-mails opposing the deal. They've agreed to extend the deadline for the decision until more public meetings are held.

Who knows what will happen with any of that? Right now Dave's got his mind on his garden. And his bees. He's placed his order for this year's two boxes. And he's planning to get down to Fairbanks in the next month or so to check out the nurseries, see what they've got for the early spring planting.

As for the basketball team, he's already collected and laundered and stored the team's uniforms till next winter, when he'll hand them back out again. That's if he comes back. That's if Fort Yukon even has a basketball team next season. They could be tremendous, with twelve players returning, and a couple of talented kids coming up from eighth grade. Some of the boys have already been asking—about whether they'll have a team next year, about whether Dave's going to coach them.

Who knows? he tells them. We'll just have to wait and see.

The basketball season's still eight months away.

So much can happen between now and then.

AFTERWORD

The boys won the Spring Carnival tournament—and the jackets—coming out of the loser's bracket to beat Earl Cadzow's team twice.

The Alaska State Legislature issued a proclamation honoring Fort Yukon's boys' basketball team for their achievements the past seven seasons. The proclamation was followed by an announcement that the school would receive $4.3 million in state funds for renovation and expansion of its gymnasium.

With the announcement of that funding, the school board assured that Fort Yukon will field a basketball team, at least for the 2006 season.

Dave Bridges was named Coach of the Year for the state's Region 2, which includes thirty-eight Class 1A, 2A and 3A schools between Fort Yukon and Homer—among them, 2A state champion Cook Inlet Academy.

Matt Shewfelt was named Honorable Mention All-State. He and his cousin Russell were arrested in July at the Fairbanks International Airport for possession of one-eighth ounce of marijuana. They were each fined two hundred dollars and placed on one year's probation. Matt plans to attend the University of Alaska–Fairbanks in the fall.

Josh Cadzow also plans to attend UAF.

The proposed land swap between the U.S. Fish and Wildlife Service and the Doyon Corporation had still not been decided as of the end of the summer.

The wolf that was roaming Fort Yukon never returned. But Earl Cadzow still keeps his gun in his truck.

Standing (left to right): Josh Cadzow, Wes James, Chris Engler, Matt Shewfelt, Derek Carroll, Aaron Carroll, Johnny Adams, Justin James, Wade Fields.

Standing (rear): Tim Fields, Kyle Joseph.

Seated (left to right): Bruce James, Tim Woods, Zach Carroll.

2005 Fort Yukon Eagles

(24-4)

Anderson	W 86-33	Tanana	L 62-49
Anderson	W 72-36	Tok	W 73-70
Anderson	W 66-40	Galena	W 56-44
Houston	L 50-38	Wainwright	W 81-36
Nikolaevsk	L 63-48	Tanana	W 65-44
Mat-Su Christian	W 57-49	Tanana	W 60-51
Anderson	W 81-23		
Susitna Valley	W 63-58	**Regional Tournament**	
Tok	W 65-54	Huslia	W 48-18
Allakaket	W 81-41	Allakaket	W 68-51
Allakaket	W 57-49	Tanana	W 61-44
Mat-Su Christian	W 69-35		
Mat-Su Christian	W 71-42	**State Tournament**	
Huslia	W 91-30	Russian Mission	W 53-38
Tanana	W 83-54	Newhalen	L 71-48
Allakaket	W 63-47	Atqasuk	W 56-48

NOTES, SOURCES AND ACKNOWLEDGMENTS

I first learned about the phenomenon of basketball in rural Alaska as a newspaper reporter in November of 1992, when I traveled with an inner-city high school team from Norfolk, Virginia, as they flew to Anchorage to take part in a tournament there. I returned the next spring to the village of Kotzebue to write a magazine profile of a bush basketball star named Butch Lincoln. I promised myself at that time that I would come back to Alaska someday to spend a winter following one village team through an entire season.

That time came in the winter of 2004. I decided upon Fort Yukon for a number of reasons. First, the town's school had a strong tradition of successful basketball teams. Second, it had a coach who had been there a number of years. Finally, the village itself had a history that encompassed the myriad issues facing Native communities throughout rural Alaska.

I flew to Fort Yukon in the spring of 2004 to meet some of the people in the village and to arrange a place to live for the following winter. I talked at that time to the school's principal and to the basketball coach, Dave Bridges, who told me it was up to the players themselves whether they wanted to have an outsider shadow them through a season of practices, traveling and games. I was welcome to return for the winter, he said, but he couldn't guarantee what the team would decide.

At that time, I also wrote a letter to the village's chief and its Tribal Council, to introduce myself and explain my plans. This is what I wrote:

To: *The Gwich'yaa Zhee Gwich'in Tribal Government*
From: *Mike D'Orso*

Thank you for the opportunity to explain my intentions.

I am a journalist, a nonfiction writer specializing in human interest subjects and stories. I am not an academic professor, or a teacher, or a politician with a particular agenda. I approach every story I write with the intention of getting at the heart of the subject, and I do not use that term "heart" lightly. Beyond simply gathering facts, my goal with each story I write is to get at the soul and the feelings of the people who agree to let me into their lives— not my feelings, but theirs. My mission with each book I write is to garner a true understanding of the people and place about which I am writing, so that the reader will come away from the book with a deeper, fuller and richer appreciation of the subject than he had before he read it.

I am painfully aware of how often people like yourselves trust a writer like me, invite him (or her) into their lives, into their world, and find that the writer was not interested in the truth or humanity of your world but was rather intent on finding his truth, the truth that fits his own agenda, his own needs. Believe me, the Gwich'yaa Zhee community is not the first to be burned by a writer such as this. I learned early in my career that the most difficult stage of most of my stories is often in the beginning, when I have to earn the trust of people whose trust has been betrayed by writers who have come before me.

That said, I can tell you that I approach every subject I write about with a great amount of humility. I am the outsider. I am the guest. I am the ignorant one. I have to be patient. I have to listen. I have to watch. I have to learn. I have to let the people who agree to bring me into their world show me the way. And from beginning to end, I have to honor the enormous responsibility of sharing with the world the lives of very real human beings who have agreed to trust me to get it right.

This is what I promise to do with the story I'd like to pursue in Fort Yukon. My hope is to follow the school's basketball team

*through an entire season, from the first day of practice to the final
buzzer of the season's last game. The kids on the team (and the
coach) will of course be the book's main characters. But the village
too (its rhythms, its people, their lives) will obviously be at the
heart of the story as well, as the basketball season unfolds.*

*Again, I can assure you that the dignity and integrity of your
lives and your community will be honored and accurately reflected
in the book I hope to write. I look forward to hearing from you
and will be happy to answer any questions you might have.*
Sincerely,
Mike D'Orso

The chief, Adlai Alexander, responded by welcoming me to come
spend the winter in their village.

I flew to Fort Yukon that October, settled into my rented cabin, and
spent the next five months getting to know the people of Gwich'yaa
Zhee. By the time the preseason began at the end of November, the
boys—and their coach—had agreed to allow me to attend every practice, to join them in the locker room before and after each game, to sit
with them on the bench during the games, and to travel with them on
road trips—sleeping where they slept, eating where they ate, going wherever they went.

It is, of course, the boys and Dave Bridges whom I must thank first,
for so completely opening their world to me. Without their trust and
honesty, this book could never have been written.

The same goes for the people of Fort Yukon. They have not always
been treated kindly nor fairly by outsiders. It took courage and faith for
them to accept me into their community. Again, without their trust and
guidance, I could not have written this story.

Beyond the individuals whose names appear on the pages of this book,
there were numerous people who helped guide me as I worked my way
through various aspects of this book. They include Gary Lawrence, exec-
utive director of the Gwich'yaa Zhee Gwich'in Tribal Government; Stan
Swetzoff, acting chief of police for Fort Yukon; Jed Lowell, former propri-
etor of the now-defunct River in the Sky Lodge in Fort Yukon; Steve

Klaich, head basketball coach at the Nikolaevsk School; Daryl Frisbee, head coach at the Anderson School; Gary Matthews and Carrie Spackman with the Alaska School Activities Association; Jack Rasmussen with the Fairbanks Borough Public Library; and Rick Thoman, lead forecaster with the National Weather Service in Fairbanks.

Here at home, I must thank my editor, Colin Dickerman, whose enthusiasm and support during my reporting of this story and whose guidance and insight during its writing were more than any author could hope for. His assistant, Marisa Pagano, was also a great help as this book took its shape.

As always, my agent, David Black, and his staff were there for me during the coldest and—literally—darkest days.

Finally, I must thank Joy and Alex for keeping the house warm and our hearts connected while I was away.

Si se puede.

All scenes, incidents and conversations contained in this book occurred as described. In almost all cases, I was there to witness and record them. If I was not, they are re-created from the recollections and accounts of those who were, as well as from documented sources.

The following list of books, as well as newspaper and magazine articles, provided information on a variety of subjects discussed on these pages.

BOOKS

Agnew, Eleanor. *Back from the Land.*

Alexander, Ginny. *Life on the Edge of the Arctic Circle.*

Anderson, James, and Jim Reardon. *Arctic Bush Pilot.*

Balikci, Asen. *Vunta Kutchin Social Change: A Study of the People of Old Crow, Yukon Territory.*

Balzer, John. *Yukon Alone.*

Beaver, C. Masten. *Fort Yukon Trader: Three Years in an Alaskan Wilderness.*

Berger, Judge Thomas. *Village Journey: The Report of the Alaska Native Review Commission.*

Berry, Mary Clay. *The Alaska Pipeline: The Politics of Oil*.

Campbell, James. *The Final Frontiersman: Heimo Korth and His Family, Alone in Alaska's Arctic Wilderness*.

Carlo, Poline. *Nulato: An Indian Life on the Yukon*.

Carroll, James. *The First Ten Years in Alaska: Memoirs of a Fort Yukon Trapper, 1911–1922*.

Coates, Peter. *The Trans-Alaska Pipeline Controversy*.

Crisler, Lois. *Arctic Wild*.

Dean, David. *Breaking Trail: Hudson Stuck of Texas and Alaska*.

Dorris, Michael. *The Broken Cord*.

Fast, Phyllis Ann. *Northern Athabascan Survival*.

Feies, Claire. *Villagers: Athabaskan Indian Life Along the Yukon River*.

Freuchen, Peter. *Book of the Eskimos*.

Harper-Haines, Jan. *Cold River Spirits: The Legacy of an Athabascan-Irish Family from Alaska's Yukon River*.

Haskin, Pamela. *Deliberate Life: A Journey into the Alaskan Wilderness*.

Herbert, Belle, as told to Bill Pfisterer, with Alice Moses. *Shandaa; In My Lifetime*.

Jans, Nick. *The Last Light Breaking*.

———. *A Place Beyond*.

Jenkins, Peter. *Looking for Alaska*.

Kollin, Susan. *Nature's State: Imagining Alaska as the Last Frontier*.

Krakauer, Jon. *Into the Wild*.

MacKenzie, Claire. *Wolf Smeller: A Biography of John Fredson, Native Alaskan*.

Maclean, Norman. *Young Men and Fire*.

Madsen, Ken. *Under the Arctic Sun: Gwich'in, Caribou and the Arctic National Wildlife Refuge*.

McPhee, John. *Coming into the Country*.

Miller, Debbie S. *Midnight Wilderness: Journeys in Alaska's Arctic National Wildlife Refuge*.

Nelson, Richard K. *Hunters of the Northern Forest*.

O'Neill, Dan. *The Firecracker Boys*.

Ruppert, James, ed. *Our Voices: Native Stories of Alaska and the Yukon*.

Shore, Evelyn Berglund. *Born on Snowshoes.*

Stuck, Hudson. *The Ascent of Denali.*

Vyvyan, Clara. *The Ladies, the Gwich'in and the Rat: Travels on the Athabasca, MacKenzie, Rat, Porcupine, and Yukon Rivers in 1926.*

Wallis, Velma. *Raising Ourselves: A Gwich'in Coming of Age Story from the Yukon River.*

———. *Two Old Women: An Alaska Legend of Betrayal, Courage and Survival.*

Webb, Melody. *Yukon: The Last Frontier.*

NEWSPAPER AND MAGAZINE ARTICLES

"AFN Rejects Vote on Drilling Issue." *Anchorage Daily News*, October 20, 1996.

"Alaska Natives Improve Status." *Anchorage Daily News*, May 29, 2004.

"Alaska Voters Have Sent Mixed Messages on Marijuana." *Anchorage Daily News*, October 25, 2004.

"Alaska: Politicians and Natives, Money and Oil." *Harper's*, May 1970.

"Alaska's '04 Suicide Numbers Highest Ever." *Fairbanks Daily News-Miner*, January 9, 2005.

"Alaska's Road Warriors." *USA Today*, February 21, 2001.

"Alaska's Wildfire Costs Could Top $106 Million." *Anchorage Daily News*, October 30, 2004.

"An Alaskan Hot Spot, Even at 50 Below Zero." *New York Times*, March 4, 2002.

"Alaskans Have Hooped It Up for Years." *USA Today*, August 17, 1993.

"Alcohol and 'Special Populations': Biological Vulnerability." *International Center for Alcohol Policies*, November 2001.

"The Amazing Don Young." *Anchorage Daily News*, November 1, 2004.

"ANWR Issue Pops Up in Races Across Nation." Associated Press, October 23, 2004.

"A Bad Mix in the Bush." *Anchorage Daily News*, August 9, 1989.

"Ballot Measure to Decriminalize Marijuana Fails." *Fairbanks Daily News-Miner*, November 3, 2004.

"The Battle for Fish and Survival Along the Yukon." *Christian Science Monitor,* May 24, 1994.

"Between Two Worlds." *Juneau Empire* (series), January 1999.

"Blaze Levels Café, Home in Fort Yukon." *Fairbanks Daily News-Miner,* January 31, 2004.

"Blazes 'Help a Lot of People': Hundreds of Alaskans Find Work Battling Fires." *Anchorage Daily News,* July 11, 2004.

"Breaking Up Is Hard to Do: Traditional Tripod Set to Signal Spring." *Fairbanks Daily News-Miner,* March 7, 2005.

"British Walker Still Slogging Along." *Fairbanks Daily News-Miner,* February 11, 2005.

"Caribou Culture Clashes with Oil Age." *Christian Science Monitor,* November 24, 1995.

"The Climate of Man." *New Yorker,* April 25, 2005.

"A Culture in Crisis, A People in Peril." *Anchorage Daily News,* January 10, 1988.

"A Culture out of Balance." *Fairbanks Daily News-Miner,* December 7, 2004.

"Cycle of Native Despair Likely to Go On, Report Says." *Anchorage Daily News,* January 21, 1989.

"Death Spurs Village to Ban Booze." *Anchorage Daily News,* August 15, 2004.

"A Deep Wound, Slow to Heal." *Anchorage Daily News,* January 11, 1988.

"Drilling in ANWR Tops Bush Agenda." Associated Press, November 10, 2004.

"Drugs, Alcohol, Violence Erode Way of Life in Fort Yukon." *Northland News,* April 1998.

"Eagles End First-Round Futility." *Fairbanks Daily News-Miner,* March 28, 2003.

"Evaluation and Review of a Proposed Land Exchange and Acquisition of Native Lands." U.S. Fish and Wildlife Service, February 2005.

"Even the Great White North Has Reached 100 Degrees." Associated Press, August 21, 2001.

"Fiddlers Rosin Up Their Bows for Annual Festival." *Fairbanks Daily News-Miner,* November 9, 2004.

"A Fight for Sovereignty in Alaska's Native Villages." *Christian Science Monitor,* June 26, 1997.

"For Native Alaskans, Tradition Is Yielding to Modern Customs." *New York Times,* August 21, 2004.

"Fort Yukon City Manager Fires Police Chief, Investigator." Associated Press, February 12, 2004.

"Fort Yukon Comprehensive Plan." City of Fort Yukon, 1996.

"Fort Yukon Gets Grant for Police Department." *Fairbanks Daily News-Miner,* June 30, 2003.

"Fort Yukon Hockey League Starts Small." *Fairbanks Daily News-Miner,* August 1, 1998.

"Fort Yukon Man Charged with Allowing Prisoner to Escape." *Fairbanks Daily News-Miner,* October 24, 2003.

"Fort Yukon Man Charged with Attempted Murder." *Fairbanks Daily News-Miner,* December 14, 2001.

"Fort Yukon Man Gets 21-Year Sentence for Murder of Cousin." *Fairbanks Daily News-Miner,* October 30, 2001.

"Fort Yukon Man Hurt in Shooting." *Fairbanks Daily News-Miner,* March 19, 2004.

"Fort Yukon Man Recipient of Ecotrust." *Fairbanks Daily News-Miner,* November 15, 2004.

"Fort Yukon Residents Vote to Stay 'Wet.'" *Anchorage Daily News,* April 14, 1998.

"Fort Yukon Shoulders Great Expectations." *Fairbanks Daily News-Miner,* March 27, 2003.

"Fort Yukon Soldier Glad to Be Home." *Fairbanks Daily News-Miner,* August 8, 2004.

"Fort Yukon Super Sub Sparks Win." *Anchorage Daily News,* March 18, 2005.

"Fort Yukon's Ex-Mayor Charged in Embezzlement." Associated Press, February 1, 2004.

"Four Tragedies in Small Village." *Anchorage Daily News,* July 8, 1996.

"From Deep Childhood Wounds, a Memoir Rich in Detail." *Seattle Times,* January 10, 2003.

"From Humble Roots, Gonzales Reached Great Heights." *Dallas Morning News,* November 13, 2004.

"Frostbite Turns Spaniards from Adventure." *Fairbanks Daily News-Miner,* January 22, 1993.

"Golden Game: Bartlett Star Can Focus on Winning a State Title After Committing to Kansas." *Anchorage Daily News,* January 13, 2005.

"Governor Questions Oil Companies' Interest in ANWR." *Fairbanks Daily News-Miner,* March 1, 2005.

"Here, the City Sells It." *Anchorage Daily News,* January 16, 1988.

"History of Alcohol in Alaska." *Breining Institute College for the Advanced Study of Addictive Disorders,* 2002.

"Holding Court: Russian Old Believers Adjust to Sporting Life." *Anchorage Daily News,* March 25, 2001.

"Hundreds Rally Against Drilling in ANWR." *Fairbanks Daily News-Miner,* March 4, 2005.

"In Fairbanks, the Light Fantastic." *Los Angeles Times,* April 15, 2001.

"In Much of Alaska, Games Mean an Odyssey." *New York Times,* March 2, 2004.

"In Venetie, a Matter of Control." *Northland News,* April 1998.

"Injury, Illness Hit Natives Harder." *Anchorage Daily News,* December 6, 1991.

"Inupiat Eskimoes, Gwich'in Indians Disagree About Oil." *Christian Science Monitor,* July 30, 1991.

"Junket or Fact-Finding Trip? Senators Fly to ANWR." *Fairbanks Daily News-Miner,* March 4, 2005.

"K-9 Helps Hub Village in Fight Against Drugs." *Anchorage Daily News,* November 25, 2002.

"King of the Hill and the Highway." *New York Times,* April 4, 2004.

"Land Trade Would Allow Drilling Refuge." *Los Angeles Times,* October 22, 2004.

"Leaning Towers of Snow Explained." *Fairbanks Daily News-Miner,* February 27, 2005.

"Leg Wrestlers and Muskrat Callers Join the Party: Midsummer at Normally Frozen Fort Yukon." *Financial Times,* July 18, 1998.

"Lives Go Up in Smoke." *Fairbanks Daily News-Miner,* December 6, 2004.

"The Long and Icy Road." *USA Today,* February 21, 2001.

"Man Accused of Sex Attack on Cousin." *Fairbanks Daily News-Miner,* January 17, 2004.

"Marijuana Smuggling Seizures Up." *Fairbanks Daily News-Miner,* November 29, 2004.

"Murkowski Declares Disaster in Kaktovik, North Slope." *Fairbanks Daily News-Miner,* January 16, 2005.

"Mystery Surrounds Outdoorsman's Death." *Anchorage Daily News,* October 24, 2004.

"Natives of North Ready to Take on Anti-Fur Groups." *Journal of Commerce,* July 19, 1990.

"New Tanana Chiefs President Finds Strength in Village Life." *Fairbanks Daily News-Miner,* March 21, 1999.

"No Wimps Here: It's America's Last Frontier." *Newsday,* May 22, 1988.

"Northwest Passage." *Time,* August 31, 1942.

"Nothing Else Compares to Arctic Refuge." Universal Press Syndicate, March 18, 2001.

"Oil Drilling in Alaska Looms." *Wall Street Journal,* January 12, 2001.

"The Oilmen's Last Frontier." *Financial Times,* March 19, 1987.

"Once, Caribou People Followed Ancient Ways; Then Television Arrived." Associated Press, May 27, 1999.

"Outage Has Kaktovik in Deep Freeze." *Fairbanks Daily News-Miner,* January 11, 2005.

"Panel Fears 'Two Separate Alaskas.'" *Anchorage Daily News,* June 24, 1999.

"Permits Issued for Wolf Control near Tok." Associated Press, December 10, 2004.

"Poll: Majority in U.S. Oppose ANWR Drilling." *Fairbanks Daily News-Miner,* December 22, 2004.

"Power Struggle Far from Finished," *Northland News,* April 1998.

"Pride in Fur Is Promoted by Alaskans." *New York Times,* March 20, 1990.

"Professor Brought to Ground: Bootlegging Scheme Nets Economist a

Year Behind Bars." *Fairbanks Daily News-Miner,* December 18, 2004.

"Pump Dreams." *New Yorker,* October 11, 2004.

"Record-Breaking Lightning Ignites Interior Wildfires." *Anchorage Daily News,* June 19, 2004.

"Redoubt Volcano Erupts Again; Fiery Display Lights Up West Side of Inlet." *Anchorage Daily News,* January 3, 1990.

"Report Assesses Arctic Warming." *New York Times,* November 1, 2004.

"Report Looks at Status of Alaska Natives." Associated Press, January 8, 2005.

"Republican Calls ANWR First Priority." Associated Press, January 7, 2005.

"Riding an Ideological Divide; Man in the News—Alberto Gonzales." *New York Times,* November 11, 2004.

"Salmon Apologizes for 'Devil' Comment." *Fairbanks Daily News-Miner,* March 4, 2005.

"Salmon Failure 'A Disaster for the People.'" *Fairbanks Daily News-Miner,* July 15, 2000.

"School Fire Leaves Big Void in Fort Yukon." *Fairbanks Daily News-Miner,* February 11, 1995.

"Scientists Keep Eye on Alaska Volcanoes." Associated Press, January 12, 2005.

"Seventeen Flat Tires." *Fairbanks Daily News-Miner,* October 26, 1946.

"Shareholders Speak Out Against Doyon Land Swap." *Fairbanks Daily News-Miner,* March 22, 2005.

"Snowmachine Collision Kills Man." *Fairbanks Daily News-Miner,* November 27, 2001.

"Somewhere in the Thick Ground Fog." *Fairbanks Daily News-Miner,* November 13, 1953.

"Sorlie Keeps on Sloggin': Leader's Dogs Keep Pace Through Deep Snow, Warm Days." *Anchorage Daily News,* March 13, 2005.

"State of Alaska, Department of Education and Early Development, Report Card to the Public, 2003–2004." Alaska Public Schools, 2005.

"State Sale of Leases Success." *Anchorage Daily News,* May 20, 2004.

"State's ANWR Lobby Effort Reorganized." *Fairbanks Daily News-Miner,* February 20, 2005.

"Stevens Cool to Conclusion of Global Warming Study." Associated Press, November 18, 2004.

"Study Considers Yukon Flats Gas." *Fairbanks Daily News-Miner*, December 21, 2004.

"The Surrender of Fort Yukon." *Beaver*, Autumn 1969.

"Tanana Lays Down the Law." *Northland News*, April 1998.

"TCC Honors Native Businesses." *Fairbanks Daily News-Miner*, December 16, 2001.

"They Said It Shouldn't Ever Flood Here, but Don't Try to Tell That to Fort Yukon." *Fairbank Daily News-Miner*, May 12, 1982.

"Tok First Stop on Itinerary." *Fairbanks Daily News-Miner*, December 22, 2001.

"Tribes Oppose Yukon Flats Land Swap." *Fairbanks Daily News-Miner*, March 11, 2005.

"A Troubled Melting Pot Brews on Kenai." *Anchorage Daily News*, May 1, 1988.

"Turner, Wilson, Cadzow—It's Your Pick." *Fairbanks Daily News-Miner*, February 23, 1995.

"Vanishing Alaska." *Time*, October 4, 2004.

"Wandering Old Believers Find a Home in Alaska." Associated Press, July 20, 2004.

"Wicked Wonderland: For over a Century, America's War Vets Have Taken to the Outback." *Guardian*, March 30, 1991.

"Wildfires Smoke Out Fairbanks." *Anchorage Daily News*, June 29, 2004.

"Wintry Ordeal on the Yukon: Vivid Story of Athabascan Life." Associated Press, December 26, 1993.

"Wolf Kill Foes Resume 'Howl-Ins.'" Associated Press, November 6, 2004.

"World Walkabout." *Fairbanks Daily News-Miner*, December 10, 2004.

A NOTE ON THE AUTHOR

Michael D'Orso is the author of more than a dozen books, including *Like Judgment Day: The Ruin and Redemption of a Town Called Rosewood* and *Plundering Paradise: The Hand of Man on the Galapagos Islands*. He lives in Norfolk, Virginia.